Jane & Me

MY AUSTEN HERITAGE

Jane & Me

MY AUSTEN HERITAGE

Caroline Jane Knight
JANE AUSTEN'S FIFTH GREAT-NIECE

Jane & Me: My Austen Heritage

Published by
The Greyfriar Group
852 Canterbury Road
Box Hill South
Victoria 3128
Australia
www.austenheritage.com

First published in 2017

Written by Caroline Jane Knight
Cover and text design by Susannah Low
Additional photographs by Dr Julia Grantham

National Library of Australia
Cataloguing-in-Publication entry:

Creator: Knight, Caroline Jane, author.
Title: Jane & me : my Austen Heritage / Caroline Jane Knight.

ISBN: 978-0-648-08050-3 (hardback)
ISBN: 978-0-648-08051-0 (paperback)

Subjects: Knight, Caroline Jane.
Austen, Jane, 1775-1817--Influence.
Austen, Jane, 1775-1817--Homes and haunts
Printed in Great Britain by Clays Ltd, St Ives plc

For my family

CONTENTS

FOREWORD

Caroline Jane Knight's *Jane & Me: My Austen Heritage* is not a work of fandom or fantasy. It is the authentic and extraordinary story of a life interwoven with Jane Austen's in many compelling ways. Caroline grew up in Chawton House, the sixteenth-century manor inherited in 1798 by Jane Austen's brother Edward Austen Knight—Caroline's fourth great-grandfather—a home that had been in Caroline's family for many generations. But when Caroline's grandfather died, it was no longer possible to maintain the family home of four hundred years, and Caroline was forced to leave it behind—she was seventeen, and she didn't want to hear anything more about Chawton *or* Jane Austen. How Caroline came to terms with the troubling heritage she was left with and eventually founded the Jane Austen Literacy Foundation is the arresting personal narrative running through these chapters.

This book is a major contribution to the now vast library of works about Jane Austen. It sheds a great deal of light on country-house life in England in the early twentieth century, as well as on the Knight and Austen families, and includes much information that will be thrillingly new to Jane Austen's readers and scholars. The last of the close family memoirs, Caroline Austen's *My Aunt Jane Austen*, was published in 1867. How wonderful it is that in the twenty-first century those family recollections are now being complemented and transformed in this contemporary and dramatic story.

– John Wiltshire

INTRODUCTION

I have spent most of my adult life trying to forget Chawton and avoiding all reminders of my heritage, my ancestors and Chawton House, which I miss so dearly but which can never again be my family home. For more than twenty years, I chose not to tell my colleagues or friends that I am Jane Austen's fifth great-niece and the last descendant of the Austen family to grow up in Chawton House, the ancestral home of the Knight family for four centuries and fifteen generations. But in 2013, the widely celebrated bicentennial of the publishing of *Pride and Prejudice* started a chain of events in my life that would take me back to my roots and reunite me with my 'very great' great-aunt, Jane Austen. It was difficult at first, for the loss of Chawton still weighed heavy on my heart.

In Melbourne, where I now live, I talked to a group of women at the local Jane Austen Society and a packed crowd at a National Trust event, and I was astounded by the level of interest in me and my family. Jane Austen fans wanted to know every detail of my connection with the world-famous author and my life at Chawton—from the rooms, furniture and crockery in Chawton House to the local walks and family traditions I shared with Jane. Historians were interested in my memories of the last years of Chawton House as a family home. The demise of the Knight family's ancestral estate is typical of the demise of many English country manors, but Great Aunt Jane's extraordinary literary talent and her increasing popularity globally—particularly over the last twenty years—has ignited a special interest in Chawton. Many people suggested I write a book about my memories, but I dismissed the idea—I had no idea where or how to start.

I am often asked what it was like to live at Chawton House, why I had chosen not to tell anyone about my family connections and famous relative, and why I started the Jane Austen Literacy Foundation. These are all difficult questions to answer in just a few sentences, for I find it impossible to talk about Chawton without sharing stories—so many stories—of the most notable of my Knight and Austen ancestors, of working in Granny's tea room, of hosting community events, of the family library and bookplates and of my relationship with my grandfather Edward Knight III—the fifteenth squire of Chawton—who rarely spoke to me. It is difficult to explain why my heart had ached for Chawton, why the mere mention of Jane Austen had been more than I could bear, and why I had jumped at the chance to move to the other side of the world, as far away as possible, to be anonymous. And it is difficult to articulate why I now feel so compelled to honour Jane's legacy by harnessing the Austen community to increase literacy rates in the world's poorest communities.

Many writers and historians have documented the history of Chawton House and the Austen and Knight families, but little is known about the last decades of Chawton House as my family's home. Montagu Knight, the thirteenth squire of Chawton, was the last family member to write a book about the house, and that book was published more than one hundred years ago. During a short visit home to my parents' house in 2014, I read a copy of Montagu's book and savoured every word—I had not seen the book for years. I wished then that I had an original version of my own and that Montagu had written about his own life. By the end of my visit, I had decided to write this book, adding my memories to the rich history of the Knight family of Chawton—with my branch, the Austens.

Jane & Me: My Austen Heritage would not have been possible without the support of my friends and family. I am forever grateful to my loving family for the privilege of growing up in Chawton House, for supporting this book and for patiently answering my never-ending questions. I would particularly like to thank John Wiltshire, who has been extraordinarily generous with his time, advice and encouragement; my dear friend Amanda for the highs and lows we have shared; and Marilyn, who has taught me how to be happy. Lastly, I would like to thank my wonderful husband, Roger, for believing in me.

My story starts on Christmas Eve 1986.

CHAPTER ONE

'Ah! there is nothing like staying at home for real comfort'

Emma – Chapter 32

CHRISTMAS EVE WAS MY favourite night of the year at Chawton House, and Christmas 1986 was no exception. I didn't know then that it would be the last Christmas our family would spend together, happily enjoying our festive traditions in the Great Hall.

I was sixteen, and a few months earlier, I had started attending the local sixth-form college where I was studying A-level mathematics, economics and psychology. But after five years at an all-girls convent school, I was struggling to settle in. I was easily distracted from my studies and had fallen behind. But it was the Christmas holidays, so I pushed all thoughts about college to the back of my mind and concentrated on the night ahead. I had attended and enjoyed this most traditional family event every year since I was born. I would not have missed it for the world.

A few days earlier, my father, my older brother, Paul, and I had followed the path through the woodlands on the south-western edge of our country estate in search of holly packed with bright-red berries to decorate the largest room in our Elizabethan manor house. In the springtime, a carpet of bluebells would stretch from the hollow tree at the bottom of the woods all the way to the flint-walled orchard garden at the top. On a cold midwinter's morning, though, there was little colour to be seen, and frost crunched beneath our boots. Many of the trees had shed their leaves, and the woods appeared lifeless, save for the pheasants and red-breasted robins. This year, as with every other year, our extended family would be joining us in the Great Hall for celebrations and a game of Snap-Dragon, as enjoyed by generations of our family.

The receding winter undergrowth revealed the traces of the once manicured gardens: paths, long unkempt and overgrown; life-size stone statues of Adam and Eve in the Garden of Eden; and ornamental plaques, depicting coats of arms and foreign travels, set into the brickwork of the walled garden. My fifth great-aunt, Jane Austen, must have walked these paths many times and stopped, perhaps, at the most advantageous points to admire the avenue of trees and rolling pastures of her brother Edward's home. For the last eight years of her life, Jane lived just four hundred yards from the 'Great House', as she referred to the manor, in a cottage in the centre of the village of Chawton in Hampshire in the south of England. Jane was a frequent visitor to the Great House and mentioned it in many of her letters. 'I went up to the Gt. House between three and four, and dawdled away an hour very comfortably,' Jane wrote to her sister Cassandra on 13 June 1814. I had often heard it said that Jane's access to the inner workings of her wealthy brother's country estate, manor house and library assisted her writing.

My father and Paul, who was twenty-one at the time, often walked through the woods to feed the pheasants or to attend to fallen trees and took note of the best holly growth, so it didn't take long for us to find our prize and to collect berry-laden boughs. I had rugged up warmly with a jumper and a padded coat, but as usual, I had not brought thick enough gloves, and the sharp spikes of the holly pricked my hands despite my best efforts to be careful as I gathered them up.

With armfuls of waxy green leaves and red berries, we emerged at the top of the woods in front of the walled garden to the south and walked down the sweeping lawns to the house. Our boots left a trail in the grass, crisp and shimmering with ice crystals from the morning frost, like faint footsteps in the snow. No snow had fallen that year, much to my disappointment. The long, wide lawns to the southwest provided the perfect gradient and safe landing for a toboggan, tray or even an empty feedbag, and were irresistible when covered in snow. As a child, I loved the rush of wind on my face as my father and I hurtled down the lawn, but as I didn't want to crash into the bushes at the bottom, I often leapt off the back of the toboggan before we reached them. It was impossible not to be in fits of giggles as I rolled in the soft snow.

When my father, Paul, and I reached the side door of the house, we stomped our feet to remove as much debris as possible before walking along the inner hallway and into the nursery. It wasn't actually the nursery; it was the Great Hall. The name 'nursery' had come about when my father, Jeremy Knight, as a young boy had played cricket and other games with his siblings in the large open room. For nearly four hundred years, the Great Hall had hosted official visitors, social occasions, community events and the Knight family's private celebrations.

Chawton Great House was built by John Knight around 1585 (the first major build would have taken a number of years) two and a half centuries after the Knight name was first recorded in Chawton. Fanny Knight, Edward's eldest daughter and one of Jane's favourite nieces, wrote to her old governess Miss Chapman in 1807 describing the Great House:

> This is a fine large old house, built long before Queen Elizabeth I believe, & here are such a number of old irregular passages &c &c that it is very entertaining to explore them, & often when I think

myself miles away from one part of the house I find a passage or
entrance close to it, & I don't know when I shall be quite mistress
of all the intricate, & different ways.

The house had been subject to continuous change, with additions, renovations and alterations ever since it was built—a four-storey extension to
the north wing added in the Victorian era had been the last major works.
The result was a labyrinth of staircases, passages and rooms. The dark interior
and numerous interconnecting doors only added to the confusion. The layout
was complicated, and it is difficult to describe—visitors frequently got lost.

The house sits at the end of the village halfway up a hill, with the garden
and grounds reaching up further still behind the house. A straight gravel
drive led down from the road to Chawton Church, St Nicholas, on the right
and the stables on the left, before going up the hill to the front entrance. The
natural dip in the landscape around the house had once provided a moat and
later a ha-ha—or dry moat—a recessed fence that provided boundaries but
did not obscure the view.

The front entrance is approached from the west by five stone steps up to
a large archway, above which carved stone heraldry proudly declares this the
home of the Knights. The carving depicts a shield, or coat of arms, with a lozenge design running diagonally down from left to right and the motto *Suivant Saint Pierre* (Follow St Peter) in bold letters below. The arms are topped
with a knight's helmet and the family crest: a sixteenth-century monk named
'the Greyfriar'. The house had never been sold, passing from one generation
to the next. If the squire had no heir, a relative was chosen—a male cousin or
nephew perhaps—on the condition that the name of Knight was taken upon
their inheritance so that the family name and the heraldry would live on.
Edward Austen, Jane's brother and my fourth great-grandfather, was adopted
by the Knights to become the eleventh squire of Chawton Great House.

My grandfather, Edward Knight III, Edward Austen's great-great-grandson, was seventy-six and had been squire of the once vast 2,500-acre estate for over fifty years. After decades of financial pressures and asset sales, only the manor house and twenty-four acres remained. The east and north wings of the house had been converted into self-contained flats for tenants, who used the rear entrance. Three branches of our family lived in the house: my grandparents—Edward and Elizabeth Knight—with their youngest son, Uncle Robert; my father's older sister, Penny, with her husband, Dougie, and their three children, all older than me; and my parents, my brother, Paul, and me. Christmas Eve celebrations were rarely missed by any of us. Other aunts, uncles, cousins and close family friends were invited to join us, and the house was filled with excitement.

Preparations for our celebrations had begun days before. Granny ran a tea room in the Great Hall during the summer months, and the tea room's numerous tables and chairs had been rearranged to allow plenty of room for the family to mingle, talk and play games rather than be formally seated. Granny's tea room attracted visitors to the house every year. Tourists came to the village of Chawton to visit Jane's cottage (Jane Austen's House Museum), and they often liked to retrace Jane's steps by taking the short stroll from her home in the centre of the village to her brother's manor house for tea. Jane would have walked south past the same village green and cricket pitch before walking up the drive towards the steps of the manor.

The large archway at the front entrance to the house leads into a covered porch to shelter visitors from inhospitable weather. Beyond the oversized oak front door is a hallway, with a door on the right to the study, lined with bookshelves. Two doors on the left open into the Great Hall: a large oak-panelled room with a grand open fireplace with a cupboard to its left (once used to store wood), two stone leaded-light windows with views down the front drive and a door at the opposite end of the room, which led to my immediate family's living quarters.

The Great Hall was in my grandparents' quarters, which included the study and the main entrance to the house. A large inner hall beyond led to the servants' passage behind the Great Hall, Granny's kitchen, the library and a grand suspended staircase which led to the bedroom chambers above and the Oak Room—a lady's morning room that had long been used as a bedroom. It is said that Jane liked to sit in the Oak Room and enjoy the magnificent view of the long driveway, where she was able to see all who approached.

It was now midwinter, and the tea room had been closed for months. Throughout the year, my father, Paul and Granny's part-time handyman, Mr Humphries, cut wood from fallen trees and branches on the estate woodlands and stacked it in the large wood store at the back of the house. A pile of seasoned logs sat ready next to the large stone fireplace.

As young children, Cousin Fiona, who lived with her family on the top floor of the house, and I would spend hours sitting at a table by the fire, cutting brightly coloured paper into strips to make streamers. It was like a scene I later read in *Persuasion*: 'On one side was a table occupied by some chattering girls, cutting up silk and gold paper…the whole completed by a roaring Christmas fire.' I used to like the colour schemes of the streamers to be coordinated and the loops to be neat.

Now that we were older, we were not as careful with our handiwork, but we still enjoyed the annual ritual. It was easier to make the decorations than it was to hang them. Blu Tack and sticky tape have limited success when used on oak-panelled walls, and drawing pins were out of the question. Luckily, the large stag antlers above the panelling provided convenient anchor points, and we draped the streamers from one set of antlers to another.

We cut sprigs from the newly cut holly boughs and spread them around the room to complete the decorations—on the fireplace mantle, on the lip above the panelling, above the doors and on the window ledges. Mistletoe was harder to find, but Paul, a tree surgeon, had cut a thick bunch from one of the woodlands where he had worked a few days earlier, which we hung in the doorways so guests would be greeted with a kiss. A large Christmas tree took pride of place. Freshly cut from a neighbour's woodlands, it was decorated with baubles of different shapes, sizes and colours and with 'white-man's beard'—wispy white threads that hung from the bows like snow. Presents to be opened on Christmas Day were piled under the tree.

An enormous pewter charger had been retrieved from its home above the panelling in the inner hall to be warmed in front of the fire for Snap-Dragon, the main event of the evening. Granny said the chargers were very old, but she didn't know how old. 'Though I like praise as well as anybody, I like what Edward calls "Pewter" too,' Jane once quipped, determined to make some money from her writing, but I didn't know whether this was Edward's pewter.

I loved to help Granny prepare food for the evening, and I had accompanied her days before Christmas to Alton, the nearby market town on the main route between Farnham, nine miles to the northeast, and Winchester, sixteen miles to the southwest. We had bought butter and filling for the mince pies, raisins and brandy for Snap-Dragon and drinks for the children and adults. I watched while she rolled out the pastry, layering with thick butter over and over, to make her legendary flaky puff pastry.

Once the pastry cases were cut and placed in the baking tray, it was my job to fill each case with mincemeat and top and glaze them. 'Put plenty of filling in,' Granny would say with encouragement, as I tried not to lick my fingers before she handed me the pastry brush and egg wash. I waited impatiently for twenty minutes before carefully taking the sizzling, golden, crumbly pies out of the oven and burning my lips with the first bite of the festive season. The crumbly butter pastry melted in my mouth before the rich fruit filling gave me that undeniable taste of Christmas.

Then Granny would give me other jobs—sometimes I swept and dusted the Great Hall, which hadn't been used since the Christmas carol service a few weeks earlier. Then the tables needed a wipe, and the eclectic mix of antique bone china—from traditional Willow to vibrant Aynsley designs—and the glasses and cutlery needed to be brought through from the cupboards in Granny's kitchen. The original house kitchen in the east wing was now disused. There had been no servants or cook in the house for decades, and the kitchen was far too big for domestic use. A small kitchen, built in my grandparents' quarters for Granny, was accessed from the servants' passage behind the Great Hall.

Before I began to get ready for the evening's celebrations, I walked to the church to see the festive decorations. I liked to go into the church when it was empty. The latch on the thick wooden door clanged loudly as I let myself in. Immediately inside the doorway was the stone font where I was christened. Rows of pews up the nave led to the crossing with a pulpit on the right and a door to the vestry on the left. Beyond the crossing was the chancel. The church was decorated with holly and handmade decorations that I assumed were from the village school's nativity performance.

I played Mary in the nativity when I was five. The service began with all the children sitting in the back pews behind the congregation for prayers and hymns. After the hymns, I walked up the central aisle to the front of the nave and took my place next to the manger, ready for the play to begin. Suddenly, I realised I had left Jesus behind on the back pew (or rather the doll we were using). I called out to my mother that I had 'forgotten the baby', and she quickly retrieved the doll and brought it to me at the front before she slipped back into her seat. The congregation laughed affectionately, but I was embarrassed and felt my cheeks turn pink.

I liked the stillness of the quiet church, and I loved to read the inscriptions and plaques dedicated to the Knights and the Austens—records of the centuries of our ancestors in Chawton. At the very back of the church, on the right wall of the chancel, Sir Richard Knight reclined in marble. He had been installed three centuries earlier on what appeared to be the mantelpiece of a grand fireplace.

He wore battle dress and a wig like the judges' wigs on *Crown Court*, a television courtroom drama my grandparents watched daily. The marble behind Sir Richard was carved in relief with suits of armour, swords and helmets. The monument was finished at the top with the Knight coat of arms, crest and motto. The date '1679' marked his death and was all I could make out from the Latin inscription below the mantel. The Knight arms were featured in the stained-glass window next to Sir Richard on the back wall of the chancel.

With too many 'greats' for me to calculate—about ten, I thought—I had decided to consider myself Sir Richard's great-granddaughter. A more accurate description of the relationship between us, with the house having passed to numerous different branches of the family, seemed difficult to determine and unnecessary. He was a Knight from Chawton, and so was I; therefore, he was my great-grandfather—simple.

Sir Richard had a serious face, and I tried to imagine what sort of man he had been. The faces of our many ancestors were depicted in oil paintings throughout the house, but this was the only three-dimensional statue. It was as if he were frozen in time, lost in the eyes of Medusa, his white marble skin smooth and flawless. He looked well fed and healthy.

When he left provisions in his will for the monument to be constructed, did he think that three hundred years later, his descendants would still be living in Chawton House? Sir Richard could not possibly have imagined that this estate would one day boast a world-renowned writer as one of its own. And especially not a woman! Jane would have known Sir Richard just as I did; much of the old wooden church had been destroyed by fire and rebuilt in 1872, but the chancel and family vault underneath had remained intact, and Sir Richard had not been disturbed.

I thought about how the world had changed since the seventeenth century. In Sir Richard's time, the horse-drawn carriage had offered the only means of transport, and the most adventurous of explorers had had to take to the seas in search of new lands. I had watched on television old newsreels of men landing on the moon in 1969—the year before I was born.

Sir Richard, an educated and well-travelled man of means, had not known of the great southern land of Australia where my mother would later grow up, as Captain Cook had not yet landed at Botany Bay. In Sir Richard's time, hundreds of women were accused of witchcraft—perhaps it was Sir Richard who had carved the witches' marks in the sides of the fireplace in the Great Hall to prevent witches from entering the house. The industrial revolution, Charles Darwin's theory of evolution, the discovery of penicillin, two world wars and three centuries of history separated our life experiences, but Sir Richard and I shared this—our home. We had trodden the same floors, been warmed by the same fireplaces, joined family celebrations in the same Great Hall and tobogganed down the same lawns—I liked to think Sir Richard would have jumped on a feedbag when he was young.

In 1644, when Sir Richard was five, Oliver Cromwell enforced an Act of Parliament which banned Christmas celebrations in England, as Christmas was considered a wasteful festival that threatened core Christian beliefs. The ban was not lifted until Sir Richard was twenty-one, although many people had continued to celebrate Christmas in secret. I hated the thought of Sir Richard missing Christmas as a child and hoped his family had marked the occasion, even if behind closed doors. I assumed that was why Granny placed a sprig of holly in his hand every year—to ensure Sir Richard didn't miss out on any more Christmases.

In the late afternoon, I started to get ready for the evening's festivities. My parents, Paul and I lived in the north wing, accessed through the far door of the Great Hall or via the rear entrance to the house, which we preferred to use. On the first floor was our sitting room, originally the grand dining room of the house. Across the hall, three steps led to the small door into my parents' bedroom, once used as the gentleman's smoking room. It had leaded-light windows to the rear of the manor and a low ceiling, unlike the rest of our quarters, and it was lined with mismatching oak panelling, which I assumed had been recycled from elsewhere in the house or from another property. There was a door through to a back staircase, which my parents kept locked.

On the same floor were my family's kitchen and my bedroom—a long, narrow room with an especially high ceiling, painted walls and a large sash window overlooking the back entrance to the house. At one end was a fitted sink and across the other end a fitted wardrobe, above which my father had installed a mezzanine, complete with mattress for a bed and a wooden ladder for access.

A doorway from the hall of our quarters led up a sixteenth-century staircase to the Tapestry Gallery, a vast landing with a door to my brother's bedroom, long known as the Blue Room, above our sitting room. There were no tapestries hanging on the walls; my father said his father had sold them to pay for school fees, but I was never sure whether this was a joke.

A room outside the Blue Room, a dressing room perhaps, had been divided and converted into two bathrooms, one now used by my immediate family and the other by tenants. The bathroom, fitted with an old-fashioned white porcelain sink and cast-iron bath, was always cold. Wind often whistled through from the Tapestry Gallery. The water was hot enough to keep me warm, but as soon as I clambered out of the bath, I wrapped myself in a thick dressing gown and, without dawdling, quickly made my way back down the stairs, through the kitchen and into my bedroom.

I often wore a dress from my mother's wardrobe for family occasions, but not this year. I had recently borrowed her sewing machine and made a mid-calf blue corduroy skirt from fabric she had purchased for me at a fabric shop on Crown Hill in Alton. Alton was famous in the eighteenth century for its manufacture of paper and dress fabrics as well as for its breweries for which it remains well known today. Jane and Cassandra visited Alton frequently and would sometimes visit Henry Austen's bank on Crown Hill.

I teamed my newly made skirt with a blue and white striped cotton blouse with an upturned collar and then draped a jumper over my shoulders. The oil-fired central heating radiators installed throughout the house were highly inefficient, and layers of clothing were essential. As I readied myself for the evening, I listened to Blondie on my cassette player and sang along at the top of my voice. I dried my hair with a large round brush into a fashionable Princess Diana–inspired bouffant style and applied a little mascara and lip gloss. I finished my outfit with sensible navy shoes with a small heel. We all dressed smartly for celebrations in the Great Hall, and I am sure Jane did too—a best dress perhaps, with hair freshly pinned and smart shoes to change into when she arrived; it wasn't far to walk from the cottage.

From my bedroom, I walked down the dark panelled hall—past the oil portraits of the sixth, seventh and eighth squires of Chawton House—and into our sitting room. The middle of the room was furnished with a sofa and two comfy armchairs with yellow floral upholstery upon a large Persian rug. The sofa and chairs had originally been gold in colour, but my mother had made new covers for them. Dark wooden furniture dressed the edges of the room and included a long bookshelf topped with photographs in assorted silver frames; a tall, deep corner cupboard for serving spirits; an antique desk; and a piece of furniture that looked like a square table with cupboards underneath but was, in fact, a commode—no longer used of course. The polished dining table bore the faint scars of inkwell stains.

My father was seated in an armchair by the fireplace, while I sat on a window seat with a clear view of the front entrance to the house and peeked through the curtains to watch the guests arrive. My grandparents had six children between them, three of whom lived away from Chawton. Uncle Richard, my grandfather's eldest son and heir to Chawton, lived in Gloucestershire with his wife and three children. Aunt Margaret—my godmother—lived about half an hour away in Hampshire with her husband and two children, and Aunt Ann lived in Buckinghamshire with her husband and two children.

It was a particularly wet English winter, and the leaded-light windows rattled in the cold wind. I could hear the faint sound of a hairdryer as my mother finished styling her hair and applying her make-up in the bedroom across the hall. I hadn't seen Paul all afternoon but wasn't concerned; I knew he would not miss Snap-Dragon. With large rooms separated by thick walls, passages, hallways and galleries—all accessible by a choice of entrances and staircases—we often didn't see each other come and go. Paul was largely independent, although he still ate dinner cooked by our mother every night—even if it was heated up hours later.

At six o'clock, we opened the heavy door from the north wing and walked into the Great Hall. A fire flickered in the large open hearth, the curtains were drawn, and the room was warm. Mince pies, cocktail sausages and a cheese platter took pride of place on a high refectory table pushed to the wall on the right of the fireplace. Plates and cutlery for self-service were at one end, glasses, mulled wine and drinks at the other. The small black bats that occasionally flew around the top of the room were nowhere to be seen.

Within half an hour, all the guests had arrived. Granny suffered from arthritis by this time, but she rarely sat down at these events and, assisted by my mother and other willing helpers, ensured that everyone had a glass in hand and a mince pie with brandy butter or cream. Top-up supplies were collected from Granny's kitchen, carried along the servants' passage and through the inner hallway and into the Great Hall or, when an accomplice was there to receive them, passed directly from the servants' passage via the hatch of the old wood cupboard. The smell of Christmas was unmistakeable: chestnuts on the roaring fire, spices in the mulled wine and brandy warming in a jug by the fire. The room soon hummed with lively conversation, laughter and anticipation.

Once we were all gathered, my grandfather, Edward Knight III, joined the party and exchanged quiet conversation with Granny and other adults in attendance. He was known as Bapops to us, a nickname given to him by my eldest cousin when she was a toddler. Bapops had grown a beard by this time because he could no longer shave, but he was smartly dressed with a collar and tie, as always. I was in awe of him as the resident squire and figurehead of our family.

As Bapops stood quietly, I watched him and wondered about his thoughts. Did he enjoy his family gathered around him, or did he wish Christmas was over so he could return to the privacy of the library where he spent most of his time? Bapops was accessible to only a small inner circle of the family and trusted advisers, and he conducted his business as squire behind closed doors in the library and in private meetings with his accountant, solicitor or doctor, or with Uncle Richard on his annual visits. Events like Snap-Dragon were the only times I saw Bapops smile. I wondered why, but I didn't ask. I didn't know how to approach him, as we hadn't exchanged more than the odd word since I was born. We had never had a conversation.

Cousins shared stories and personal news and talked about the festivities planned for the next few days. We reflected on the year just gone—1986 had seen Margaret Thatcher's reputation damaged by the resignation of Michael Heseltine over the Westland affair. The future of space exploration and nuclear power were in question following the Space Shuttle Challenger disaster and the catastrophic accident at Chernobyl. Prince Andrew and Sarah Ferguson had married that year, and there had been a devastating fire at Hampton Court. We empathised, imagining how upset we would be if our heritage had been destroyed by fire.

'Can you imagine if there were a fire here? If the Knight Family Pedigree book were lost?'

'Or the portraits.'

'Or the Austen Knight dinner service!'

'Some things just can't be replaced.'

An hour into the evening, Granny appeared with the warmed jug of brandy—the signal that it was time for Snap-Dragon to begin. The pewter charger had been piled high with raisins, and it now took pride of place on a round table in the centre of the room. We gathered around the table, and the lights were turned out. Granny poured the brandy over the raisins and lit a match. As the alcohol in the brandy ignited, a burst of blue flames lit up the room with a flickering light, making our happy, excited faces suddenly appear ghoulish and sinister.

The room filled with laughter and excitement as we put our hands into the flames to grab the brandy-soaked fruit. As a young child, I had been frightened of being burnt. But my desire to do as my older brother and cousins did outweighed my fears, and I eventually discovered that as long as I was quick and immediately put the raisins in my mouth, it didn't hurt at all. It was as if we were eating fire! Watching Paul put his hand into the flames again and again without any sign of fear or hesitation encouraged me to be braver. It was over in a matter of minutes, but the adrenaline lasted much longer.

My ancestors had played the same game. 'Different amusements every evening! We had Bullet Pudding, then Snap-Dragon,' Fanny wrote in her diary in 1806. Did Jane join in and put her hands into the flames, or did she choose to stand back and watch? I like to think that Jane joined in, as she is reported to have been great fun. 'Don't be afraid, Fanny, proceed in a determined and speedy fashion and you will not be harmed,' I imagine Jane saying quietly in kind encouragement before she led the chant:

> Here he comes with flaming bowl,
> Don't he mean to take his toll,
> Snip! Snap! Dragon!
> Take care you don't take too much,
> Be not greedy in your clutch,
> Snip! Snap! Dragon!
> With his blue and lapping tongue
> Many of you will be stung,
> Snip! Snap! Dragon!
> For he snaps at all that comes

Snatching at his feast of plums,

Snip! Snap! Dragon!

But Old Christmas makes his come,

Though he looks so fee! fa! fum!

Snip! Snap! Dragon!

Don't 'ee fear him but be bold

Out he goes his flames are cold,

Snip! Snap! Dragon!

Snap-Dragon was popular in England from the sixteenth to the nineteenth centuries. Had my family played Snap-Dragon since Shakespeare's time, when the house was built? Did Sir Richard secretly play during the seventeenth-century Christmas prohibition? Or was it introduced by Great Aunt Jane herself? I would never know.

In a more modern addition to the celebrations, after the flames had died down and the charger had been cleared away, we heard sleigh bells outside, and Father Christmas, complete with a sack of presents, entered the Great Hall. After we had opened our gifts, Bapops quietly slipped away. Others stayed and talked, played parlour games and finalised plans for the coming day. By half past eight, most of the family and guests had left, and after we had helped to tidy up and carry dirty plates and glasses to Granny's kitchen, Paul and I went to join friends at a local country pub to continue the festive celebrations. Paul, with his bleached-blond hair spiked up, was dressed eccentrically in ripped jeans and Bapops's old red hunting tails, and I had changed my shoes for leather boots. We left in high spirits.

It was dark as we drove through the village. Jane's cottage, in the middle of Chawton village, had closed a few months prior for the winter and could only be seen in the glow from the street lights and The Greyfriar pub opposite. Jane lived at the cottage for only eight of her forty-one years, but they were the last eight years of her life when she had finally realised her dream and become a professional writer.

On sunny days, I would occasionally sit in the garden at Jane's cottage and wonder what Jane would think of all the visitors who had made the pilgrimage to her home. I watched as people went in and out of the cottage, but I rarely ventured inside—perhaps a couple of times a year. The artefacts didn't change and seemed similar to the furniture and heirlooms we had at home, except for Jane's tiny twelve-sided walnut single-tripod table. I sometimes sat at the little table and imagined Jane as she worked, hour after hour, to create her characters and polish her stories.

Jane had lived with her mother and sister, Cassandra, in Southampton on the Hampshire coast with her brother Frank before Edward offered the Austen ladies the choice of their own home on either his Godmersham or Chawton estate. The ladies chose to stay in Hampshire. 'Everybody,' wrote Jane from Southampton, 'is acquainted with Chawton, and speaks of it as a remarkably pretty village, and everyone knows the house we describe.' On 7 July 1809, the Austen ladies along with their close friend, Martha Lloyd, moved into the newly renovated bailiff's house, Chawton Cottage, situated in the middle of the village.

The village of Chawton is indeed remarkably pretty, with the Great House on a hill at the southern end and the estate's dower house at the northern end towards Alton. The village is complete with a church, cricket pitch, public house and school and is filled with estate cottages and country houses. Other than tourists visiting Jane's cottage, Chawton is a quiet village, but in Jane's time, all travellers on the roads from Winchester and Gosport to Alton passed through Chawton, right past the cottage. Jane was pleased with her new home, and wrote to her brother Frank:

Our Chawton home – how much we find
Already in it, to our mind,

And how convinced that when complete,

It will all other Houses beat

That ever have been made or mended,

With rooms concise or rooms distended

Jane Austen arrived in the village of Chawton as an unpublished author. Her eight short years in the village were her most productive, and at the time of her early death in 1817 Jane's dream had come true. Jane Austen had published four books to high acclaim and had secured her position as an accomplished author. The cottage became a museum in the late 1940s, and the village of Chawton became known as Jane's literary home. For me, Jane was an inspiration and a role model, and I was very proud of what she had achieved.

Paul and I didn't stay long in the village that night as we were eager to join our friends at The Sun, a pub in a nearby village. Paul had been a regular at The Sun for a few years, and for the last few months I had tagged along. I was too young to drink and didn't like the taste of alcohol anyway, but I enjoyed the atmosphere, fun and laughter.

Christmas Eve was the happiest day of the year, when the traditions of our heritage were most celebrated, followed by much merriment with my friends in the pub. I loved everything about Chawton: the village, the security of the Great House, the home of the Knight family. 'Ah! there is nothing like staying at home for real comfort,' Jane had written, and I knew what she meant. I couldn't imagine living anywhere else and liked to think we would play Snap-Dragon in the Great Hall for generations to come.

But the following year our lives would change forever. On 8 October 1987, my grandfather, Edward Knight III, the fifteenth squire of Chawton—Bapops—would die, leaving a depleted estate in financial ruin and in desperate need of restoration.

CHAPTER TWO

'Family connexions were always worth preserving,
good company always worth seeking.'

Persuasion – Chapter 16

MY PARENTS, PAUL AND I lived in the north wing. We were a typical family in many respects. My parents were in their twenties when I was born, and they worked hard to raise their two children in a comfortable, joyous and secure environment. My father worked as a leather craftsman for an artificial limb company in Alton. My mother also worked in Alton, as an administrator and physiotherapy aide at the Lord Mayor Treloar Hospital, which specialised in orthopaedic surgery. My mother worked school hours, from nine o'clock in the morning until three o'clock in the afternoon.

My father was clever and resourceful, a hands-on problem-solver rather than an academic and always had one project or other on the go; he cleared overgrown gardens, made improvements to our quarters and carried out many patchwork repairs to other parts of the house. He enjoyed the company of friends at dinner parties and liked to engage in lively conversation about the issues of the day. My mother was more reserved and down to earth, with a strong work ethic and high moral standards.

She grew up in Australia and did well at school, but she chose to marry and have a family rather than continue with her studies—otherwise she could have easily gone to university.

Most of the manor has three floors, some with cellars underneath, except for the north wing which has four floors, including the basement quarters down an internal flight of steps close to the original house kitchen—'below stairs'. The basement quarters included a corridor and four rooms once used for storage, including a knife room, a linen store for the housekeeper and a china room, which housed dinner services and tea sets. The rooms were half underground; the base of the high windows in each room was at ground level. Bapops had a kitchen and a bathroom installed in the 1950s to provide accommodation for Mr Munn and his wife, the only staff retained in my father's youth other than nannies for the children. Mr Munn had worked in and around the house as a handyman, while Mrs Munn worked as a cook and undertook domestic work.

With the Munns long since departed, my parents and Paul moved into the basement before I was born. With only one bedroom, the basement was not big enough, and my father hatched a plan to extend it. A disused boiler room on the other side of the kitchen wall offered the solution. My parents undertook the job together, using sledgehammers to knock a door-sized hole through the 36-inch-thick wall of the kitchen to the double-depth room beyond, where the old boiler was still in place on the floor deep underground. Joists were installed above the boiler and floorboards laid and, because the newly created room did not extend the full width of the boiler room, walls were constructed. After a door was fitted to allow entry to and from the kitchen, my mother made curtains for the windows. Carpet was laid, the room was decorated, and it was finally ready for Paul to use as a bedroom.

I was born late afternoon on 28 August 1970, a few weeks before Paul turned five. With older cousins named Jane and Cassandra, I was named

Caroline Jane—Caroline after Caroline Austen, a niece of Jane's who had later written and published her memories of her aunt, and Jane after Jane herself. I was christened in Chawton Church, and the occasion was followed by tea and cakes in the Great Hall.

Paul and I shared his bedroom until, when I was a toddler, my father knocked through the wall of the boiler room to the gunroom beyond to add yet another bedroom to the basement flat. A door was fitted, the room was plastered and decorated, and carpet was laid on the stone floors. Because of limited funds, my parents once again completed the renovations, with help from a neighbour when more hands were needed.

The bedrooms were not big in comparison to others in the house, but the living accommodation was spacious with a large kitchen, bathroom and sitting room, the latter complete with open fireplace and plenty of room for a dining table and chairs to seat eight. My parents loved having the company of friends for dinner, and they had the perfect surroundings for entertaining. They grew vegetables in an extensive vegetable plot they had created in the walled garden and liked to use as much home-grown produce as possible so they could give their guests a delicious meal and an enjoyable evening.

The walled garden was at the top of the south-west lawns that swept up behind the house and past the large copper beech tree, which took pride of place at the edge of the woods. The beech's huge crown of red in the autumn was spectacular against the green backdrop of lawns and woodlands, and its immense convoluted trunk provided hours of make-believe and enjoyment. Beyond the beech tree sat a large weeping willow in front of the top terrace walk.

The neat path along the edge of the lawns between the house and the terrace had long ago been claimed by grass and overgrown bushes, but it could still be made out underfoot. At the top, there was a marvellous view, and being far from the road, it was a quiet place to enjoy the unspoiled sounds of the birds. Pheasants, rooks, jackdaws, pigeons, blackbirds, thrushes, jays and sparrows were in abundance, and in the winter, robins with their red breasts could easily be seen against the bleak winter background.

My father recalls having seen, as a young boy, murmurations of starlings twisting and changing direction at a moment's notice as if interconnected, but there were few starlings remaining in my childhood. I also recall my father saying Jane mentioned starlings in *Mansfield Park*, and it was easy to imagine Jane and Cassandra, after lunch at the Great House, taking a walk to the top of the lawns to be treated to a mesmerising display of starlings swooping and diving.

The path continued to the rose garden on the left or straight ahead to the open parklands stretching towards Farringdon, a neighbouring village. Jane would have known these fields and paddocks to be part of her brother's estate. The edge of the woodlands marked our south-western boundary. The estate parklands had been sold decades earlier to be farmed with crops and livestock. The walled garden had once been at the front of the house, but Edward Austen Knight had it moved—Jane included garden improvements in *Mansfield Park* as well.

On the far side of the rose garden, two large ornate wrought-iron gates led to a fully enclosed flint-walled garden. It had once been an orchard, with dozens of fruit trees when my father was a boy, but it had long since been abandoned and become overgrown.

When I was too young to remember, by parents devised a plan to turn the walled garden into a vegetable garden. A farmer friend helped to clear the ground with a tractor and rotavator. The vegetable garden provided far more growing space than my parents could manage alone, so they shared the garden beds, work and crops with two local couples. My mother had become close friends with two of the physiotherapists she worked with at the hospital, Trish and Daryl. Daryl and her husband moved to South Africa when I was about nine, but Trish and her husband, Dennis, continued to share the garden with my parents year after year and became great family friends. They lived only ten minutes away and visited most days from spring through to harvest at the end of each summer to tend the vegetable garden.

I loved to spend time with my father in this garden, helping with the weeding, picking runner beans and collecting potatoes. While turning the soil with a fork, he would explain why some crops had grown better than others, and he would share his next plan for the garden—he always had a plan. I helped sprinkle seeds as he made furrows in the soil with a tool he fashioned from an old fork handle.

About a dozen apple trees, a couple of pear trees and some plum trees remained from the days of the orchard and provided fruit for cooking and for eating fresh, along with newly planted strawberries and rhubarb. The garden was divided into plots for different crops and rotated yearly. One plot was used for root vegetables: potatoes, parsnips, carrots, onions and leeks. Another was used for cabbages, cauliflower, broccoli and Brussels sprouts. Lettuces and other salad greens were planted under rows of glass cloches to protect them from the occasional frost. Rows of tepees made from bamboo, cut from the cluster in the woods, allowed French beans and runner beans to climb. Courgettes and marrows grew to gargantuan sizes, but as with beans and carrots, they were usually picked smaller when at their sweetest and most tender.

I wanted to talk to my father more than I wanted to garden and usually left him to it after an hour or so when the chatter died down and the hard work began. I would often return at lunchtime to walk with him to the house for a sandwich or later in the afternoon with cold refreshments on a warm day.

Beans, peas and other suitable vegetables were blanched before being frozen for use in the winter months. This job seemed to take my parents days— huge boiling pots were used, and the vegetables were drained in the largest colanders I have ever seen. Every vegetable had to be chopped, boiled, cooled, bagged and labelled, and my parents heaved a sigh of relief as the last bag was sealed. Our family's winter supplies were stored in large chest freezers in the old house kitchen. Other crops were also prepared for long-term storage. My father carefully laid apples on sacks in the old apple store at the back of the house so as not to touch each other, before being covered and kept fresh for up to five months, while my mother froze or preserved in jars the berries, plums and other soft fruits.

I always had good intentions to help my parents, but I quickly tired of this repetitive work and left them to it. I was expected to keep my room tidy and to help clear up after dinner, but my parents never insisted I join them in the hours of work they put into the estate or the garden.

At least a couple of times a year there was a power cut, sometimes lasting a few days. My parents, worried that their home-grown produce would spoil, would cover all the freezers with blankets, but I thought power cuts were exciting and fun. On such occasions, we cooked and ate our meals by candle-light, huddling around the open fire for warmth and light. 'What game would you like to play first?' my mother would ask, to which I would always reply, 'giant dominos' and reach for the box of large tiles, each bigger than a playing card and with brightly coloured spots. I liked board games and cards. My father and I played cribbage together regularly, but we played giant dominos as a family only when the power was off.

The rest of the house was rather unnerving when the lights were out: the dark oak-panelled walls, the creaky floors, the stories of resident ghosts, and the many portraits of our ancestors with eyes that followed me as I walked past. I was easily spooked in my grandparents' quarters at night and felt re-lieved that we lived tucked away in the corner of the house, half underground. Our living quarters in the basement had white walls, carpeted floors and no portraits, and I was sure the ghosts that roamed 'above stairs' would not ven-ture into the servants' quarters. I had never seen any trace of the Grey Lady, who was said to walk through my father's old bedroom in my grandparents' quarters, or the poltergeist that was said to inhabit the Blue Room, but I was wary none the less.

As a very young child, I did not give our home, the grounds or our family heritage much thought. But this changed when we moved to the first-floor quarters of the north wing when I was twelve. Our new quarters were 'above stairs'—rooms built for the squire and his family to occupy—and were opulent in comparison to the converted storerooms below.

My mother told me about the move at the beginning of the summer in 1983, a few months before my thirteenth birthday. Paul had already moved to the Blue Room, a vacant bedroom on the second floor of the north wing. I was keen to have a larger bedroom, so I was excited by the news. I had rarely been into the rooms on the first floor of the north wing because they had been occupied by tenants since I was born.

When my father returned from work, just after five, my parents and I walked up the stairs to the first-floor corridor to have a look at our new quarters. Portraits in oil were set into the oak-panelled walls. I was most struck by the portrait of a woman in a sumptuous blue taffeta gown, with white ruffles at the sleeves and around the plunging neckline—to preserve her modesty, I assumed. The other portraits were of men.

The woman in the blue taffeta gown was called Elizabeth, my father said. With a double chin, pink cheeks and dark hair pinned away from her round face, she looked well fed. I decided she had been an important woman, the mistress of the house dressed in her luxurious robes, her elbow resting on a velvet cushion. She wasn't terribly pretty, and like the *Mona Lisa*, her expression was difficult to read and open to interpretation. Her eyes were slightly squinted as if she could see something or someone behind the artist that displeased her, or perhaps she was frustrated at having to spend her time sitting for a portrait. Elizabeth looked like a woman not to be trifled with—much like Granny, I thought; she could be very forthright.

Opposite the portrait of Elizabeth was a door to the original dining room of the house, which would become the sitting room of our new quarters. At one time, the squire's quarters would have encompassed these rooms, but my grandfather had separated off the north wing decades before. Equally as splendid as the Great Hall next door, our new sitting room was complete with a large stone-mantel fireplace, floor-to-ceiling oak panelling and leaded-light windows to two aspects with beautiful views across the front of the estate— our basement windows had not offered any views to speak of.

From a window seat, I could see across the front of the house to the south-east lawns. Overgrown woodlands on the other side of the lawns partially blocked what would otherwise have been an uninterrupted view across the estate parklands. With clear sight of the front entrance of the house, the window seat offered a perfect spot to view who came and went. This, coupled with the above-stairs decor, gave the quarters a different atmosphere to the basement, where it had been easy to forget the main house. Only one flight of stairs separated our old and new quarters, but the difference was pronounced. We were now in the squire's quarters, and the grandeur was plain to see.

The dining room had hosted dinners for generations; only a short distance from the house kitchen via a passage, it was convenient for service. The bell to summon the servants had been disconnected long ago, but the button was still in place in the dining room, and the brass bell still hung in the servants' passage.

How wonderful it would have been to go back in time—just for a minute—to see the silver service in full flow. 'We four sweet Brothers & Sisters dine today at the Gt House. Is not that quite natural?' Jane wrote to Caroline Austen in March 1815. It was easy to imagine the room filled with lively conversation and finely dressed guests seated around Edward Austen Knight's grand dining table. Did Jane and Cassandra always sit in the same seats, or did their position at the dinner table depend on other company present? The table had long since been removed from the dining room; my father had found it in pieces in the old house kitchen, where Granny had been using it for sorting her washing! My father had rescued the table and reassembled it in the Great Hall, where it was used for family lunches with Granny and Bapops.

A striking wooden carving graced the wall above the fireplace mantel, towering up to the high ceiling. Carved in relief from oak to match the panelled walls and fireside columns, a wide central panel showed a shield with four quarters on the left and two halves on the right. Two of the four quarters on the left, with diagonal lozenges, were instantly recognisable as Knight arms. In traditional style, the arms sat above the family motto and below a knight's helmet with an effigy of the Greyfriar topmost, all surrounded by foliage, just like the arms above the front entrance to the house. In bold relief below the motto was a date—'1895'.

To the left, a narrower panel featured flowers and leaves, and the initials 'MGK'. A matching panel to the right carried the initials 'FK'. My father explained that 1895 was the twenty-fifth wedding anniversary of Montagu, the thirteenth squire, and his wife, Florence. The left of the arms in the middle panel were Montagu's four quarters: Knight, Austen, Leigh (Jane Austen's mother was a Leigh) and Knight again—the same as those of his grandfather, Edward Austen Knight. Florence's arms were on the right. Did Montagu design and install the carving secretly and, once it was in place, surprise Florence? Or had they planned it together? Did Florence influence Montagu's flamboyant design choices? Either way, it was the most romantic gesture of love I had ever seen.

The rest of our new quarters lay down the hallway in the extension, which had originally added a billiard room with an open fire and windows to two aspects. The billiard table and lights had long since been removed and the room split into two to provide another spacious sitting room and a kitchen beyond. My father was planning to fit a new kitchen into a corner of the sitting room and convert the kitchen into a bedroom for me.

The Tapestry Gallery upstairs provided access to not only Paul's new bedroom and our new bathroom but also the back of my grandparents' quarters, the tenants' quarters above the billiard room, the backstairs that led to the house kitchen on the ground floor, and the staircase up to my cousins' quarters on the top floor.

A door at the corner of the Tapestry Gallery opened to the top of the backstairs, a convenient route from our basement quarters to Fiona on the top floor, without the need to walk through my grandparents' or any of the tenants' living quarters. Despite having used these stairs many times, I had never before noticed in the dim light of the stairway a dark oak door on the right at the top of the stairs. The door wasn't easy to open, but when my father gave it a firm shove to move whatever was blocking access, I was surprised to see that the door opened to the north-west end of Suicide Alley. It was actually the picture gallery, but we called it Suicide Alley because the passage was so cluttered that one risked injury simply by entering it.

The wide unused corridor, originally built for servants to move around the first floor without the need to go through the family's bedroom chambers, was crammed with unused and broken furniture, dusty boxes, picture frames, books, riding boots, coats and ornaments—decades of family possessions stored with good intentions for later use or disposal. I had seen only the south-east end of Suicide Alley on the first-floor landing of my grandparents' quarters. I hadn't realised that the door visible at the far end, behind all the boxes, opened at the top of the backstairs.

My father pulled back a curtain behind some discarded furniture to reveal a large leaded-light window I had never seen before. It overlooked the inner courtyard and depicted six shields in stained glass that traced the coats of arms of each successive owner of Chawton House. There was a second set of six behind another curtain around the corner on my grandparents' landing, which also overlooked the courtyard. The windows had been installed by Montagu, and they were beautiful—just like the carving above the fireplace. Under each vibrantly coloured shield were the names of the squires with their arms and the date of their inheritance of the house. The stained-glass windows became my favourite record of the names and dates of my ancestors.

Multiple squires were listed underneath a few of the shields in the stained-glass windows, but most shields listed only one squire. Although each shield was a different combination of arms—evidence of families joining through marriage, inheritance and adoption—every shield included the gold lozenges set diagonally on a green background. Some of the squires were of particular note and familiar to me, but other names I knew little about. From the first squire to the last, each was named Knight.

Long before I first saw the stained-glass windows, I had seen in my grand-parents' quarters an iron fireback marked 'JK 1588'—the name and date under the first glass shield was 'John 1583'. John Knight was the principal builder of the house. I was about seven when I first calculated that my family had owned Chawton for nearly four centuries—it was such a long time, it might as well have been forever. I later discovered that the Knights had been in Chawton for over six and a half centuries and had held land in the parish since at least 1307.

The Middle Ages were impossible for me to imagine, but I could picture England in the sixteenth century. I had seen repeats of the 1971 BBC series *Elizabeth R* with Glenda Jackson playing Queen Elizabeth I. The interiors of the buildings in the series were very similar to those in Chawton House, and I could imagine how John Knight might have dressed and spoken; he contributed £50 to the funds raised by the Queen to defend the realm against the Spanish Armada, commemorated by the fireback, and I pictured him as a serious man with great presence. John died leaving no heir, and his brother Stephen became the second squire of the new manor house.

The stained-glass windows made it easy for me to establish just how many squires there had been. 'John 1583', 'Stephen 1620', 'John 1627', 'Richard 1636' and 'Sir Richard 1641' completed the names under the first three shields. Sir Richard inherited Chawton estate in 1641 when he was only two. In practice, his mother managed the property on her young son's behalf. This is believed to have saved the house from being burnt to the ground during the English Civil War, as other manor houses in the area, such as Basing House, were destroyed by Oliver Cromwell's army, the 'Roundheads'. 'Richard was so young, Cromwell couldn't tell what shape his head was,' My father once joked. I couldn't believe how lucky we had been—Chawton House could so easily have been lost.

King Charles I, guarded by a strong body of troops, came through Chawton village on his last sad journey from Hurst Castle on the Hampshire south coast to Windsor on his way to the Palace of Whitehall where he was executed. It was hard to imagine such an important but sombre procession in our pretty village. Were the streets empty, or did people come out of their houses to watch?

Richard was the only 'sir' in the family. At the Restoration of the monarchy in 1660, when Richard had just come of age, his name appeared on a list for the proposed new order of the Knights of the Royal Oak. The idea was later abandoned by Charles II, but Richard did receive the honour of a knighthood on 10 January 1667, and I was super proud of him. I assumed Uncle Richard had been named after Sir Richard—Bapops keen to ensure his heir was given a traditional and respected family name as he had been. Sir Richard left no children and chose another Richard—Richard Martin, his aunt's grandson, as his successor on the condition that he took the name of Knight. The name 'Richard' was obviously of some amusement to Jane. At the beginning of *Northanger Abbey*, Jane tells us that Catherine Morland's father was 'a very respectable man, though his name was Richard.'

'Richard 1679' and 'Christopher 1687' were under the next shield, which included a quarter of arms with three birds (at least that is what they looked like to me). Both Martin brothers were also childless, making three childless squires in succession. 'Who decides who the next squire will be?' I asked, and my father explained that it was the duty of each squire to name their heir, usually their eldest son. If the squire had no children, it was his responsibility to find the most suitable male relative to continue the family legacy and prepare him for the responsibilities he would inherit.

The fifth and sixth shields were startlingly different from the others. Under the fifth shield were the words 'William Woodward Knight Elizabeth Knight 1702 1ST Husband', while under the sixth were 'Bulstrode Peachey Knight Elizabeth Knight 1702 2ND Husband'. I was surprised when my father said that neither William nor Bulstrode had inherited the house. It was Elizabeth Martin—Richard and Christopher's sister—who had inherited the house from her brother the same year Queen Anne inherited the Crown. I was shocked to learn that a woman had run the estate; I had always thought only a man could inherit Chawton. Both of Elizabeth's husbands took her new surname, such was the importance of the Knight name remaining in control of the estate. On each marriage, a new shield was created, with Elizabeth's arms on the left and her husband's on the right.

Elizabeth ran the estates for thirty-five years and occupied a central position in the history of Chawton. She was a woman of strong character, masterful but affectionate, with a keen sense of the duties and the dignity required of the resident landowner. I had assumed that the woman with the pink cheeks and blue taffeta gown in the portrait in our new quarters had been the wife of a squire. But in fact, she had been in charge; she was Elizabeth Martin Knight, a highly competent woman, who secured and expanded the estate as effectively as the most capable of male squires.

I had accepted without question the succession of men to the position of squire, assuming it the ancient laws of the land. But it wasn't. Perhaps the family had adopted the tradition after Elizabeth, or perhaps an exception had been made for her. Whatever the circumstances, I believed Elizabeth served as proof that a woman could do equally as good a job as a man. I thought about it some more, unsure whether this was a sensible measure for the success of the estate or simply unfair. My Uncle Richard was Bapops's firstborn, so the question of succession when a daughter is the eldest child had not arisen.

I wonder what Jane thought of Elizabeth—Jane must have known how well she managed the estates in the eighteenth century. Did Fanny Knight, denied the opportunity due to her gender despite being Edward Austen Knight's firstborn child, feel the injustice? Jane and Fanny were very close; was it discussed? Perhaps Fanny saw the burdens her father had endured with legal challenges to his ownership of Chawton (from Hinton and Baverstock, descendants of the Martins, who believed that under some conditions of inheritance for Chawton they had a right to the estate—I didn't know the details) and the associated financial losses, and was happy the responsibility had passed her by.

However, I didn't need to look as far back as Fanny to see this tradition in action. I was again taken by surprise when my father explained that Aunt Betty, my great-aunt who lived in Alton and who was the only regular visitor I knew Bapops to have, was Bapops's older sister. I was curious to know how Aunt Betty, another Elizabeth, felt about visiting the childhood home that would have been hers to inherit if she were a man or if the tradition of male succession had not existed? Did she wish she had been squire or was it a relief not to have inherited the responsibility? But she never talked about it, and I never would have asked Aunt Betty such personal questions.

I was not sure who would have been known as 'the squire'—Elizabeth or her successive husbands. I decided to count Elizabeth as the eighth squire—after all, she was the one who had inherited and run the estate from 1702 to 1737. Like her brothers, Elizabeth had no children and chose as her successor her second cousin Thomas from the Brodnax branch of her family. Thomas was also heir to Godmersham Park, and his succession brought the estates together under the same squire. Elizabeth seemed as significant to the family's landholdings as Queen Anne had been to Britain. Under Queen Anne's reign, The Acts of Union passed by the English and Scottish parliaments in 1707 led to the creation of the United Kingdom of Great Britain, governed by a single monarch.

Thomas had already received his inheritance from the May family and, as a condition, had changed his name to Thomas May by an Act of Parliament, as was required. When he sought another Act of Parliament to change his name once more—to Knight, to inherit Chawton House—it was flippantly suggested in the House of Commons that a law be passed to allow Thomas to call himself whatever he liked. 'Or whatever he *May*,' my father quipped.

This was the Thomas Knight who was second cousin to George Austen and who appointed George the Rector of Steventon, a parish Thomas had also inherited from Elizabeth Martin Knight. Like all previous shields, Thomas's shield included the Knight arms of gold lozenges set diagonally on a green background but with the addition of a small flower towards the bottom left. The arms were altered to signify the distance of the blood relationship between Elizabeth and Thomas. 'Thomas 1737' and 'Thomas 1781' were the names under the next two shields. Thomas left the estates to his son, Thomas II, who was childless and who, at the end of the eighteenth century, chose Jane's older brother, Edward Austen, my fourth great-grandfather, as his heir. In 1791, Edward married Elizabeth, daughter of Sir Brook Bridges, a British baronet and Whig politician—so my grandparents were not the first couple named Edward and Elizabeth Knight to have run the estate.

'Edward 1794' was under the next shield. I was a little confused because I had previously heard that Jane's brother had been squire from 1798, so my father explained that Thomas had died in 1794 but his wife, Catherine, had run the estates for four years after his death before passing control to Edward.

He was commonly referred to as Edward Austen Knight, despite never having carried both surnames, and Edward's heraldry included both the Knight and Austen arms. The Austen arms, a red chevron with three black bear paws, came from John Austen Esq. of Broadford in Kent. In his book, Montagu Knight describes Broadford as 'a picturesque Elizabethan residence'. Over the fireplace in the entrance hall are the Austen arms, with the date '1587'— only a year earlier than the 'JK 1588' fireback in my grandparents' quarters. The Austens had equally as long a history as the Knights.

When Edward Austen inherited the Chawton estate, the Knight arms of lozenges with a small flower were altered once more, with the addition of a red square in the top-left corner to signify the fourth-cousin blood relationship between Thomas II and Edward. In 1812, Edward changed his name—and thus my own—to Knight. 'Papa changed his name about this time in compliance with the will of the late Mr. Knight and we are therefore all <u>Knights</u> instead of dear old <u>Austens</u> How I hate it!' noted Fanny in her diary. Jane drily commented in a letter to Martha Lloyd, 'I must learn to make a better K.' But Jane did pay her respects to the Knight name, my family said, and appreciated the circumstances that had led to her life in Chawton village. The hero of her fourth novel, *Emma*, written in Chawton three years later, was a perfect English gentleman named Mr Knightley.

The next two shields depicted the two marriages of Edward II, the eldest son of Edward Austen Knight. A portrait of Edward II hung opposite the stained-glass windows directly outside Granny's bedroom door. I had seen the portrait many times. He was a tall, proud man with a huge unruly moustache, a top hat and a cane. He had a serious face and eyes that followed me as I walked past. With portraits throughout my grandparents' quarters, I was always under the watchful eye of one ancestor or another—it could be most disconcerting.

The portrait portrayed none of the scandal or mystery that surrounded Edward II. He eloped with his first wife, Mary Knatchbull, and they subsequently had seven children. Mary died in 1838 at the young age of thirty-one, leaving Edward with her six surviving children, including four sons. Edward had nine children with his second wife, Adela Portal; the eldest died in infancy, only five weeks after his younger brother Montagu was born. Montagu George Knight, the second-born son of Edward II and Adela, became heir and inherited the estate upon his father's death in 1879. I wondered why Edward II's surviving sons from his first marriage were overlooked in favour of their younger half-brother. Were none of them suitable for the job, or did Adela assert her influence upon her husband? I couldn't help but think of Adela when I later read *Sense and Sensibility*—Mrs John Dashwood showed exactly how persuasive a wife could be.

After six years of marriage, Montagu and Florence had not had children, and for the eighth time in our history, the squire did not have an heir. Montagu chose his brother's firstborn son, Lionel, Bapops's father, to succeed him. From my observations, Montagu had been a proud squire. The history of the house had been enhanced by the installation, under his stewardship, of both the carving above the fireplace and the stained-glass windows. In 1911, he co-wrote a book, *Chawton Manor and Its Owners: A Family History*, with his cousin William Austen Leigh (who went on to write *Jane Austen: Her Life and Letters, A Family Record*, published in 1913). Even his grave was the most elaborate in the family section of the church graveyard. Clearly, Montagu celebrated his custodianship of Chawton and wanted to leave his mark. Perhaps, because his brother's descendants were to continue the family legacy, he wanted to ensure he was not forgotten. Or perhaps he had something to prove.

My mind burst with all the twists and turns of the inheritance of the house over the centuries—for me, the convolutions of the family tree were as confusing as the layout of the house. Chawton estate passing from father to eldest son was said to be tradition, but our history showed this not to be the case for the majority of the squires. Since John Knight—the first squire in the stained-glass windows—the house had been passed from father to eldest son on only five occasions, the last being from Lionel to Bapops, the fifteenth squire, in 1932.

The final stained-glass window depicted Montagu. Some of the portraits in the house were labelled, and I had heard most of our ancestors' names or read them on the church wall plaques, but I had not previously understood how they were all connected. The stained-glass windows explained the line of succession. There were other windows on the landing ready for more stained glass to be installed, but neither Lionel nor Bapops had added their own names. Neither used their heraldry or a coat of arms or installed grand gestures of their position; it was as if they didn't care to be remembered. The eyes that had watched me all these years were leaders who generation after generation had succeeded in retaining the estate, despite the challenges they faced. These were our forefathers, and I understood the weight of responsibility on Bapops's shoulders to continue their legacy.

The precise connections between the different branches of the family were difficult to understand, complicated by the intricate web of marriages and succession choices. I tried to fathom the relationship between my father and Thomas Knight II, who had adopted Edward Austen. Edward was my father's third great-grandfather, and Thomas was Edward's fourth cousin. I was unable to solve it and gave up. Besides, it didn't matter—we were all Knights from Chawton.

My father's family had lived in the same location for generations, living off wealth and fortune built over centuries. In sharp contrast, my mother's family were on the other side of the world. My mother was the eldest of five children born to Alfred and Florence, a builder and his wife, who had migrated from the East End of London to Australia in 1950 when my mother was three and her brother was an infant. The young family eventually settled in Caltowie, located on the road between Jamestown and Laura in the Mid North region of South Australia. In the mid nineteenth century, during the early years of European settlement, Caltowie was used as a camping ground for teamsters hauling timber, the creek providing a good place for the animals to water. Travellers going north to the forests or south to the copper mines would stop to revive. By the 1950s, Caltowie had grown into a small but bustling town.

My Australian grandparents went on to have three more children. Their fourth child tragically died in infancy. Alf, as we called my grandfather, built residential properties in the region, which often took him away from home for extended periods. Although he worked hard to support his family, they lived a modest life, struggling to make ends meet at times. But the children were well cared for, and the bills were always paid—eventually.

I loved the story of how my parents, from such different backgrounds, had met and fallen in love—I found it so romantic. As was customary, my father travelled after completing his education. He set off by ship from South-ampton to Melbourne. Soon after my father arrived in Melbourne, he was introduced to Dud Sparks, who was looking to hire a farmhand in exchange for board and wages. For two years, my father worked on Dud's farm in the Jamestown area and became proficient in managing both arable land and large herds of sheep.

One Saturday evening, my father went to a dance in Caltowie, a quar-ter-hour drive from Jamestown, and there he met my mother, Carol. My mother, who was in her last year at Jamestown High School and would soon start nursing at Jamestown Hospital, was instantly taken with the handsome young English gentleman. Their love blossomed, and they were married in Caltowie before taking a brief honeymoon near Port Pirie. In September 1965, my brother, Paul Edward Knight, was born in Naracoorte in the south-ern region of South Australia. My father had taken a position 340 miles south on a farm that offered better accommodation for a young family. My mother had no option but to abandon her nursing course.

Within a few weeks of Paul's arrival, Granny flew from England to Australia to meet her new daughter-in-law and grandson and suggested they return to England with her to visit the family in Chawton. My father had mentioned that his family owned a large country house in England, and he carried a crumpled photograph of the manor in his wallet, which my mother had briefly viewed. But the photograph offered no sense of scale, and without any point of comparison, she thought perhaps all houses in England were much like that!

Granny traded in her return airfare in exchange for four tickets to travel home by ship. On the four-week journey to England, Granny took it upon herself to educate my mother—an eighteen-year-old girl from country Australia—in preparation for life in England. Granny delivered a crash course in the etiquette she thought necessary, including dinner-table protocol, and encouraged my mother to sample many alcoholic drinks in search of one she might like—a soft drink over dinner would not do!

Granny was direct and to the point and could not hide her dismay when an instruction was not followed correctly. Having seen cruise ships on television and photographs of Granny when she was younger—a tall, handsome, well-dressed woman with a confident smile—I imagined the most glamorous of voyages. But my mother was not fooled by extravagance and glamour and valued people based on their behaviour and the pleasure of their company, not wealth or position. She believed in personal responsibility and the need to do what must be done. Granny was very fond of my mother.

One cold morning in December 1965, when Paul was only three months old, my mother saw Chawton House for the first time; she was a couple of years younger than Elizabeth Bennet was when she first saw Pemberley. I asked my mother what she had thought as they came up the drive, but she had no clear memory of the moment. After four weeks on a ship and being far away from her remote Australian home and family for the first time, everything was extraordinary, and she was obviously not able to absorb it all.

Although the visit to England had been intended as a holiday, my parents decided to stay and rented a cottage in a nearby village before moving into the basement quarters at Chawton House. In the summer of 1973, my mother took Paul and me to visit our Australian family, and I had my third birthday in South Australia. I couldn't remember it, but I often looked at my mother's few photographs of the trip and dreamed of travelling to Australia again. We were there for the whole of Paul's six-week school holiday from Chawton Primary School, from mid July through to early September. We visited Dud Sparks's farm in Canowie Belt where my father had worked. My mother said Paul and I loved our visit to the farm. We helped with the lambs, we saw where my father had slept, and we sat in the truck he had driven. When the time came to leave Australia, both Paul and I were upset and wanted to stay longer. But our lives were in England now. Paul would soon be returning to school for the commencement of the year, and I was due back at nursery school. We returned as planned.

During my mother's early years in Chawton, the only regular contact she had with her family in Australia was by letter. She was homesick, of course, and missed them. But she fell in love with Chawton, and within a couple of years, my mother was settled. Despite the cultural differences, Granny and Bapops made my mother feel welcome and were sensitive to how far away she was from her family—Bapops even made sure my mother spoke to her parents in Australia on the telephone at least once a year. Telephone exchanges stopped work during the postal workers strike of 1971, but Bapops used his influence to ensure my mother didn't miss the annual call—because family connections are important and always worth preserving.

CHAPTER THREE

'Those who do not complain are never pitied.'
Pride and Prejudice – Chapter 20

I MIXED WELL WITH THE other young children at nursery school, where I enjoyed painting and collage, making pom-poms, and looking at books. However, I was unable to throw a ball in the playground with any degree of accuracy and quickly learnt that I had no sporting talent whatsoever. I was curious as a child. I always had something to say and was frequently told to 'stop talking' when I 'should be listening'. I was impatient to learn to write. I thought my mother's joined-up writing was the cleverest thing I had ever seen, and I would write squiggles along the lines in my exercise book as I pretended to be the author of a recipe book—'Whisk three egg whites in a bowl'—or perhaps even a great novelist—'It is a truth universally acknowledged'. I had carefully inspected Jane's letters in Chawton Cottage, but I couldn't read her writing at all.

My earliest memory is of the day my mother brought a basket of puppies into the nursery school, located in the grounds of the hospital where she worked. My father's gun dog Candy, a black Labrador, had given birth to ten puppies—five yellow and five black—which my father had bred for sale.

My nursery classmates were delighted to see them, and there was much excitement as the tiny black and yellow bundles huddled together, eyes tightly shut. One of the puppies, a yellow male, had no fur on its nose and was difficult to sell. But Granny was rather taken with him, and 'Flash', as she called him, became her faithful companion for the next fifteen years or so.

Flash was my grandparents' only pet, other than Granny's chickens. Dozens of them roamed the inner courtyard of the house and the large coop at the edge of the lawns. Granny rose at dawn every day and let the chickens out to wander freely around the lawns and woodlands. She shut them back in their coops before dusk each night to keep them safe from the foxes that ranged over the estate. A cunning fox would occasionally dig its way into the coop, and Granny would wake to a massacre, much to her chagrin. She was not at all squeamish about animal husbandry and would slaughter and pluck chickens without a second thought. The cockerels delivered their familiar crowing across the estate each morning and ensured Granny's brood laid well and produced chicks in abundance. Granny collected dozens of eggs daily for cooking and baking; she was always baking for something or other.

For as long as I could remember, I had spent a couple of hours a day with Granny at the weekends; I liked to help her cook and run errands. Granny also looked after Paul and me during the school holidays. When my parents went out for an evening, I slept in Granny's bedroom, or the Green Room, which was identical in both size and shape to the library directly below. The leaded-light windows on two aspects of Granny's bedroom overlooked the lawns, the terraced garden and 'The Bottles'—trees clipped into the shape of wine bottles. There were two double beds, a screen, a wardrobe, two chests of drawers, a large mirror, a couple of mismatched chairs and an ironing table covered in a blanket. On the wall hung an original 1783 silhouette by William Wellings of London (who famously painted a silhouette of Pitt the

Younger) which showed George Austen presenting his son Edward to Thomas and Catherine Knight.

'Time for bed, Mabel Lucie,' Granny would say at seven o'clock sharp and give me a biscuit and a glass of milk for supper. We all had nicknames. I assume I was named after Mabel Lucie Attwell (1879–1964), a British illustrator or, more likely, after her cute drawings of dimpled children (I had a dimple on each cheek), but I never asked. I have no idea why Paul was called William and other cousins were called Beetle and Bun. It was a long-held tradition—Jane Austen had been called Jennie by her family, and Edward Austen Knight was known as Ned.

I felt safe and secure tucked in to Granny's spare bed. When the lights went out, it was silent except for the occasional sound of an owl or a fox, and I slept soundly.

When the Chawton cricket team played at home, Granny provided the cricket teas for both the Saturday and Sunday home matches for some years— and on just one of the two days for the other years. By the time I had dressed and arrived to help at about nine o'clock, two cakes were already baked, cooled and ready to ice. Granny was an instinctive cook, calculating most measurements by eye, except when she baked cakes. Then she would use her cast-iron balance scales to weigh the flour, sugar, and butter. These were put into a large Mason Cash cane bowl with some eggs and mixed by hand or with a handheld electric beater—Granny's only modern appliance. The mixture would be poured into cake tins that were floured but never washed. I would butter rounds and rounds of white bread, to be filled with ham and egg. I mixed coffee essence with softened butter and icing sugar and filled the coffee cake. The Victoria sponge was sandwiched with jam and sprinkled with sugar, and chocolate icing was poured over the chocolate cake.

Granny didn't ask about my schoolwork, academic achievements or friends. She encouraged me to be 'accomplished'. I learnt to play the piano, sew, cook, draw, and paint. I also learnt various handicrafts, such as decoupage, and I would proudly show her what I had made. We talked for hours as we worked. She told me many stories of her 'coming out' as a debutante—I assumed it was a time she remembered with fondness.

When sharing her memories with me, Granny told me the facts only, such as her attendance at a ball where she was presented as a young woman formally ready to consider marriage—within a select circle. She didn't tell me how she felt about anything, and she spoke in a manner that did not invite probing questions or encourage a granddaughter with a curious mind to enquire beyond the superficial. Having seen photographs of Granny as a younger woman, I knew she had been attractive and had obviously had an expensive custom-made wardrobe. I asked about the fine dresses she had worn, but she ignored my question as though she didn't want to remember. Granny was sixty-six at the time, tall and heavy, and she seemed to take little notice of her appearance. Her hair was white, and she never wore make-up, but her face lit up when she smiled.

Granny had been raised in privileged circumstances, but both her parents died when she was a girl—I didn't know the details. Her mother was from the respected Heywood–Jones family of Yorkshire, descended from Edward III of England, and her father was from the Scottish clan of Hay. My father had a tie made of the bright orange Hay tartan. Granny was well educated and well travelled. She had attended finishing school in France and trained as a chef. She was a capable woman and able to turn her hand to most tasks. She had ridden horses and been quite a good shot by all accounts—legend has it Granny once felled two pheasants with one shot. An aunt told my mother that she and Granny had once driven past Bletchley Park near Milton Keynes, the central site for Britain's codebreakers during the Second World War, and Granny, who was fluent in French, commented that she had worked there, but she didn't elaborate.

It was a special time being alone with Granny, uninterrupted in her kitchen for a couple of hours. Granny told me stories about her younger life, but she never once mentioned Bapops, or the diminishing estate, or what would happen to her if Bapops died. Granny didn't talk about personal things, and I never plucked up the courage to ask. I didn't know whether she was content with the life she had and the responsibilities that fell on her shoulders.

I don't know how much input Bapops had behind the scenes, but Granny appeared to run every aspect of their daily lives. She looked after Bapops, shopped, cooked, ran errands, prepared for family events, managed Mr Humphries, dealt with tradespeople and the local community for events held at the house, ran a tea room, liaised with tenants and ensured the house ran smoothly on a day-to-day basis. She seemed happy enough going about her business, other than the physical discomfort of arthritis, and never spoke a bad word about Bapops. Occasionally I would see Granny and Bapops reach across from their armchairs and affectionately hold hands under the side table, so I hoped she had no regrets.

One Sunday morning, I suggested that the cricketers might enjoy some lettuce or tomato with their ham sandwiches. 'Salad isn't for sandwiches!' Granny responded as if it were the most preposterous of notions. I changed the subject and asked Granny what India was like. My father had told me that Granny had visited India in the 1940s with her first husband, who had died while they were away. Bapops, a major in the British Army at the time, was also in India, and that is where Granny and Bapops first met. I didn't know the details and hoped Granny would tell me, but she ignored my question and didn't talk about India at all. As I buttered the bread for the *plain* ham sandwiches, she told me that Jane had turned down a good offer of marriage and what an extraordinary decision this had been, given her circumstances. Granny didn't talk about Jane often, so I was quite surprised.

Jane was born in Steventon in 1775 and had a happy childhood in the rectory. In 1801, when she was twenty-six, Jane's father suddenly announced his intention to retire and move his wife and daughters from Steventon to Bath, sixty-five miles away. Jane's brother James was to take over the Steventon parish. 'The whole World is in a conspiracy to enrich one part of our family at the expense of another,' Jane wrote to Cassandra on 21 May 1801. Legend has it that Jane fainted upon hearing the news, but that is hard to believe. No doubt she would have been very sad to leave her childhood home and her friends, whom she was unlikely to see very often, but Jane did not have such a 'delicate constitution'. The familiar surroundings and memories of her family home would be lost of course, but the tranquillity and open space of the Hampshire countryside would be replaced with the hustle, bustle and excitement of a city.

The house in Bath was much smaller than the rectory, and many of their possessions had to be sold, including most of George's extensive collection of books. The library was my favourite room in Chawton House, and yet I looked at the books only occasionally. For a writer like Jane, who read many of her father's books, this must have been a huge loss. Jane also sacrificed her piano. Granny had given me a second-hand piano as a Christmas present when I was five, and I had played ever since. Playing music was one of my biggest joys, and I couldn't imagine the frustration of being without an instrument. I decided it would be wise to learn to play a portable instrument and chose the guitar.

Jane must have known that her father would likely retire one day, and with her brothers no longer at home, the day would come when they would leave the Steventon Rectory. But she may not have thought that far ahead or she may have assumed they would remain living in the village—or at least in Hampshire in familiar surroundings. I could not bear to think about my family ever having to leave Chawton; perhaps Jane had felt the same way.

Whether Jane had thought about it or not, the family left Steventon in 1801. It was commonly believed that Jane didn't like Bath, but as with many things said about Jane's feelings and personality, this was speculation; how could anyone know for certain? Even when reading Jane's letters in which she wrote of her feelings and views, it can be difficult to determine whether she was purposely being amusing or enjoying a private joke with her correspondent.

In December 1802, Jane was visiting some friends in Manydown House near Steventon and received a proposal of marriage from her friend's younger brother, Harris Bigg-Wither, who was nearly six years Jane's junior. We laughed at how different it would have sounded—*Pride and Prejudice* by Jane Bigg-Wither, although there would have been little chance of her devoting her time to writing had she married. Jane accepted the proposal, and the house celebrated. After what must have been a sleepless night, Jane changed her mind and withdrew her acceptance the next morning. Jane shared a bedroom with Cassandra, as she had all her life. I desperately wanted to know why Jane changed her mind—it was such a pivotal decision for Jane's future and our family heritage. But Granny said no one would ever be certain what Jane thought, except perhaps Cassandra, who no doubt had talked it through with Jane overnight. How I wish I could go back in time and listen to that conversation.

The marriage would have offered Jane a secure future, as Harris Bigg-Wither had become heir following the death of his older brother. Jane would have eventually become the mistress of Manydown House, an ancient manor dating back to the fourteenth century, surrounded by 1,500 acres of parklands and 400 acres of plantations. Manydown was not far from Steventon, so the marriage would also have returned Jane to the Hampshire countryside.

Caroline Austen, daughter of Jane's brother James, described Harris as not attractive—he was a large, plain-looking man, aggressive and almost completely tactless in conversation, hardly a good match for Jane. But a marriage to Bigg-Wither would have offered relief from poverty, a stately home, security for her parents and sister, and many advantageous associations for her brothers. Jane had a choice: all the practical advantages and lifelong security that would result from marrying a man she didn't love or remaining in Bath in relative poverty with no imminent prospects of her or her parents' situation improving. Jane had no way of knowing whether she would receive another offer of marriage. They had been in Bath for only a year, so perhaps she thought there would be other opportunities for marriage, or perhaps she loved someone else. If Jane were in love, I don't think it was with Tom Lefroy, who she had supposedly fallen for six years earlier in Steventon as Montagu's book tells a different story:

> In the early years of her womanhood she had composed at all
> events the first drafts of three of the six novels on which her fame
> rests.... Then follow six or eight years of almost absolute silence.
> Shortly before the beginning of this period occurred, probably, the
> one romance of her life. We have it on the authority of her sister
> that about that time Jane met in the West of England a young
> man between whom and herself was formed a mutual bond of
> attachment, soon to be snapped asunder by his death.

There was no mention of Tom Lefroy.

Granny and I worked in silence for a while as I pondered Jane's decision. Perhaps Jane had known that marriage would bring responsibilities that would consume her time and make it difficult for her to write, and perhaps she was not prepared to make that sacrifice. My mother had sacrificed her home and nursing career and moved to the other side of the world for love. Did marriage always involve such sacrifice, whether or not it was for love?

I would never know Jane's reasons, but in a letter to Fanny Knight, who had asked for advice about a serious relationship, Jane wrote, 'having written so much on one side of the question, I shall now turn around & entreat you not to commit yourself farther, & not to think of accepting him unless you really do like him. Anything is to be preferred or endured rather than marrying without affection.' Jane had the determination to follow her heart against the expectations of her friends and family, and I admired her courage. Jane wanted marriage to be a consequence of love, not a means to material security. Jane lived at a time when women were not encouraged to write professionally or earn an income, but Jane did not bow to pressure. She didn't need someone else to secure her future; she would secure her own.

I commented to Granny how brave this ancestor of Bapops had been. 'It's not just Edward; I am a relation of Jane's, too,' she responded unusually sharply and with some annoyance, so I did not pursue the conversation any further. Besides, I had just realised my grandparents were related. I didn't know anyone else with grandparents who were related, and I decided not to tell anyone. I realised much later that this was not unusual for my grandparents' generation and social class.

I helped Granny pack the sandwiches, cakes, scones, butter, and jam into bread crates for Uncle Robert to take to the cricket ground. Robert had been a talented cricketer, but his sporting ambitions had been thwarted by the early onset of psoriatic arthritis in his twenties. He remained passionate about the game, was heavily involved with Chawton Cricket Club and had maintained the pitch for years.

Granny was a member of the Women's Institute, and every week she baked cakes, which she would take to the fair in the community centre in Alton. The women at the institute appeared to be Granny's only company outside the family—my grandparents had no social life. After we delivered the cakes and two trays of eggs to the Women's Institute fair at the Alton Community

Centre, I went with Granny to the post office and to her favourite shops, such as Joyce and Lucas Butchers and Delicatessen, which looked like it had been in the high street for decades. The shop owners called Granny 'Mrs Knight' and seemed to treat her with the highest respect. People outside the family and our closest friends seemed to have varying impressions. It was never directly discussed with me, but it was obvious some could see that the family's fortune was long gone and that other than our surroundings, we were not privileged; both my parents worked, and finances had to be managed carefully. Others clearly thought we were still very wealthy and perhaps eccentric in our choice of budget cars and camping holidays.

I first became aware of other people's opinions when I started at Chawton Primary School in September 1975. The school was a short distance from the end of the back drive, the drive my parents tended to use. At that time, Chawton House had two approaches—the back drive, as we called it, took an earlier turn off the road in Chawton, skirted past the Home Farm buildings, and arrived at the back entrance of the house. Chawton Primary had around fifty pupils across six school years. Five boys and four other girls started school that year, some from Chawton, others from neighbouring villages or Alton.

With my birthday on 28 August, only four days before the new school year, I was the youngest in the class, just as I was the youngest at home. The year groups were so small that each of the three teachers taught two years together in one of the three classrooms. The original Victorian flint schoolhouse was used for the younger classes, with a modern extension added for the older children, each complete with a blackboard and desks. The small hard-surface area at the front of the school was marked with both a football pitch and a netball court. At playtime, I played hopscotch and French skipping—jumping up and down on long elastic ropes—with other girls.

Mrs Potter was my first teacher, a fair and no-nonsense woman who expected concentration and effort. I enjoyed my first years of school. I learnt to read and write and discovered I had a talent for mathematics. I recited my times tables regularly and liked to solve maths questions; it felt like a fun game, and I was good at it. My sporting talent did not improve, much to my disappointment. I couldn't run fast or catch and throw a ball, and I cringed at the thought of team games. I was always the last picked and rightly so—I was hopeless. I also struggled to concentrate in silence for long periods, and I was often reprimanded for talking in class. My end-of-term report cards were consistent: Mathematics 'A'; everything else 'could try harder'. For my sixth birthday, I was given a Mr Men book—Mr Chatterbox!

For a fun competition, the children were all asked to bring to school one of their baby photographs. The photographs were displayed on a board, and everyone had to guess who was who. I was convinced that no one would guess my photograph correctly as my dark hair had been blonde when I was very young. But mine was the easiest for everyone to identify; I was crawling on oak floorboards, and the panelled walls and large doorway in the background gave it away. I was not happy about it at all and complained bitterly to my mother when I got home.

At the end of one school day when I was six or seven, as parents arrived to collect their children, I overheard two mothers from the village discussing their children's performance in class in comparison to that of their peers. As I collected my things and turned to leave, one of the mothers remarked, 'She doesn't count—anyone with her advantages would do well.' I was surprised by her bitter tone and turned to look at her. She stared straight at me with an expression of disdain and failed to drop her stare, even when it was obvious I had heard. I was embarrassed and left as fast I could.

I never understood what advantages they believed I had; many of my classmates came from families with far more wealth and opportunity, regardless of their family's past or the size of their bedroom. They had lots of new clothes, holidays abroad and the latest gadgets—a girl in the village had a new video game called Pong, a table-tennis game that she played on a television. I made my assumptions, just as they did. I concluded that, for some, my family's earlier history as the chief landowners in the area and employers of many local families, was in living memory and had left a sense of division. Others assumed we were wealthy, and for some, the British class system still defined us. Or perhaps it was nothing to do with any of that—perhaps they just didn't like me. I tried to tell Granny what had happened, but she stopped me before I could finish. 'Don't take any notice. It's just tittle-tattle,' she said and moved the conversation on to something else.

It was around this time that Granny's daughter Penny, along with her husband and children, moved into the top-floor apartment built into the eaves of the house. Our nearest neighbours were too far away for me to visit alone as a young child, and Paul and I didn't have many other children to play with, so I was very excited. Formerly used as the estate offices, the top floor had been converted into tenants' quarters decades earlier and had recently become vacant. A long, wide corridor down the centre led to many small rooms with oak beams so low in places that adults had to duck to go under them. Most of the rooms afforded views across the front of the estate. Cousin Jane was the eldest of my generation and a few years older than Robin, who was the same age as Paul. Born just seven days apart, Paul and Robin had become great friends—like brothers. Fiona was a couple of years older than me and went to junior school in Alton, but we often saw each other when we arrived home from school. I loved having other children in the house.

In the summer months, Granny's tea room was open in the Great Hall on Saturday and Sunday afternoons. The long, high wooden refectory table along the wall provided a counter for the display of homemade cakes. Edward Austen Knight's grand dining table, with a few extension leaves removed so as not to be too long, seated about eight and was pushed to the north wall of the room. Five or six other tables were dotted around the room, each seating four or six people. The crockery was a collection of various types that Granny had assembled over the years. Each table would be set for tea, with odd Wedgwood plates and perhaps some Willow cups and saucers. The old wood cupboard to the left of the fireplace was used as a serving hatch from the kitchen and was plenty big enough for a chair, a duplicate invoice book with bright-blue carbon paper and a cash box.

As well as her cakes, Granny was famous for her scones made from the sourest of milk that would be left to ferment in milk bottles along a ledge in her kitchen. By today's standards of health and safety, Granny's tea room would not pass muster, and she ignored modern ideas of reducing fat and sugar. But there was something completely delicious about everything she cooked. The flavours were authentic and the textures just right; it was simply impossible to have just one of anything.

In between preparing orders in the kitchen, Granny would walk along the servants' passage and enter the Great Hall to check that everything 'front of house' was as she wanted. This was her tea room; visitors had entered her home to eat her home-cooked food, and Granny expected a certain level of behaviour and decorum. She didn't hesitate to reprimand anyone who overstepped the mark. As a matter of principle, Granny would not allow people to choose the type of cake they would be served. If customers ordered cake, they would be served whichever slice she wanted to give them. I wondered whether she had a system. Did she distribute the slices of cake in such a way as to ensure all cakes were used evenly, or did she reserve her favourite cake for the people who made the best impression? I couldn't fathom it. I never asked Granny about her reasoning—for this or for anything else. Granny gave her instructions with confidence and absolute authority.

When I was very young, Granny humoured me and allowed me to 'help' serve customers in the tea room with Fiona. Visitors to the tea room often referred to the long history of the Knights of Chawton as well as to Jane and her works, characters, and quotes. Our heritage and connection to Jane was never more discussed than on Saturday and Sunday afternoons in the tea room. When I was about five, I proudly told Chawton visitors that 'Jane was a pioneer' even though I had no idea what a pioneer was—I had heard someone else say it.

I gradually took on grown-up tasks until I was old enough to work as a waitress. I set the tables ready for customers; took orders; carried trays of tea, sandwiches, and scones; and collected money. It was a family affair, and over the years my mother and cousins all worked front of house in the tea room. But the kitchen was Granny's domain. From time to time, a customer would ask to look at the cakes on the refectory table to choose which one they wanted. When Granny was in the kitchen, I would say yes, but I would ask them to be quick; Granny would reprimand me if she saw me allowing customers to take such liberties.

Most visitors to the tea room had been to Jane Austen's House Museum and understood that the resident family at Chawton House were descended from Edward Austen Knight. Occasionally, a highly enthusiastic Austen fan would be overwhelmed by the opportunity to speak with Jane's family. One Saturday afternoon, I approached two American couples—friends on holiday together, I assumed—and proceeded to take their order. They enquired whether the Knight family were at home, and I replied, 'Yes, *we* are.' I introduced myself and explained that Jane was my fifth great-aunt.

The darker-haired woman immediately looked up and stared at me. Her eyes filled with tears as she rose to her feet. She grabbed my hand, shouted something about how she had never been so close to Jane, wrapped her arms around me and pulled me in close. I dropped my order pad and pen on the floor, and the tea room came to a hush as everyone turned to view the commotion. I tried to hide my embarrassment and willed the heat in my cheeks to subside. I was quickly released and smiled at the woman who had regained her composure.

I held my emotions in check and proceeded to take the order—tea and cake for four—before I returned to the privacy of the wood cupboard. My heart raced, and my stomach was in my throat. The sudden and intimate nature of the interaction had taken me by surprise, and I had been startled for a moment, but I quickly realised her good intentions. I did not want her to know that she had scared me. Nor did I want her to be embarrassed—for both her sake and mine. I didn't want to dwell on the incident any longer than necessary, so I took a few deep breaths, stood tall and called 'order' through to the kitchen. I was busy again soon enough, and the incident was forgotten.

When the tea room was open, Bapops stayed in the library, the room my grandparents used as a sitting room. On rare occasions, visitors to the tea room would see Bapops on their way to the bathroom if he happened to walk along the servants' passage, and they would later ask me who the elderly gentleman was. I would proudly say that he was Edward Knight, my grandfather, and quickly move the conversation on to avoid any questions about him—I would not have been able to answer them.

I knew more about my Australian grandfather, Alf, than I did about Bapops. Alf came to England every few years or so and usually combined his visit with a trip through Asia or Europe. He liked going to the pub and had been known to go out and not come back for days. With his sun-aged skin, Australian drawl and walkabout ways, Alf was different from anyone I had ever known. I loved talking to him and looked forward to his visits.

Alf was adventurous, had travelled the world and didn't seem scared of anything. But one year, when I was about eight or nine, Alf stayed a couple of nights in my father's childhood bedroom, just off the Tapestry Gallery where the Grey Lady was said to roam. I knew something had happened, but all my parents would say was that he was more comfortable sleeping in our quarters. I later discovered that something had woken Alf in the night. He told my mother he wasn't sure whether it was a bird in the chimney, but it made the hairs on the back of his neck stand up. Alf didn't want to admit he was afraid, so my mother moved him into our basement quarters just to make sure the 'bird' didn't disturb him any further.

Some of the visitors seemed to think we were wealthy, but it was plain to see that the significant fortunes of the Knight family had gone. Other than the Great House itself, most of the estate land, property and valuable possessions that would have been familiar to Jane had been sold. Why, when or by whom I didn't know—I had never heard it discussed. My parents had told me the estate was financially broke and that we were unlikely to be able to stay in Chawton after Bapops died. But it was difficult to know the truth, and I didn't know what to think. Although all the evidence pointed to the contrary, it was easier to believe that Bapops had a secret fortune hidden away and to dream of the riches that would save the house. It was too difficult to consider the repercussions for Richard and the future of the Knight family in Chawton if what my father said was true.

We were rich in so many other ways, if not financially. We had our heritage, an extended family, acres to roam and most of the house to play in. From time to time, the house was used for filming and appeared on television—the Great Hall was used by *Blue Peter* (now the longest-running children's television programme in the world) to film a segment about Jane Austen. The English band Level 42 used the front drive and entrance to film the video for their chart-topping hit *Something About You*.

I used the house and gardens as my own and moved freely between my family's quarters in the north wing, my grandparents' public and private quarters and all the in-between rooms and passages. The tenants in the rented apartments in the house changed from time to time. Some tenants I would simply acknowledge, but others I became more acquainted with and would visit, including a young couple with a baby and a small group of twenty-something sharers. I spent time with my cousins and tenant friends in various parts of the house. I played for hours in the house kitchen, attic rooms and disused servants' hall, the latter piled high with old wooden furniture and broken chairs; wooden shoe trees; picture frames; rolled-up maps and documents; tatty boxes and old trunks; large wooden shields with painted coats of arms (perhaps made for a play); deck quoits and wooden skittles; bows and arrows; old cricket bags, bats, and pads; riding boots and clothes; and family possessions and keepsakes—all covered in dust.

In the warmer weather, twenty-four acres of gardens and woodlands, along with the outbuildings and the church, provided hours of entertainment. From the middle of summer until the first frost of winter, blackberry bushes in the woods grew thick with delicious fruit. Sometimes I would take a trug and pick enough blackberries for my mother to make a fruit crumble or a blackberry and apple pie. But most of the time, I just popped them straight into my mouth. Towards the top of the woods, a bamboo thicket planted decades prior grew in a neat circle. I liked to stand inside the circle and pretend I was in a far-off exotic land.

In the autumn, shiny conkers fell from the horse chestnut trees in the four-acre paddock in front of the church. A couple of times, Fiona and I cleaned the Knight gravestones in the churchyard and dared each other to stay overnight among the graves—but we never did. In the four-acre paddock, we once found some brass candleholders that had fallen off the chandeliers, which thieves had stolen from the church the night before. The police were called, and we proudly showed them what we had found, not realising we had contaminated the evidence by handling it. Lucky for us, the thieves had dropped a few more pieces as they made their escape across the paddock, so all was not lost.

The only places I didn't go on the estate were the tenants' apartment on the first floor of the servants' wing (it had been rented since I was born to tenants I didn't visit) and near the old wooden gamekeeper's hut in the woods at the top of the lawns. My cousins had teased me with stories about a witch living in the hut, so I always gave that part of the woods a wide berth. I was often gone for hours in the afternoon, either alone or with Fiona, but my parents knew I would not leave the grounds without their permission, and I could easily be found. A loud whistle from my father or a high-pitched holler from Granny could be heard across the estate and was my signal to return to the house for tea. The bell that would have been rung in the past to call the estate workers to the house still hung at the top of the house, but it hadn't been rung for years for fear the old bell tower would collapse.

During the summer, tourists came up the drive most days, despite the 'Private' notice attached to the entrance gate on weekdays when the tea room was closed. In the main, visitors would sweep up the drive, stop for a few seconds and then sweep back down again to the church. Occasionally a party of day trippers would bring out their picnic blanket and set out their picnic-ware on our front lawn. From his bedroom at the front of the house, Paul could see intruders much quicker than Granny and Bapops, who were tucked away in the library. He would mischievously wait until the blanket and picnic were spread on the lawn before telling Granny, who would burst out of the side door waving her walking stick in the air to gain their attention before telling them politely, but in no uncertain terms, that they were to be gone, much to Paul's amusement. I never saw anyone argue with Granny. Not only was she the mistress of the house, but she also had an air of authority. She was not to be trifled with, and if pushed, the tone of her admonishment was not lost on anyone; even the most rebellious were a little intimidated by her. Granny took her responsibilities seriously, but she was also kind and generous.

I had so many questions I wanted to ask Granny. What had Bapops been like as a younger man? Were they wealthy when Granny first arrived at Chawton? Did Bapops have a secret fortune stashed away? When did Bapops become so withdrawn from society? I had never known them to leave Chawton for even one night, let alone for a holiday.

I loved going on holiday. Every summer my parents took Paul and me camping for a week or two, and Granny would be left to cook on her own. My father had been reluctant to go camping at first, but when I was about five, he agreed to give it a try and had a wonderful time—we all did. It was to be the start of many years of carefree camping holidays. We particularly enjoyed Wales and Cornwall, and we often camped on farm sites where the only facilities were a tap and a sewage tank. Supplies from the local shops were expensive, so my mother would shop for all the non-perishable groceries in our local supermarket and pack them into the trailer. It was all very basic, with my mother kneeling on the ground to cook on the gas rings. We made many new friends among the other families staying at the campsites, and we played for hours. Looking back, I realise it was refreshing that no one knew about Chawton. We were just an everyday family on a camping holiday, cooking sausages on the camp stove and building sandcastles on the beach.

In the summer of 1979, we were invited to camp in the grounds of Uncle Richard's farm near Cirencester. Richard and his then wife, Anna, had three children: Adam, Cassandra and Benjamin. I used to see Richard and his family on their annual visits to Chawton House. Fiona and I would play 'sardines' with our cousins, a variation on hide and seek where only one person hides and many seekers look. When the hidden person is found, the seeker joins them in the hiding place and waits for the other seekers to find them. The loser is the person who is last to find the hiding place. It was great fun.

Richard was warm and friendly, and nothing he said or did ever made me feel awkward or inferior. However, I was conscious that he would one day own Chawton, and this left me feeling rather intimidated and my emotions conflicted. On the one hand, I liked and respected my uncle; he was a decent man, a gentleman. On the other hand, he would eventually inherit our home and everything I loved. I longed to ask questions: What was Richard planning to do with Chawton House? Was he planning to live there? Would we be able to continue living in the north wing (he couldn't possibly need the whole house)? Would Richard have his portrait painted and his own coat of arms as had previous squires? All these questions I pondered in silence. But Richard and his family were exceptional hosts, and with Chawton House far away in another county, I was able to forget my questions—instead, I rode horses, played with my cousins and had a wonderful holiday.

CHAPTER FOUR

'I shall be miserable if I have not an excellent library.'

Pride and Prejudice – Chapter 11

BAPOPS SPENT MOST OF his time in the library, the room my grand-parents used as a sitting room. Two large leaded-light windows provided the library with a double aspect over the sweeping lawns, the terraced gardens and The Bottles to the side of the house. An oil portrait of my father's younger sister, Ann, hung above the fireplace on the only clear wall in the room. Floor-to-ceiling bookshelves, packed with books, covered the other walls. The art deco wooden clock on the mantel above the open fire governed the rhythm of Bapops's day. He sat in an armchair in the corner to the left of the fireplace and opposite the television, which was usually on. He liked to watch horse racing, current affairs programmes and *Crown Court*. Granny's armchair, sep-arated from Bapops by a small, high wooden table piled with newspapers and racing guides from weeks gone by, also faced the television. Granny and Bapops studied the racing form in the newspaper and made bets between themselves for pennies.

Two large upholstered sofas set against the opposite walls faced Granny and Bapops and provided seating for Uncle Robert, who lived with my grandparents, and for visitors. Oak side tables, low drop-leaf coffee tables and a telephone table and chair at the side of the room completed the furniture. Family photographs of weddings and christenings and of grandchildren in their school uniforms were proudly displayed in a variety of silver frames on the bookshelves. The oak floors were covered with a large, plain, beige carpet that almost reached the edges of the room. The Axminster rugs that had once covered the floors were now threadbare and considered too dangerous for young children and an ageing squire.

During the school holidays, when my parents were at work, I usually joined my grandparents for lunch. On Sundays, or for a special family lunch, Granny would roast a large leg of lamb or joint of beef and serve it with crispy roast potatoes, heavenly Yorkshire pudding and gravy. The leftover meat was made into a shepherd's pie or meat rissoles for a midweek lunch. I liked watching the minced meat squirm onto a plate as I cranked the handle of the metal meat grinder round and round. Lunch was served when the mantel clock in the library struck one o'clock. Granny often cooked brains especially for Bapops—sweetbreads she called them—but they looked disgusting to me.

If there were only a few of us for lunch, we didn't dine in the Great Hall; we ate off our laps in the library. After lunch, Bapops would quietly watch television, read the newspaper or study the day's racing guide. When Granny or Robert spoke to him directly, he would respond with a few words but rarely continued the conversation. I often flicked through the pages of country-house architecture and gardens in *Country Life*, the glossy magazine that was delivered weekly. I knew to be quieter than usual when Bapops was in the library. No one had specifically said he was not to be disturbed—I instinctively knew.

I saw my aunts, uncles and older cousins talk to Bapops, but I never saw him engage in animated conversation. He sometimes smiled, but he was a man of few words from my observations. I thought it was his place, as head of the house, to talk to me if he wanted to; I didn't have the courage to start a conversation with him. I didn't know whether his distance was usual for a man of his position, as I had no one with whom to compare him. We lacked the finances to socialise with other people who lived in grand houses, and no one I knew had a grandfather who was a squire. So I accepted the distance between us. I saw it as a mark of his superior position and respected him for this, although I would have been overjoyed if he had taken an interest in me. I was in awe of Bapops—'king' of everything I could see. If he wandered into a room in which I was alone, such as Granny's kitchen or the study, I would discreetly leave so as not to be in his way.

I never saw Bapops or Granny look at any of the books in the library. It was as if the spines of the books were merely decorative wallpaper. My grandparents went to bed early, and the library was often empty at night. I would sneak in sometimes, pull a large book off one of the many shelves and peek inside. Some of the spines cracked as I levered open the hard leather covers. I particularly liked the books with beautiful hand-painted illustrations of flora and fauna from around the world. As I carefully turned the pages over one at a time, I would marvel at the pictures—bright and clear as the day they were printed. I couldn't help but run my fingers over the thick pages. I kept a listen out so that I could quickly put the book away if anyone came into the room, which they rarely did. All I could hear was the familiar ticking of the mantel clock and the occasional hoot of an owl.

Most of the books were extremely old, and many were in languages I didn't understand. Tales of foreign travel; illustrated natural histories; books of letters; volumes of poetry; novels; and books on politics, law, sport, history, estate management, art, and religion were interspersed with estate records, family history and our Chawton heritage. Many of them were complete with a bookplate inside the front cover, indicating which of my ancestors had been their original owner.

I was fascinated by each ancestor's choice of bookplate design—and books—because I considered their choices an indication of personality. Edward Austen Knight's bookplate was much plainer than Thomas Knight's. Unlike the rest of the family, who appeared to have satisfied themselves with one bookplate design, Montagu had three—and each was elaborate and bold. I particularly liked Montagu's round design; it was the only circular bookplate I had seen. Sitting side by side on the bookshelves were the personalities and preferences of generations of Chawton squires. I knew the faces of most from their portraits, but the bookplates brought my ancestors to life. There were no bookplates for Lionel or Bapops, so the library provided me with no clues about their personalities. Bapops spent his days sitting in the library—what I considered the heart of our heritage—but he seemed so disengaged from it all.

The library was very much a male domain, despite the fact that a woman—Jane—was the celebrated and much-revered literary member of the family. The bookplates showed that the collection had been largely put together by the men of the family, and most of the books had been written by men. The journals of foreign travels were of gentlemen's journeys—photographs and illustrations focused on men's achievements and interests, not women's. Jane would have known the older books, either at Chawton or in the library at Godmersham Park before they were moved to Chawton. I could imagine her browsing through the eclectic mix of books, perhaps to gain knowledge and inspiration for her writing.

I wondered which books had been Jane's favourites. Was Jane, the most talented writer in the family, resentful of the lack of female representation in the library? When I later read *Persuasion*, I couldn't help but notice that Jane perhaps shared her own views through the voice of Anne Elliot in a lively conversation with Captain Harville about the fickleness of women: 'I could bring you fifty quotations in a moment on my side the argument, and I do not think I ever opened a book in my life which had not something to say upon woman's inconstancy. Songs and proverbs, all talk of woman's fickleness. But perhaps you will say, these were all written by men,' says Captain Harville. 'Perhaps I shall,' responds Anne. 'Yes, yes, if you please, no reference to examples in books. Men have had every advantage of us in telling their own story. Education has been theirs in so much higher a degree; the pen has been in their hands. I will not allow books to prove anything.'

My mother had modern copies of Jane Austen's works, but I didn't see any copies of Jane's novels, new or old, in the library. Years later, I discovered that four of Jane's books were listed in the Godmersham Park library catalogue of 1818, the year after she died. At the very end of the catalogue, in a small section labelled 'Drawing Room', the novels published in Jane's lifetime were listed: *Sense and Sensibility* (1811), *Pride and Prejudice* (1813), *Mansfield Park* (1814) and *Emma* (1816). They were recorded as having been printed in London, as sitting on shelf six and as comprising three volumes each. The volumes were originally sold unbound and would likely have been bound with Edward Austen Knight's bookplate. Much of the Godmersham collection was moved to Chawton when Godmersham was sold. A set may also have been held in the Chawton collection, but first editions of Jane's work would have been valuable, and I could guess what their fate would have been.

I could see from a photograph of the Great Hall in Montagu's book that Chawton House had once been full of opulent possessions: dark antique wooden tables, chairs with barley-twist legs and high backs, and tall candlesticks by the side of the fireplace. I recognised a couple of pieces of furniture and was certain they were still in the house. I could clearly see the miniature coats of arms still in place around the top of the panelling and the large ornate wooden carving that depicted a scene of Abraham about to sacrifice his only son, with both a mosque and a church in the background, high above the doors.

But most of the portraits that had once hung between the antlers were gone, as were the plates that had shone so brightly in the daylight streaming in through the windows of the Great Hall. I was unable to tell from the photograph whether the plates had been pewter, brass or china. Paul told me about a beautiful and extensive collection of fossils and shells kept in narrow drawers in a dresser in the servants' passage. He had played with the collection for hours when he was young, but one day it was gone, and no one ever mentioned it.

Despite the obvious loss of valuable possessions, Bapops kept certain standards and was always smartly dressed in tailored trousers, white shirt and tie, and a gentleman's cardigan. His dark hair, regularly cut by a visiting barber, was slicked back with Brylcreem, and he was always clean-shaven. But Bapops had always been old and frail to me—he walked quietly and slowly, but always upright. From time to time, I would pass him in a hall or passage, and he would usually make some acknowledgement—a brief hello or nod of the head before he continued on his way. He didn't stop to talk.

It was impossible for me to imagine Bapops as a young and active man, so I asked my father what he had been like. Bapops had never worked in the traditional sense—that is, he had never had a job, not as my parents did. There had been business ventures, such as commercial flower growing, my father said, but nothing had taken off. Bapops had been a keen photographer. He had taken friends on photographic safaris in Kenya, and large black-and-white prints in narrow dusty frames hung in the disused servants' hall at the back of the house. He had also taken cine film of my father and his siblings as they ran around on the lawns. The reels were occasionally projected onto a pull-up screen when our extended family came to visit. I had also seen a photograph of Bapops as a younger man sitting in the driver's seat of an open-top car. I guessed it was taken when he was in his thirties. He looked confident and dapper, with slicked-back hair and a sharp suit—like a character from *Bugsy Malone*, I thought.

One Christmas, my parents invited their long-standing friends, Jake and Amber, to join us for the festive period. Many years earlier, when Jake was a young vet, he had rented the north-wing quarters that would later become our quarters. Being of similar age to my parents, they had become great friends. My grandparents knew Jake and his then girlfriend, Amber—they later married—and we were all invited to join Granny and Bapops in the library for six o'clock drinks a couple of days before Christmas. Bapops went to pour the drinks from a secret cupboard behind a row of book spines. I saw him take a swig of whisky before he harmlessly but unmistakably flirted with Amber. It was only for a brief moment, and I don't remember what he said exactly, but I was struck by how cheeky and funny he was. I had never seen this side of his personality before, and I never saw it again. For a few seconds, he showed a glimpse of his former self, and I could imagine what a charming man he had once been.

The only other photograph I had seen of Bapops as a younger man was in his military uniform. In the far left corner of the house kitchen was a staircase that led to the attic rooms. Behind the bottom of the stairs was a large alcove full of old military uniforms—coats, boots, trunks and bags—all piled on top of each other. Everything was covered in dust and looked as though it had not been touched for decades, or perhaps centuries. Paul, who had thoroughly explored every corner of the house, had looked through the pile and said it was like a time machine—as he had dug deeper into the pile, the uniforms had been older, going further back in time as he peeled back the layers.

I was too wary of spiders to rummage as Paul did. Paul had ventured up the staircase to the attic rooms and turned the first of them into a den for himself. He had painted it blue and installed an old sofa and a CB radio, and he spent hours there talking to people over the airwaves. Being high up at the top of the house, he could pick up signals all the way from the Isle of Wight.

In their early years together, Granny and Bapops had enjoyed a busy country-estate life and hosted dinners, shooting parties and hunt meets. But other than family lunches, Granny and Bapops had given up entertaining a long time ago. When my parents arrived from Australia as a married couple, Bapops gave them the 'Austen Knight china', as we called it, as a wedding gift. Before my parents' arrival, the china had been stored for years in boxes in the attic above the servants' wing, but now it was being used for dinner parties once again. The grand dinner service had been commissioned from Wedgwood by Edward Austen Knight on a visit to London with Jane and Fanny. Jane wrote of the occasion in a letter to Cassandra from Henrietta Street on Thursday, 16 September 1813—'after dinner'. In the letter, Jane first gives Cassandra a horrifying account of their companions, Lizzy and Marianne, friends of the family who were staying at Chawton House, receiving dental treatment before the visit to Wedgwood:

> and poor Marianne had two taken out after all...Fanny, Lizzy
> and I walked into the next room, where we heard each of the two
> sharp and hasty screams...I would not have had him look at mine
> for a shilling a tooth and double it. It was a disagreeable hour.

I winced as I imagined the pain. My mother had taken swift action when my teeth started to overcrowd and become crooked. Our family dentist in Alton had removed five of my baby teeth and four of my adult teeth over the years. I knew the extractions would help straighten my teeth, and each tooth was pulled with the help of a local anaesthetic, but I still dreaded every visit. I could only imagine how scared Marianne would have been.

'We then went to Wedgwoods,' Jane continued 'where my Bʳ & Fanny chose a Dinner Set...the pattern is a small Lozenge in purple, between Lines of narrow Gold;—& it is to have the Crest.' I approved of Edward's choice. The pattern was beautiful and far more tasteful than many of the other bright and garish antique designs I had seen. Clearly inspired by our Knight heraldry, the dinner service had been made specifically and uniquely for Edward

Austen Knight, and it must have taken Wedgwood months to make. Made of thick white porcelain, each piece was hand painted with a narrow border of lozenges in purple, edged with gold leaf. A tiny gold flower had been painted in the middle of each lozenge, reminiscent of the lozenges and flower on Edward Austen Knight's coat of arms. The pattern, which trimmed the outer edge of each piece, was interrupted with a single image of our Knight crest, the Greyfriar, intricately painted in miniature.

It had been a substantial dinner service. I didn't know how many dinner plates had been broken in the 170 years it had been in the family, but thirty-six plates remained. Small and large plates, soup bowls, a range of serving dishes (some with lids), large meat platters and three grand soup tureens had largely survived intact, although some pieces were damaged, and clearly some items were missing.

For some reason, Bapops and Granny must have decided they didn't want to entertain on a grand scale, which I could not understand at all—I loved it. My parents used the china on very special occasions and only with a small group of familiar and trusted guests. Some pieces were too damaged to use, but others were in mint condition and were the perfect backdrop for delicious home produce cooked to perfection by my mother.

The estate had hosted pheasant shoots for generations, and my father and Uncle Robert continued this tradition. Shooting and hunting were still popular pursuits in the English countryside. From the first day in October until the end of January each year, invited friends and acquaintances would bring their guns and join shooting parties through the woods. The 'guns' and 'beaters' would meet in the Great Hall for a tot of whisky early in the morning before setting off down the back drive to enter the woods at the bottom. Sometimes I joined the beaters.

Lined up together, twenty feet or so apart, we walked slowly through the woods in front of the guns and waved sticks, beating the ground to make as much noise as possible to encourage the birds to take flight. The guns were careful to point their weapons high into the air to ensure no beaters were accidentally shot. Fallen birds were collected by gun dogs and then tied and carried in pairs by the guns, who took the majority of their kill home. Throughout the autumn, my father would traipse through the woods in all weather to feed the pheasants, ensuring our stocks on the estate remained plentiful.

Once the shooting party was over, my father would hang his pheasants undrawn—that is, complete with guts and feathers—in the old kitchen for a week to allow the meat to tenderise and develop a gamey aroma before the birds were plucked, gutted and trimmed. My parents preferred a medium intensity flavour; others liked their game 'high' and hung it for longer. At the end of a good season, we would have a dozen brace of pheasants in our freezer for dinner parties. Roast pheasant was delicious, but a pheasant pie with moist gravy and a pastry top was even tastier.

The Hampshire Hunt still held meets at the front of the house occasionally, and Bapops would stand on the front steps to watch. Paul and Fiona sometimes went out with the hunt on friends' horses, but I wasn't a good enough rider and could only look up at the horses and smart riders in their black coats and red riding tails.

My father had ridden since he was a young boy, but he didn't ride much anymore. As a child, he had kept his pony, Rusty, in the stables and enjoyed riding across the paddocks and around the estate during the school holidays. He laughed as he recounted riding his horse through the house—from the lawns, in through the side door, along the servants' passage and out the back door—much to Bapops's chagrin. Bapops had occasionally taken him hunting on a lead rein until my father was old enough to ride alone. Bapops had been a keen and talented horseman and had kept his best hunters at Hall Farm in the nearby village of Bentworth. I knew of Hall Farm—about five miles away—as Paul was friends with the family that lived there. I don't know why Bapops chose not to keep the horses in our stables, which were only a short walk down the drive.

The stonework above the front door of the stables was dated 1593. When I was young, the stables were still fitted out with old-fashioned boxes, and although they had not been used for decades, it took little imagination to picture them bustling with life—Edward Austen Knight's mount being prepared for his ride around the estate and horses being hitched to a coach in the rear yard. Perhaps on a cold day, Jane, Cassandra and Fanny waited in the Great Hall for the coach to take them all to a dance at the Assembly Rooms in Basingstoke. Edward's horses were stabled at Godmersham, but he brought a carriage and riding horses with him on his annual visits to Chawton.

We had no horses of our own, so Paul and I were excited to look after two ponies for an aunt who was travelling overseas one summer. We kept the ponies in wooden boxes behind the stables and rode them daily in the four-acre paddock in front of the church. The stables had been sold towards the end of the 1970s and converted into a family home. I had played in the old boxes for hours, and it seemed a significant loss. Bapops had rented out apartments in the wings of the house for as long as my father could remember, but this was a sale, not a tenancy. It happened quietly and without explanation; Granny didn't mention it, but I remember it well. For the first time, the gate at the end of the long gravel drive did not mark our boundary. The first half of the driveway was now shared with the residents of the newly converted stables, and the edge of our estate was only yards from our front door.

In the past, Bapops had ridden his own horses in point-to-point steeplechases organised by the local hunts. Most years, Uncle Robert, my parents, Paul and I—often joined by various friends and family—went to the point-to-point race event held at Hackwood Park near Basingstoke where Bapops himself had ridden as a younger man, but this year Bapops came with us. Cousin Georgina was riding. Bapops had left the grounds of Chawton House only once in my lifetime, as far as I could remember.

Granny and Bapops travelled in Robert's car, and we parked the two cars side by side on the edge of the course and unloaded chairs and blankets to sit on. Picnics packed into cool boxes and baskets were served from the car boot. I enjoyed the atmosphere of the day and walked around the show stalls. I looked at the horses in the parade ring and joined the family sweepstake for each race. For much of the day, Bapops sat in the car. He joined us at the back of the car to watch the races and for a homemade sausage roll. He seemed content enough but didn't say much. He looked pleased as Georgina rode her mount over the brush fences. Was it a joy for Bapops to be back at the racecourse where he had raced in a former life when he was active and connected with the outside world?

My father had gone to boarding school from a young age, so he was unable to tell me much else about those days at Chawton. With term times at school and a few weeks annual holiday at the seaside with the nannies, my father had spent only nine weeks or so each year at home in Chawton. When he was eight, my father did spend a year at home when a burst appendix put his life in danger. The family were very concerned, and like Jane in her last weeks, he travelled from Chawton to Winchester for treatment. Fortunately, my father returned home where he remained for a year until the family doctor deemed him fit enough to return to boarding school. My father fully recovered and went on to break the high-jump record at Milton Abbey, in Dorset, where he was boarding. He remembered that Bapops came to see him play rugby at school, but they were not close. I was so grateful not to be sent away to school. I couldn't imagine being away from Chawton for months on end—it was our home.

Although my parents didn't want either my brother or me to attend boarding school, in the end it was the only option for Paul. After he left Chawton Primary, Paul went to Amery Hill Secondary School in Alton. Everything seemed fine for a couple of years until I was eight and Paul was thirteen. For weeks, I had sensed something was not right. My parents had attended meetings with Paul's school, and I was aware of private phone calls made in quiet tones but didn't attempt to listen. Paul never returned to Amery Hill, and for the next few weeks he remained at home. I could see the concern on my mother's face as she read leaflets and filled in forms.

One Sunday afternoon about a month later, my parents explained to me that Paul had a learning difficulty called dyslexia. It was 1978, and I had never heard the term 'learning difficulty', let alone 'dyslexia'. My mother explained that Paul found it difficult to learn by reading, so he would have to go to a special boarding school that was able to teach him. I was upset and cried for Paul. I was scared for him: What did it all mean, and would he be all right? I was also sad for myself that Paul was going away to boarding school; our home would not be the same without him.

My parents explained the sacrifices that would be made to meet Paul's school fees. Horse riding and piano lessons, my only regular activities outside the estate, would have to stop, and we would be 'economising'. A moment of disappointment was quickly replaced by the realisation that these were small inconveniences for me in comparison with Paul, who had to leave Chawton. I was upset to see him go.

After a few months, Paul settled in at Slindon College, an independent boarding school on the West Sussex coast. A converted manor house, Slindon College was grand and imposing, much like Chawton House, and Paul seemed happy enough. The headmaster's racehorses were kept in a stable at the school. Paul was a talented rider and worked the horses every day. I missed Paul during term time and looked forward to sports days at his school. I beamed with pride as he ran past the finish line first in the hurdle race.

Paul had got into some fights at Amery Hill, and I did not want to follow in his footsteps, so when it was time for me to leave Chawton Primary, my mother arranged for me to take the entrance exam for the Convent of Our Lady of Providence in Alton. The prospect filled me with excitement and horror—only the highest performers would be offered a place. I had no sense of my intelligence in comparison with others, and I didn't know whether I would pass the exam or not. I was known as the girl who talked too much and who frequently got into trouble for chatting to the person next to me in class, and I didn't think this reputation was likely to stand me in good stead with a new school. To top it all, my talent on the sports field had not improved.

I completed the exam, and after an agonising wait, my mother opened the letter confirming a place for my senior years—just as we had hoped. It was my first experience of personal achievement; I had passed a fair and equal examination where everyone was judged by the same standard, regardless of their circumstances, and I liked it. My mother was thrilled, and I knew my parents were proud of me as well as relieved. The convent offered a good education locally; boarding-school fees were out of the question. I was relieved as it was an all-girls school, which I thought would be nice, and I would not need to leave Chawton. I was glad I would be attending the same school as my friend, Bronte, who also lived in the village.

I wasn't particularly popular at school, but I did have a few friends. Bronte, the friend I played with the most, lived with her parents and sister in a large thatched cottage at the other end of Chawton, opposite Alphonsus House, a monastery that had originally been built as the estate dower house by Montagu in 1810. Bronte lived close enough for me to bicycle to her house, as long as my mother knew where I was going and when I would be back. Her father, who had once been in the navy but was now retired, was related to Lord Nelson, the celebrated British admiral killed at the Battle of Trafalgar in 1805. Bronte's family were proud of their heritage and equally enthusiastic about mine, and they welcomed me with warm smiles and strawberry Quikshake—milk mixed with flavoured pink powder—which I vigorously stirred into my milk in an attempt to dissolve the fine grains. Bronte and I would play for hours and listen to her Eurythmics records.

I was also relieved that I would not be the only grandchild not to go to a private school—I wanted to fit in with my cousins. Paul and Robin were away at boarding school, and Fiona went to a private school seventeen miles away in Fleet. As Fiona was older than me, she was always ahead in the milestones of life, such as going to senior school and becoming an adolescent. I looked up to her and sought her approval—much like a younger sister would do.

I settled into the convent well enough. I liked most of my teachers and classmates, although I was never part of the in-crowd and didn't mix easily with the other girls. I wished I had inherited some of my father's sporting or horse-riding talent, as I am sure that would have helped. I missed Paul terribly during term time and worried about him. My mother had explained dyslexia to me as best she could and had reassured me, but it wasn't clearly understood by the experts, and she didn't have all the answers. My father had always struggled with reading and writing, and subsequent testing showed that he too was dyslexic. I didn't know what effect it would have on Paul or his future.

But my worries were allayed a year or so later when I went to watch Paul ride in his first horse race. It was an ambition of Paul's to ride for his head-master's stables, but he had a pair of knee-length riding boots only, not the ankle-length leather jockey boots he needed, so Paul borrowed £50 from Granny and then worked around the estate over the summer holidays to pay it back.

I was allowed a rare day off school and went with my parents to Southwell Racecourse in Nottinghamshire for the day. I was in awe as Paul, in brightly coloured silks with his initials 'PEK' clearly visible on the front of his skull-cap, rode his racehorse out of the parade ring and towards the starting line. He was so high up on a tiny jockey saddle, but he looked confident in his seat as his horse danced about. I had wanted to wish Paul good luck before the race, but with throngs of people everywhere and Paul high up on his horse, I was unable to. Paul rode off towards the start, and my parents and I went to stand by the finishing line, stopping on the way at the on-track bookmakers to back Paul in an each-way bet.

The horses gathered at the starting line on the other side of the track. The starter gave the signal, and they were off. Paul had struggled to settle his mount before the start, and as the horses set off, he was facing the wrong way and had a late start. I could see that Paul was at the back, about twenty lengths behind the rest of the field. It was a long steeplechase, and the riders and horses would come by the winning post twice before the end of the race on the third pass. There was a clear gap between the pack and Paul at the rear as they came past the post the first time. Paul had caught up with the back of the pack by the time they came past the post for a second time, and we watched him work his way past the other horses as they ran the last lap and jumped the brush fences.

I had never felt such excitement as I watched Paul come round the last bend towards the winning post. My parents and I whooped with delight and waved our betting slips in the air as Paul came in second behind Mark Pitman, son of Jenny Pitman, who the following year became the first female trainer to win the Grand National. As Paul rode his horse to the winners' enclosure, we looked on with pride. I had never seen such a beaming smile on his face, and I was so very proud of my big brother and knew he would be OK. He had been determined to race, and he had done so, triumphantly.

My father didn't know whether Bapops had ever won a race—or come second or third. Bapops was so reserved that I couldn't picture him punching the air with delight. But despite his quiet nature, it was hard to imagine life without Bapops. I loved my extended family and our ancestors, and if what my parents said were true, we would have to leave our ancestral home. I didn't even want to try to imagine it—there simply had to be a solution.

I had been to Longleat House and Safari Park in Wiltshire, about an hour and a half from Chawton, with Paul and my parents. Longleat was the first stately home in England to open to the public on a fully commercial basis in 1949, and to me this seemed worth considering for Chawton House. I had seen hundreds of visitors queuing, happy to part with the entrance fee to peek inside the grand house at Longleat. But although Chawton House was still rich with our heritage and the spirit of our ancestors, the most valuable family heirlooms had gone, the village properties and viable outbuildings had been sold and, except for Granny and Bapops's quarters, every wing and floor of the manor had been rented out or had fallen into disrepair. My mother explained that the investment required to prepare the house and attract visitors was far more than they could ever afford. But why hadn't this been done when the house was still in good repair? Through my young eyes, it seemed so simple.

At the end of the summer in 1983, we moved up to the first floor of the north wing as planned. I was particularly pleased that our new quarters were big enough to house my piano as I would no longer have to play in the cold of the rear servants' passage. My favourite tunes were *Song for Guy* by Elton John, *Chariots of Fire* by Vangelis and *Yesterday* by The Beatles. I enjoyed singing along but did not like being heard by the tenants who used the back entrance to the house. I liked music and drama. The convent had an association with the London Academy of Music and Dramatic Art, and in the new school year, I would start acting classes. I had already passed my first 'Verse and Prose' speaking exams.

I liked living 'above stairs', with high ceilings, oak panelling and the portraits. I passed by Elizabeth Martin Knight every day—'We have all a better guide in ourselves, if we would attend to it, than any other person can be,' Jane had written, and I could see in Elizabeth's eyes the confidence of a woman who made her own decisions without the need for approval from others. I wondered whether Jane had thought the same as she passed Elizabeth's portrait on the way to dinner.

My parents didn't host dinner parties for a couple of months after we moved while my father made alterations to our quarters. After he had finished my bedroom, my father installed a new kitchen that included built-in cupboards he had constructed from a flat-pack kit, a fitted sink, a free-standing cooker, a refrigerator and our first microwave. My father fitted the kitchen into the north corner of the room, but no sooner had he finished the work than he took it all down and refitted it into the west corner. I didn't know why my father had decided to rebuild the kitchen, but its new location did improve the layout of the whole room. It was a large square room with a high ceiling, sash windows, ample space for a scrub-top table big enough to seat ten that had been used for generations of servants in the servants' hall, and a seating area with comfy armchairs around the open fireplace with stone mantel and a large mirror above. As soon as the new kitchen was finished, my parents were keen to entertain and invited some friends for dinner.

The first guests invited for dinner in our new quarters were Trish and Dennis and another local couple, John and Anne, who lived opposite the front gate in the rectory stables, which had been converted into a house long ago. My father had known John since childhood—at one point, they had attended the same school—and had rekindled their friendship as adults. John ran his own small business, and Anne was the manager of the health centre in Alton. Their two sons were of similar age to Paul and me, and our families socialised often.

My mother chose courses that would complement each other and utilised as much of our estate produce as possible: prawn cocktail, pheasant pie with roasted vegetables from the garden and poached pears for dessert. The pears had been harvested the month before and kept fresh in the apple store, so only the prawns and a handful of ingredients needed to be bought.

I enjoyed my parents' dinner parties as much as they did. I did not attend the dinner; that was for the grown-ups. I liked to help my mother plan and cook for the evening and retrieve produce from our freezers and stores, and I loved the trip into Alton to buy anything else we needed. My mother made sure that friends they dined with often didn't get the same meal twice. It was also important to consider what could be prepared in advance and what had to be done at the last minute. Dishes that required minimal attention in the final stages of cooking were preferred so that my mother would not be away from her guests for long periods. Both my mother and Granny were highly complimented by friends and family for their cooking skills. I wanted to cook as well as they did so that I could 'wow' my guests when I was older, and I listened intently to my mother's tuition.

My mother and I enjoyed each other's company and chatted away as we worked. Before the end of term, I had to choose what I wanted to study for my O levels. Maths, English literature and English language were compulsory, but other subjects were optional. My mother wanted me to take history, science and French, but I wanted to take art, needlework and geography. We had already talked about it a couple of times, and I didn't want to listen. I didn't want to talk about it again so chatted endlessly about other things.

For the first half hour or so I joined the party, warmed myself by the roaring fire and enjoyed the light-hearted conversation before I retreated for the rest of the evening to a comfy fireside chair in the kitchen to watch television.

By the time I was up and dressed the next morning, my father had cleared the dining table and washed the dishes. He was nowhere to be seen—already out in the grounds somewhere. I opened the refrigerator to see what delights were left over from the night before. There on a side plate, complete with lozenge border and the Greyfriar, sat the last slice of pheasant pie—my favourite. It was breakfast time, but I couldn't resist. It was the first pheasant pie of the season!

I removed the cellophane wrapping, popped the plate into my mother's new microwave, closed the glass door and pressed start. As the plate began to turn, I could see sparks flying. Within seconds, rapid flashes of bright light, like small bolts of lightning, were shooting in all directions. I suddenly realised it was coming from the gold leaf around the plate and pulled open the door. My heart was racing as I grabbed a cloth and carefully lifted it out. I didn't want to plunge it into cold water in case a sudden change in temperature cracked the plate. I put it on the draining board and inspected the damage.

Had the gold leaf come off? Had the colours faded? To my astonishment and absolute relief, there was no damage. The pheasant pie was stone cold, despite the spectacular light show. I waited a few minutes, re-wrapped the plate in cellophane, popped it back in the refrigerator, and never mentioned the incident to anyone. With so few of our precious heirlooms left, there seemed little reason to confess I had been so careless when no damage was done.

We had the perfect surroundings for entertaining—from large parties to intimate dinners and Sunday lunches, and everything in between. I would be turning eighteen in five years, and I had been hoping to host a big party of my own, but my plans would soon be thwarted.

Paul and Martin, a close friend of Paul's from school, threw a couple of parties in the Great Hall, and teenagers arrived in droves. At the last party, fifty guests became far more than a hundred, as more and more people arrived. My parents were anxious to ensure revelling guests were kept under control and did not damage the house or cause unnecessary disturbance to my grandparents, who were only a flight of stairs away. I tried to imagine what Bapops must have thought. He couldn't have been asleep in his bedroom above with the 1980s music blaring below. Was he horrified at the noise? Did he wish it was all over and his privacy restored, or did he nostalgically recall his younger days when he had hosted his own parties?

CHAPTER FOUR

The party spilled into the inner hallway of my grandparents' quarters and out onto the lawns—there were people everywhere. Luckily, the evening passed without serious incidence, other than the mess left in Granny's kitchen by a drunken partygoer. But far too many people we didn't know had attended, and it could easily have got out of hand, so my parents decided there would be no more teenage parties at Chawton House.

CHAPTER FIVE

'How shall I bear so much happiness!'

Pride and Prejudice – Chapter 55

UNTIL I WAS FIFTEEN, I had always considered myself a Knight, descended from Sir Richard. My fifth great-grandparents were Thomas and Catherine Knight, and Jane Austen was an aunt who happened to have a different surname. I had always known that Edward Austen had been adopted and had changed his name to Knight, but it was not until I read the details of Edward's adoption in Montagu's book that it dawned on me that my fifth great-grandparents were George and Mrs Austen and that I was, in fact, an Austen. At the time, my mother explained that I had very nearly been christened Jane Austen Knight. My parents had wanted to recognise our Austen heritage and honour Jane, but they decided against it out of concern that I would be teased at school. Although I understood the reason for their decision, I secretly wished I had been named after Jane—what an honour that would have been.

I had never before considered our Austen heritage. It seemed extraordinarily lucky that, two centuries earlier, Edward had been chosen as heir by his fourth cousin, who must have had other cousins and relatives from whom to choose. Thomas could easily have chosen someone else, and had it not been for Mrs Austen's persuasion, George Austen might not have let Edward go, and Chawton would not have been our home. It would not have been Jane's home either—and her novels might never have been written.

Thomas Knight II married Catherine Knatchbull in 1779 and hoped to have a family, but they did not bear children. Thomas and Catherine became particularly fond of twelve-year-old Edward, and after a visit to the Austens in Steventon, they took Edward with them on the remainder of their wedding tour of their Hampshire estates. According to Montagu's book, Caroline Austen recorded what her uncle Henry had told her in 1848 concerning Edward's early life:

> he was very clear as to the purport of the discourse which he heard between his Father & Mother on the morning when they received a letter from Godmersham, begging that little Edward might spend his holidays there... My grandfather was not disposed to consent to Mr. Knight's request. With the single eye of a Teacher, he looked only at one point, which was, that, if Edward went away to Godmersham for so many weeks he would get very much behind in the Latin Grammar. My grandmother seems to have used no arguments, and to have suggested no expectations; she merely said, "I think, my dear, you have better oblige your cousins, and let the child go;" and so he went, and at the end of the Holidays he came back, as much Edward Austen as before. But after this, the Summer Holidays, at least, were spent with the Knights, he being still left to his Father's tuition. Uncle Henry could not say when it was announced in the family that one son was adopted elsewhere—it was, in time, understood so to be; and he supposed that his Parents and the Knights came to an early understanding on the subject.

ABOVE Chawton House, 1987

ABOVE Chawton House, 1987

ABOVE
Statue of Sir Richard
Knight in St Nicholas
Church, Chawton

LEFT
Portrait of Elizabeth
Martin Knight by
Jeremiah Davison,
ca. 1730

LEFT
Village event at
Chawton House,
date unknown

ABOVE Montagu George Knight, centre front, at the
front steps of Chawton House, early twentieth century

ABOVE Bapops and Granny, ca. early 1940s

BELOW Granny and Bapops, 1980s

ABOVE My parents, Jeremy and Carol Knight, having supper in the library before uncle Robert's 21st birthday celebrations, Chawton House, 1968

LEFT
My parents on the lawn with Candy and her puppies, Chawton House, 1973

ABOVE LEFT Me in the arms of my godmother in the driveway of Chawton House after my christening in Chawton Church, 1971

ABOVE RIGHT My mother with Paul and me, Christmas 1971

BELOW LEFT Me, Christmas 1971

BELOW RIGHT Me by the fireplace in the dining room, Chawton House, 1974

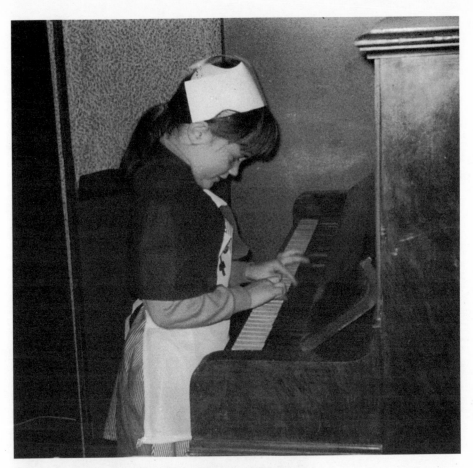

ABOVE
Me and my piano,
a gift from Granny
and Bapops,
Christmas 1975

LEFT
Me at the rear of
Chawton House,
1979

RIGHT
Me at the side
door, Chawton
House, 1984

BELOW
Me visiting friends
in Winchester,
summer 1985

It was about 1783 when Thomas and Catherine informally adopted fifteen-year-old Edward, and he became heir to the Knight fortune—there was no legal adoption process at that time. To mark the occasion, Thomas commissioned the William Wellings silhouette that I had seen so often in Granny's bedroom.

The Knights sent Edward on a grand tour of Europe in 1786 to finish his education, as had been expected of young gentlemen since the seventeenth century. He kept a journal of his travels which has since been published by the Jane Austen Society of Australia—*Jane Austen's Brother Abroad: The Grand Tour Journals of Edward Austen*. He visited Switzerland and Italy and spent a year in Dresden, where he was received at the Saxon Court. Many years later, there was an exchange of letters and presents between Prince Maximilian of Saxony and 'Edward Knight, ci-devant Austen'—as the Prince was inclined to address him. After he returned to England in 1790, Edward lived permanently with the Knights and was gradually prepared for life as squire and owner of three large country estates—Chawton, Steventon and Godmersham—further land and property in Sussex and Essex, and May's Buildings, built by Thomas Knight I, in St Martin's Lane in London.

But by the early twentieth century, Steventon and Godmersham had been sold, and most of the landholdings and properties were gone, too. The family's remaining wealth was concentrated in Chawton, and Montagu owned all but two houses in the village. I was puzzled by the contrast between the grand symbols Montagu had installed in the house and the depleted family fortune. But the Knight family presence in Chawton village had never been stronger, and Montagu may have felt more secure than perhaps he should. Wage records from 1907 show payments made to more than sixty people as Montagu increased farming across the Chawton estate. He was certainly proud of the village and his heritage, and in his book proclaims:

The beauty of the situation, the venerable age of the Manor
House, the old-world character of the village, and its literary
associations; the fact that the property (though it has been owned
by members of several families) has only once since the Norman
Conquest changed hands by way of sale and purchase—all these
advantages give the place a peculiar title to be considered as a
specimen south English manor.

There seemed to be such a dramatic contrast between Montagu, the thirteenth squire, who had celebrated his position and heritage, and his nephew
Lionel, the fourteenth squire, who had left no mark at all, not even a portrait.
Lionel was my great-grandfather and a most recent ancestor, and yet I knew
nothing about him at all. I didn't even know what he had looked like.

There was an even more dramatic contrast between Montagu's wealth
and my grandfather's. What had happened? Had there been a catastrophic
event or a poor business investment that had devastated the family's fortune?
Had Bapops been foolish or not attended to his duties and responsibilities
as squire? Had all their fortune been squandered away? It was hard to comprehend how so much could be lost in such a short period. I wondered how
Bapops had felt as he signed off the sale of one asset after another. Montagu
died in 1914, and by the 1950s, when my father was a boy, all but a few run-
down cottages and outbuildings had been sold, and parts of the house were
tenanted. My father had hoped to renovate the gardener's cottage at the back
of the estate for our family, but it was sold as well. My mother recalled there
being many more portraits in the Great Hall when she arrived in 1965, but
she didn't know when or where they had gone. Bapops was fifty-five then and
had already withdrawn into a largely reclusive lifestyle.

Fortunately, not everything had been sold. Bapops had given the Knight
Family Pedigree Book to my father when he returned to England from

Australia. My mother had explained to me that it contained all the branches of the family that had successively controlled the estates, but I hadn't taken much of an interest in it when I was younger. There were many entries referring to people I didn't know. But I had become more curious and asked if I could look at it again—I particularly wanted to look up Sir Richard and Elizabeth Martin Knight.

The old heavy pedigree book was kept in a seventeenth-century rectangular Nuremberg cast-iron Armada chest that my father had recovered from the cellar strongroom. The cellars lay under the Great Hall. A door just outside Granny's kitchen in the servants' passage opened to reveal stone steps down to the cellars, which comprised four dark rooms that had once been used for wine and safe storage. Cousin Fiona and I had often played in the cellars when we were young, creating make-believe houses between the low brick walls that divided the farthest room. Paul had used another of the rooms to race slot cars on a Scalextric track with Cousin Robin and their friends. The smallest cellar room in the south corner was a strongroom, accessed through a thick metal door.

My cousins would tease me about the unthinkable prospect of being shut in the strongroom, never to be discovered. I was certain that if I did venture in and the door did close, I would have no chance of escape. After all, the door had been designed to keep thieves out, as this was where the silver was kept, and the Nuremberg chest before it had been restored. I decided not to take the chance and never stepped inside. I could see a long metal pole leaning up against the wall inside the strongroom and had asked my father its purpose. 'It's for banging on the ceiling if you get shut in,' he said with a smile. I wasn't sure whether it was a joke or not. Would anyone hear from the hallway above? I resolved never to find out.

The Nuremberg chest—brown and flaky with rust—had sat on the floor of the cellar strongroom for years. My father had the chest restored to its original state, and the medieval dark grey gleamed. Repairs to the elaborate lock mechanism that covered the underside of the lid made it once more a usable strongbox with an impenetrably thick metal body that was much too heavy for a thief to carry. The restored chest sat in our quarters where it housed my father's most precious heirlooms. I thought the lock mechanism was terribly clever; the apparent keyhole was a trick.

I watched in anticipation as my father put the large key into the secret keyhole. I could see how difficult it was to open as he slowly levered his arm to turn the key. The lock mechanism made a loud noise as each metal rod and spring turned until the bolts retreated and the chest opened to reveal its treasures. Sir Richard's signet ring was in a small box—a rare personal possession preserved from the original line of the Knight family. The ring was tarnished and discoloured, but there was no mistaking the letter 'R' and a coronet signifying his knighthood. I wondered whether Sir Richard had worn the ring all the time or just when he was formally dressed—like when my father wore his. My father was proud of his heritage, but he rejected the traditions of superiority. He wore his signet ring on special occasions only. When we went to church, my father preferred to sit in the parishioners' pews, not in the Knight family pews at the front of the church. He insisted on being called Jeremy, not Mr Knight, and was quick to put people at ease.

Other boxes in the chest contained small items of silver, a few pictures, some small books and a large leather-bound book, which my father lifted out carefully. The Knight Family Pedigree Book, bound in red leather, covered with gold-leaf lettering and other decoration, had been given to my father by Bapops. Reverend Samuel Pegg, once the vicar of Godmersham, started the book in 1731. My father removed it from the chest and placed it on a cushion to protect the spine. It was one of the oldest and largest books I had ever seen—about the size of a large atlas. It had a faded reddish-brown leather cover and was filled with hand-drawn family trees, painted coats of arms and copious amounts of writing.

I was too nervous to touch such a precious record of hundreds of years of history that brought together the branches of the family through marriage, inheritance and adoption. My father carefully turned the thick pages. The gold leaf and vivid colours on the beautifully depicted coats of arms shone as brightly as the day they were painted. The intricately drawn family trees for the Knight, Martin, Brodnax, May, Knatchbull and Austen branches of the family were followed by pages of written entries about each person. My father turned the pages to find Sir Richard's entry, which read:

Sir Richard Knight

Sir Richard Knight, Son of ye abovesaid Richard Knight Esq,
by his wife Elizabeth, liv'd to ye Age of 40 years, when, after
some years spent abroad, & loaded with all the Provincial
Honours his Country cd. bestow on him at Home, being a
Candidate at ye County Election for Knights of ye Shire, he
died before ye Affair was determined. This was A.D. 1679
and he left his Estate by Will to Richard Martin, who took
ye Name of Knight, and was his first Cousin once removed.
The Inscription on his Monument at Chawton here follows.
There's a large Monument agst ye South Wall of ye chancel,
The Arms & Crest of Knight, with ye Motto, An Effigies lying
on a Tomb, above which, is an Inscription on Christopher
Knight Esq.
HSE Richardus Knight

I didn't read the inscription below as I recognised it to be the same Latin inscription I had tried to decipher without success in the church. I was interested to see Sir Richard's entry in the book, but I was disappointed it didn't tell me more about him.

Elizabeth's entry in the pedigree book was about a third of the way in:

Elizabeth Martin

Elizabeth Martin, afterwards Knight, & sole heiress of her brothers, mar^d William Woodward Esq concerning whom, his prior affinity to her (for they were Cousin Germans of the Families of Martin and Woodward), and their Extraction from Sr Christopher Lewkenor, by his Two Daughters, & Coheirs, Elizabeth and Frances, as set forth in ye Pedigree, I shall re: for you to ye Inscription on his monument against the North Wall of ye Chancel of Chawton Church. The Arms are Quarterly Knight (with an Inescachen of Martin), Woodward, Lewkenor, Knight, ye Crest of Woodward.

The inscription

Near this place Lyes the Body of William Woodward Knight Esq (the only son of Edward Woodward Esq. of Fosters in Surrey by Elizabeth the oldest daughter of, and Coheir to Sir Christopher Lewkenor of West Dean, Sussex) who assumed the Name of Knight, upon his marriage to Elizabeth, the only Daughter of Michael Martin Gent of Ensome in Oxfordshire (whose mother was a Knight, & heir to Sir Richard Knight of this place) by Frances, the other Coheir to Sir Christopher Lewkenor, whereby were united, their several Estates, of Lewkenors, Knights, Woodwards, and Martins. A Gentleman, dutiful to his God, true to his Country, affectionate to his wife, sincere to his Friend, charitable & obliging to all. He died, member of Parl^mt for Midhurst Sussex, Oct 26 1721 To his memory, this monument was erected By his disconsolate Relict AD 1723

Again, I skipped over the inscription before continuing to read:

> And to her second Husband Bulstrode Peachey of Petworth in
> Sussex Esq who died 14 January 1735 (he was buried at Chaw-
> ton). This lady, the Time of whose Death is omitted in the
> Inscription, departed this life AD 1737 and left her Estate unto
> Thomas May Esq of Godmersham in Kent, one of nearest Re-
> lations, obliging him to change his Name at the next Session of
> Parliament, from May to Knight, wch was accordingly done.

The name Bulstrode Peachey never failed to make me laugh. Where had the book been kept in Jane's time? Had she been equally amused? I considered the library the most likely location, although it may have been in Godmersham. Either way, I am sure Jane and Fanny turned the pages just as carefully and marvelled at the precision of the brushstrokes and the brightness of the colours. Jane obviously would not have seen her own entry. My father took a firm hold of a thick red ribbon peeking out at the top and bottom and used it to lever the book open at exactly the right spot.

The first page detailed a family tree with Jane on the right, towards the bottom. Over the page was her entry:

Jane Austen
This lady, born Dec 16 1775 is well known as the Authoress
of Pride & Prejudice, Emma and of other novels, which were
for the most part written at Chawton where she lived with her
Mother & Sister from 1809 to 1817 residing in the Cottage near
the Pond at the Junction of the Winchester and Gosport Roads.
In 1817 she removed to Winchester, for the sake of Medical
advice and died there July 18th in the same year. She was buried

in the Cathedral near the centre of the North Aisle. A large slab
of black marble marks the spot, and a Brass has recently been
placed on the North Wall adjoining, by her nephew, the Revd E
A Leigh. The Inscriptions on both marble & brass, are given on
the next page.

In Memory of Jane Austen

Youngest daughter of the late Revd George Austen formerly
Rector of Steventon in this county. She departed this life on the
18th of July 1817 aged 41. After a long illness supported with the
Patience and the Hopes of a Christian. The benevolence of her
heart, the sweetness of her temper, and the extraordinary en-
dowments of her mind obtained the regard of all who knew her,
and the warmest love of her intimate connections. Their grief
is in proportion to their affection, they know their loss to be
irreparable, but in their deepest affliction they are consoled by a
firm though humble faith that her Charity, Devotion, Faith and
Purity have rendered her soul acceptable in the sight of her Re-
deemer.

The inscription on the brass is as follows:

Jane Austen

Known to many by her writings, endeared to her Family by the varied
charms of her Character, & enabled by Christian Faith and Piety was
born in Steventon in the County of Hants Dec XVI. MDCCLXXV
& buried in the Cathedral July XXIV. MDCCCXVII
"She openeth her mouth with wisdom, and her tongue is the law
of kindness"

A school friend and I took the bus to Winchester almost every Saturday during term time to visit my first boyfriend and other friends for the day who all boarded at Winchester College, the prestigious boys' private school where Edward Austen Knight had sent his sons. My friends and I often sat in the gardens of the cathedral, but I never went inside to look at Jane's gravestone or monuments. I liked to think of Jane in Chawton and didn't want to see her grave.

The last full entry in the book was Lionel's, with the date of his sudden death in 1932 and the births of his five children, including Bapops in 1910. It was the only place I had seen Lionel or Bapops recorded in our history. Montagu Knight and William Austen Leigh had updated the book in the Victorian era with written entries, inserts and newspaper clippings, but my father didn't know who had made the final entries. The pedigree book contained the name and lineage of every squire of Chawton, and I loved it.

If the obituaries were to be believed, every squire had been highly respected and had excelled at the 'duties and dignity of the resident landholder'—as Jane described it in *Persuasion*—and many had played a prominent role in the community. Bapops didn't sit on any committees or hold office, but some traditions were maintained, and my grandparents were committed to their responsibility as the hosts of village events for the local community. I had seen old photographs of an event, hosted by Montagu I assumed, with over a hundred people on the lawn.

The house remained a centre for village festivities. Every year the Great Hall and lawns were used for many events, including the Summer Ball, the Chawton Fete and Horticultural Show, and tea and cake after the Christmas carol service in the church. This created a great deal of work, and I sometimes wondered why Granny and Bapops still hosted these events. But I loved the atmosphere of the house being so full of life and was glad they did. I liked to help with the preparations as it made me feel useful and kept me busy. There was always something to do.

Every year, on the third Saturday in July, the Jane Austen Society of the United Kingdom held its annual general meeting (AGM) in a marquee on our lawns. I presumed they had done so for decades—since the society's formation in the 1940s. A few days beforehand, the biggest marquee I had ever seen would be erected on the flat section of the lawns, close to the side door leading into Granny and Bapops' quarters. It took a whole day for a team from Carters in Basingstoke to erect the wooden poles, haul over the large canvas tent and secure it with at least a hundred guide ropes. About five hundred folding wooden chairs were delivered for visitors to sit on.

In exchange for some pocket money from Granny, Cousin Fiona and I would put the chairs in neat rows towards the temporary stage that had been built inside the marquee—it took hours. At the beginning, it seemed like a good idea, but at about 250 chairs our enthusiasm often began to wane. We would then stand on the stage in front of the microphone and pretend we were speaking to the crowd, 'I am delighted to accept this award…' When we were younger, we would play in the marquee for hours, running in and out between the poles and imagining we were in a grand ballroom or a circus big top.

On the day of the AGM, various volunteers and contractors came and went, setting up a PA system for the speakers, putting cones and tape along the driveway to direct cars into the four-acre paddock in front of the church for parking, and erecting direction notices at the house. For decades, Granny had provided tea and cake for the five hundred 'Janeites' and academics who attended for the afternoon. She would bake dozens of cakes and buy cakes from the Women's Institute Fair in Alton. To the side of the marquee, serving tables were set up with enormous urns for boiling water, cups and saucers, and serviettes to hold a slice of cake. It was a family affair, and we all helped with setting up, serving, and clearing the used crockery. But it was a lot of work for Granny, and by the time I was in my teens, caterers were used.

Early in the afternoon, visitors would take to their seats in the marquee, and the formalities would begin. Guest speakers discussed various aspects of Jane's life and literary works. I didn't listen to the speakers. When I was about eight, I had sat on an empty chair at the side to listen and found it a bit boring. But I enjoyed the buzz and excitement of the day. I helped Granny, talked to visitors and directed people who were lost.

The event attracted visitors from far and wide, most of whom were women over forty—which, at the time, seemed old to me. One year, a taxi had pulled up at the front door about half past four when it was all over. A woman had flown from America to attend the event for the day, but her flight had been delayed. She was only able to stay for half an hour before she had to jump back in the taxi and return to Heathrow to catch her return flight home. The teas had been packed away, but my father made her a cup of tea in Granny's kitchen and gave her a slice of cake and a tour of the public areas of the house, so her journey wasn't completely wasted.

In previous years, the marquee had stood empty on the lawn for a couple of days, complete with five hundred chairs before Carters returned with their trucks to take it all away. It seemed like a waste to have such a large marquee standing empty, so my mother hatched a plan. The marquee could be used for an event in the evening for a couple of hundred people, far more than the Great Hall could seat for dinner—a fundraiser for the church perhaps. It would take considerable organising. Food, entertainment, tables, plates, cutlery, staff, ticket sales and fundraising activities were among a long list of considerations. It would be hard work, but my mother was focused on the opportunity to raise money for charity and, as long as it was achievable, was not put off. She formed a committee with two local women, and they met regularly for months to plan every detail. I didn't attend the meetings but saw the file of papers she took with her get thicker and heavier as the months went on.

My mother's dream came to fruition, and the first of three Chawton summer balls was held in 1986, just before my sixteenth birthday. It was certainly not the first time the house had hosted a ball in its four-hundred-year history, but my father had no memory of one. It was the first ball I had ever attended. Some of my friends went to the Hunt Ball or the Young Farmers Ball, but I couldn't afford to go. The only dance I had been to was the end-of-school dance at the convent, which I had organised. Unfortunately, it ended with the expulsion of a girl who had invited her brother as her guest and showed him her dormitory, which was in breach of school rules. My father argued that she had not sneaked a boyfriend into the dorm, but the head teacher was undeterred.

The Chawton Ball was due to start at eight o'clock, leaving a tight three-hour window to clear the AGM and set up the marquee for dinner and dancing, with the help of friends and villagers. The dinner tables hired from Carters were covered and dressed with flowers. The chairs used for the AGM were cleared to reveal a dance floor in the centre of the marquee and rearranged around the tables for dinner. The Great Hall was set up for the food buffet. An array of cold meats, salads, breads, condiments and homemade dessert cakes were prepared by an army of volunteers under the careful direction of my mother and her committee colleagues. Some food was prepared in advance and stored in refrigerators, bags and boxes. On-the-day preparation had been happening all afternoon in the kitchen of our quarters—all unseen by the AGM guests. Lettuces were washed by the dozen. Large tubs were filled with sliced cucumber, and the roasted turkey, beef and ham were carved by hand.

Shortly before the ball was due to start, our friends Jake and Amber arrived. Amber looked elegant in a rose-gold taffeta dress with her hair pinned up on one side and cascading with curls on the other. Amber was always stylish and well dressed. Jake wore his dinner jacket 'shabby chic'. I always enjoyed their company and hoped they would stay for the weekend. Jake had opened a number of veterinary practices in the Brighton area and often had to rush back to work. As we swapped news, Jake casually mentioned that he had treated himself to a new car: 'I've been a bit naughty and bought a Ferrari.' We rushed outside to have a look. It was dark blue, very sleek and the fanciest car I had ever sat in. Jake had started out in a rented apartment in Chawton House and now owned a business that was so successful he could afford a Ferrari. He was humble, rarely spoke about his business affairs and never bragged. I had known Jake all my life and was awestruck by how successful he had become. He had always been dedicated to his work, and I was inspired.

Nearly all the men were in black tie—that is, dressed in formal black dinner suits with matching black bow ties and cummerbunds around their waists, although a few of the more eccentric guests had brightly coloured ones. The women were in evening gowns, many in taffeta creations with full skirts down to the floor. My father had liked a pink-checked taffeta dress my mother had tried on in a dress shop when we were on a camping holiday months earlier, but it was too expensive. By coincidence, my mother found the same dress for hire locally and surprised my father by wearing it on the night. My mother made my dress—white cotton with white spots, strapless, with a full calf-length skirt. It was the first time I had socialised for an evening with my parents and their friends—people I had known all my life. I felt very grown-up.

Trestle tables had been placed around the Great Hall, and volunteers stood behind them to serve the food, ensuring the food didn't run out. I served the cold meats—each person was allocated two slices of each, and I was careful to stick to the allowance. Guests came into the Great Hall to get their dinner and returned to the marquee to dine. After dinner, the charity auction was held. Local benefactors had donated items such as bottles of vintage wine, and even a stereo system. I was amazed at the amount that generous—and tipsy—diners paid for auction items as friends and neighbours tried to outbid each other in high-spirited but friendly competition. The band played, and we danced late into the night.

The ball was a complete success. The months of preparations by my mother and the committee had been worth the effort. The evening ran smoothly, was enjoyed by all and raised thousands of pounds for the church. The ball became an annual event and boosted my mother's confidence. The church organ was in need of significant repair, so the following year, as well as organising the ball, my mother and a small group of friends planned a three-day summer festival in Chawton. The festival involved the whole village, with exhibitions, stalls and open gardens. Everyone either chipped in and helped with the arrangements or volunteered for the rota to 'man' different events. Visitors came from miles around, and £8,000 was raised for the church.

Two weeks later, on the first Saturday in August, the annual Chawton Fete and Horticultural Show was held—my favourite summer event of the year. It was a family occasion, and many children from the village and surrounding areas came—I didn't often see the children who had attended Chawton Primary School with me. The Great Hall was used for the flower, produce, baking and handicraft competitions of the Horticultural Show, organised by the Horticultural Society. The tea-room tables and trestles were arranged around the edge of the room and in a row down the centre before they were covered with tablecloths and readied to display the entries for each competition class. Officials from the Horticultural Society placed cards along the tables to indicate where the entries for each class should go. Non-perishable entries such as homemade jam, dried-flower arrangements, needlework and art were all in place the day before.

I don't think I was supposed to, but I snuck into the Great Hall the night before and had a good look at all the entries. Each had a card showing its competition class. The maker's name had been written on the back of the card, which was placed flat on the table, so the judges could not identify the maker. I pretended I was a judge and made a mental note of my chosen winners.

Entries in the children's classes were displayed in the inner hall of my grandparents' quarters. A notice saying 'Private' was placed on the door to the library and on the bottom of the staircase to my grandparents' bedroom chambers. The large round hall table was usually cluttered with unopened post and other items that Granny or Bapops never put away: a wooden shoe tree, a picnic basket that hadn't been used for years and Mills & Boon romance novels that Granny had borrowed from the public library in Alton (the only books I ever saw her read). All had been cleared to the sideboard of the inner hallway, so that the table, along with some trestles, could be used to display the children's work.

The perishable entries arrived on the morning of the show. Once the freshly baked cakes and scones, fresh flowers and produce were in place, the Great Hall and inner hallway were out of bounds for a couple of hours while the serious-looking judges privately viewed, squeezed, cut and tasted. This was the only time of the year I was banished from the Great Hall, and I didn't like it at all. I didn't make a fuss or tell anyone, but I was desperate to hear what the judges were saying and how they chose the winners. I didn't try to listen—I would not have risked being caught. On the rare occasions when I did get into mischief, I wasn't harshly punished, but I didn't like being told off.

Once the judging was complete, other officials went around the tables, turning over the cards and recording the names of the winners before the Great Hall and inner hallway were opened to the public at about midday. Class winners were awarded with small silver cups, with larger cups given to the most outstanding entries, which were deemed to have won a whole category.

I had seen photographs of my father standing beside a table full of cups and holding in his hands the biggest cup awarded to the overall winner of the show. In 1976, the hottest summer in England since records began, my father entered his home-grown vegetables, fruit and flowers in the show; I was too young to remember but had heard the story from my mother. He won nearly all, if not all, the classes he had entered, and he had been awarded the large array of cups in the photograph, including the cup for the overall winner. My father overheard someone in the crowd comment, 'It must be easy when you've got gardeners to do all the work.' Nothing could have been further from the truth, and my father was embarrassed. He had carried water from the house to the walled garden in buckets every day for months in the heat-wave. My father said nothing, but he never entered the competition again. I don't remember ever entering any of the competitions; if I did, it was only once or twice, and I never won anything.

The fete was organised by a village committee, and the proceeds were used to pay for improvements to village amenities and repairs to the church. About twenty stalls were set up throughout the morning on the front lawns. The lawns were always in good condition as they were regularly cut by my father or Robert with the ride-on mower. The fete opened about lunchtime, and hundreds of people came from Chawton, Alton and the surrounding areas. Throughout the event, a compère kept everyone informed and entertained over a tannoy brought in for the day. In a marquee erected just outside the library windows on the bottom of the terrace, tea and cakes were served, organised and managed by fete volunteers. As well as the stalls and refreshments, visitors could enjoy the programme of events set for the afternoon—performances and displays by local clubs. I particularly remember dog-obedience displays and choreographed dance troops. There was archery for adults and a fancy-dress competition for children. I had once tried and dismally failed to shoot a target with Paul's bow and arrow, and I didn't want to embarrass myself in front of a crowd.

There were games of chance, such as a lucky dip and a raffle, and games of skill, such as 'splat the rat' where a pretend furry mouse, a cat toy, was dropped down a length of drainpipe and the player tried to hit it with a stick as it shot out of the bottom. Each game cost ten or twenty pence to play and offered the chance of a small prize or 'double your money'. Other stalls sold crafts and homemade jams and pickles. My parents sometimes ran the tombola stall for which they collected a hundred or so prizes from the local community—from jars of pickles to boxes of chocolates—and labelled them all with a number that ended with a five or a zero. Players paid ten pence to pick a raffle ticket from a barrel. If the raffle ticket ended in a five or a zero, they won the prize marked with the same number.

In previous years, I had helped my parents, but that year I was fifteen and wanted to run a stall of my own. I called it the 'Human Fruit Machine'. It consisted of three people sitting on a row of chairs, each with an orange, an apple, a pear, a lemon and a grapefruit in a cloth sack, instead of the reels of a fruit machine. Players paid ten pence to pull a broom handle in a downwards motion, and each 'reel' picked a fruit at random from their bag and held it up. If two of the three fruits matched, the player won thirty pence. If all three fruits matched, the prize was a whole pound!

Throughout the afternoon, I persuaded friends, family and visitors to take turns at being the reels. There was no trickery—the reels genuinely picked the fruit at random. But the low probability of two or three of the same fruit being picked ensured the stall made a profit to bump up the fete proceeds—not a great deal was raised, only twenty pounds or so. I enjoyed doing it for a few hours but was grateful when my father eventually took over.

I talked to some of the local children I knew, but mostly I walked around the stalls to see what was on offer and what had been popular, and I had a thoroughly enjoyable time. It was my favourite day of the summer. It was a day full of joy and laughter, and I felt proud of my family's heritage and role in the community.

CHAPTER SIX

'What is to become of us all?'
Pride and Prejudice – Chapter 47

AT THE END OF SUMMER when I had turned sixteen, Paul asked my parents whether he could take me to the pub with him one evening. I hadn't asked him to or expected it, and I was thrilled at the gesture. They agreed on the proviso he brought me straight home afterwards. After that night, I started going with Paul a couple of times a week to The Sun in Bentworth, six miles away. I was five years younger than Paul, but I looked older than my years, and I was articulate—I made loads of new friends. It was a joyous and carefree summer.

In September, I started at Alton College, a large tertiary college with over a thousand students. Other than in mathematics, I had achieved mediocre results at school and could have done much better, but I wasn't motivated and did just enough to pass and enrol for three A levels: mathematics, economics and psychology. I thought I might eventually study to be an accountant, and my father organised work experience for me with an accountancy firm in Alton. Everything was done by hand; numbers were written in pencil in large ledgers and added up by the accountants using calculators. Their fingers moved faster than my eyes could follow, and some could talk while they added up rows of numbers, without a single mistake. After one week of adding up numbers, I was bored and gave up any thoughts of accountancy as a career. I needed to do something much more exciting.

I liked college and met many new people, but I didn't make any long-lasting friends. My new boyfriend, Phil, was in his second year at the same college and studied far more diligently than I did. He was tall, dark and handsome in faded black jeans and Converse sneakers. I thought I had found my own Mr Darcy. I had known about Mr Darcy for as long as I could remember—visitors to Granny's tea room talked about him.

I tried to read *Pride and Prejudice* when I was about nine but managed only a chapter or two. I preferred non-fiction. The only fiction writer I liked at the time was Enid Blyton; *The Magic Faraway Tree* and *Malory Towers* were favourites. I took a well-read copy of *Pride and Prejudice* from my parents' bookshelves, opened the hard plain cover to Jane's most famous novel and started to read the small writing. 'It is a truth universally acknowledged, that a single man in possession of a good fortune, must be in want of a wife,' I read with instant recognition. I had heard this line quoted many times, but I didn't understand why people were so enamoured with it. Weren't *all* men in want of a wife? I didn't understand Jane's wit, and I struggled to follow the story. I grew weary, closed the novel and returned it to the bookcase. Jane's books were obviously meant for adults. After all, the children who came to the tea room with their parents rarely mentioned them. I concluded I was too young and should try again when I was a grown-up.

At sixteen, I considered myself a grown-up and decided to try *Pride and Prejudice* again. I took down the hardback copy from the bookshelf and sat on a Hepplewhite chair in my parents' sitting room. The upholstered seat could be lifted to reveal a commode. I felt the smoothness of the highly polished oak arms as I sat down, and I wondered who had used it—my father said it had been in the family for generations. I liked to think it had been in Fanny Knight's bedroom perhaps—definitely used by one of the women of the house.

I read the familiar words once more: 'It is a truth universally acknowledged, that a single man in possession of a good fortune, must be in want of a wife.' I needed to read some passages more than once, but the story was clear. Mr Bennet was head of the family and, as such, was afforded the same respect, privacy and deference as Bapops. Mrs Bennet and her daughters accepted the hierarchy without question. Mr Bennet had the most influence, the youngest daughters the least. They lived in a house that was to be inherited by a man who did not live there and, upon the death of Mr Bennet, Mrs Bennet and her daughters would be without a home. This was a significant cause for concern and anxiety for Mrs Bennet, who was desperate to secure rich husbands for her daughters. The Longbourn estate had been 'entailed' to a Mr Collins, who had come to visit the Bennets.

I turned to my dictionary for the meaning of 'entailed'. 'Limit the inheritance of (property) over a number of generations so that ownership remains within a particular group, usually one family,' I read over and over. I asked my father what it meant, and he explained that sometimes squires wrote into their wills certain conditions that restricted who could inherit the estates. Entails often stipulated that the eldest son inherit or the next closest male. The inheritance of the land, property and fortune by one person preserved the social standing of the family. If the conditions were ignored and an alternative heir were chosen, they were at risk of legal challenges to their inheritance by those with a greater claim under the conditions—just like Edward Austen had endured. An entail would explain why Fanny had been overlooked for her younger brother Edward II and why Aunt Betty for her younger brother Bapops. But how had Elizabeth Martin Knight, a woman, overcome such conditions to become squire? It didn't make sense.

I asked my father whether Bapops could change the heir. 'No,' he said, 'Richard is his eldest son and will inherit Chawton; that's how it works.' I didn't know anyone else whose house would be inherited by their uncle. I didn't know any other families with a named sole heir to the family home. But the tale in Great Aunt Jane's novel was similar, 'and nothing can clear Mr Collins from the guilt of inheriting Longbourn,' Mr Bennet teased his wife, for his own amusement. Richard certainly had no reason to feel guilty, and I didn't expect him to. Bapops had named Richard, his firstborn, as his successor, as was his right. Richard was the rightful heir; that was beyond dispute.

I continued to read *Pride and Prejudice* but didn't pay much attention to Mr Darcy and Elizabeth Bennet, as I was distracted by the passages that were relevant to my family: 'Daughters are never of so much consequence to a father,' said Lady Catherine de Bourgh to Elizabeth. Perhaps granddaughters were of little consequence to Bapops. Mr Bennet seemed to gain real pleasure when he spoke with his older daughters, and while he no doubt loved the rest of his family, his relationships with his younger daughters were more distant—I was the youngest in our house.

I was at first amused by Mrs Bennet's 'tears and lamentations of regret, invectives against the villainous conduct of Wickham, and complaints of her own sufferings and ill-usage; blaming everybody but the person to whose ill-judging indulgence the errors of her daughter must principally be owing.' Mrs Bennet is convinced that Mr Bennet will fight Mr Wickham and be killed. She asks, 'and what is to become of us all? The Collinses will turn us out before he is cold in his grave.'

Richard wasn't like Mr Collins at all, but I hadn't thought about the specifics of what would happen when Bapops died. If we had to leave, would it be straight away? I didn't laugh at Mrs Bennet after that—I understood her fear. 'Mr Bennet had very often wished before this period of his life that, instead of spending his whole income, he had laid by an annual sum for the better provision of his children, and of his wife, if she survived him. He now wished it more than ever.' I didn't know whether there were any provisions for Granny. Traditionally, the wife of a deceased squire would move to the estate dower house, to make way for the new squire and his family. But the dower house at Chawton didn't belong to the estate—it had been sold. I wondered whether Granny had known when she married Bapops that her home and security would last only as long as he did.

After a few twists and turns, both Elizabeth and Jane Bennet marry rich men they love. A very happy ending indeed, which secured the future of Mrs Bennet and all her daughters, but did Elizabeth consider she may have to leave Pemberley one day? Mr Darcy would no doubt have made provisions for her, and she would move to a dower house. But what if he hadn't? Were Jane's heroines beholden to their husbands to ensure they were not left destitute in old age?

That autumn, without explanation, Granny closed the tea room for the last time. I assumed it had become more than she could manage with her arthritis. I still saw Granny most days and cooked with her occasionally, but I was more interested in other things. I made clothes, covered a box with decoupage and painted, and I played my guitar every day. In the evenings, I went out with Paul, Phil and our friends, and on Saturdays I worked in a nearby village as a 'mother's help' for a couple who both worked in London. She owned a successful public relations agency, and he was an insurance underwriter at Lloyds of London.

I went to nearly all of my college classes, but I was not motivated to study, despite my mother's words of wisdom. She had told me I needed a good education for my future and had implored me to try, but I quickly fell behind. So I decided to leave college and the backlog of work behind and return to Alton convent to complete my A levels—a few girls in my year had stayed on for sixth form. My mother was not happy and questioned my decision, but I was determined, and so she reluctantly agreed and phoned the convent to make the arrangements. I pushed my academic woes to the back of my mind for the Christmas holidays and looked forward to Snap-Dragon in the Great Hall with our extended family.

In the new year, I started to read *Sense and Sensibility*. The story begins with the Dashwood family, who have been long settled in Sussex. Their ancestral home was Norland Park where 'for many generations, they had lived in so respectable a manner as to engage the general good opinion of their surrounding acquaintance.' The current custodian, Mr Henry Dashwood, had one son by his first marriage and three daughters by his 'present lady'. Due to stipulations of the will that saw Henry inherit Norwood, the property was secured for his son, and only his son, in such a way that denied a secure future for his second wife and daughters. It was all sounding rather familiar—the house was entailed.

When Henry Dashwood died, his son and heir, Mr John Dashwood, 'promised to do every thing in his power to make them comfortable'—that is, his sisters and stepmother—and decided to 'give them three thousand pounds: it would be liberal and handsome!...Three thousand pounds! he could spare so considerable a sum with little inconvenience.' But the moment Henry's funeral was over, John Dashwood's wife arrived unannounced at Norland to assert her authority as the new mistress of the house (just as Mrs Bennet had feared of the Collinses), much to the discomfort of Mrs Dashwood and her daughters who were 'degraded to the condition of visitors'.

In the second chapter, Mrs John Dashwood dissuades her husband from giving the ladies any money at all:

> Do but consider, my dear Mr. Dashwood, how excessively comfortable your mother-in-law and her daughters may live on the interest of seven thousand pounds, besides the thousand pounds belonging to each of the girls, which brings them in fifty pounds

a year a-piece, and, of course, they will pay their mother for their board out of it. Altogether, they will have five hundred a-year amongst them, and what on earth can four women want for more than that?—They will live so cheap! Their housekeeping will be nothing at all. They will have no carriage, no horses, and hardly any servants; they will keep no company, and can have no expenses of any kind! Only conceive how comfortable they will be! Five hundred a year! I am sure I cannot imagine how they will spend half of it; and as to your giving them more, it is quite absurd to think of it. They will be much more able to give YOU something.

It was impossible not to laugh at her approach. But John Dashwood and his wife had absolute power over the future security of the Dashwood ladies. When she talked her husband out of generosity, Mrs Dashwood condemned them to a life of genteel poverty. In contrast, Edward Austen Knight's generosity to his mother and sisters rescued them from relative poverty and returned them to a secure home and village life. But Edward had waited until after his wife, Elizabeth, had died, four years after George Austen had died—had Elizabeth dissuaded him from an earlier intervention?

At the end of the second chapter, Mrs John Dashwood suggests to her husband that the ladies didn't deserve to keep the china they had been left, as it was a 'great deal too handsome, in my opinion, for any place they can ever afford to live in.' It was hard not to think of the Austen Knight china Bapops had given my parents. I could read no more of *Sense and Sensibility*—it was too close to home, and I could no longer ignore the truth. We would have to leave Chawton one day.

Both my parents had talked to me and tried to prepare me for the inevitable, but I didn't want to think about a time when we, the Knight family, would no longer live at Chawton House, and I had deluded myself that the end was so far away that I need not concern myself with it. Perhaps it was not as bad as everyone said it was, and somewhere, hidden away, were the finances for Richard to maintain the house as a home, and we would stay in the north wing.

But that obviously wasn't true—the evidence was all around me. As well as the stables at the front of the house, all the old farm buildings along the back drive had been sold. There had no doubt been other sales I was not aware of—sales were not discussed, and it was difficult not to notice the letters piling up on the table in my grandparents' inner hallway. Whenever Bapops met privately with his advisers, Granny's composure and buoyant conversation as we cooked together in her kitchen had been reassuring, but, with hindsight, I now know why another heirloom or asset would often disappear. 'A large income is the best recipe for happiness I ever heard of,' I had heard quoted from *Mansfield Park*. No income and a crumbling manor house: What was that a recipe for? I couldn't bear to think what the consequences of this would be for our family.

I wondered what Richard thought about it all. Did he resent us, the family of his father's second marriage who lived in the house? Richard had been a young boy when his parents divorced and he and his mother left Chawton. I saw Richard every year on his annual visit to Chawton, and I didn't sense any ill feeling—quite the contrary, in fact. Richard would often join my parents in our quarters for an evening drink, which I would attend for a short time, or a family lunch would be organised. Richard was good company, and I enjoyed our brief conversations, although the light topics of discussion gave me no clues on his thoughts about or intentions for Chawton. I wasn't sure whether he was lucky to be the heir or not. On the one hand, he would inherit the house and be the squire of Chawton, but that wasn't necessarily a good thing given the financial demands of the estate, the lack of funds and the level of restoration required.

I went back to the convent in the middle of January. I tried to study, but my efforts were not enough to pass my subjects, and as the months went on, I became more and more disillusioned with it all. About ten girls had stayed on for sixth form, but the few friends I had previously had at school had left to study their A levels elsewhere. I was lonely and did not look forward to classes.

I spent as much time as I could with Paul, Phil and our friends. On closing time at the pub, the party would often head back home—slipping in via the backstairs so as not to wake my parents or grandparents—and congregate in Paul's bedroom. We listened to music and talked; there were no computer games or mobile phones, and the World Wide Web was yet to be invented. I became good friends with Martin, whose eighteenth birthday had been held in the Great Hall three years earlier, and I regularly visited his terraced cottage in Alton. I had known him since I was about nine, and he was like a brother to me. I sometimes ironed Martin's clothes for some extra pocket money to supplement the income from my Saturday job.

Easter 1987 was particularly warm. On Easter Monday, I went to the Hackwood Park point-to-point horse races as usual, but this time, instead of going with my parents or Robert, I went in the back of a VW van with Paul, Robin, Phil, Martin and some other friends. We walked around the stalls in the afternoon sunshine and placed our bets, but most of the afternoon was spent in the beer tent with old friends we bumped into every year at the races. After the last race, we drove to The Sun, stopping at one or two village pubs on the way for a game of pool.

I stayed at the convent until June, the end of the school year, but I had remained uninspired by education and had been handing assignments in late, if at all. I didn't want to go back for the second year; I was too far behind and didn't have the motivation to catch up. I started to have dreams in which I was in a street in the middle of a town I didn't recognise. It was dark, in the early hours of the morning, and I was walking around on my own—lost with nowhere to go, as tears streamed down my face. It was a short dream that lasted only a few seconds, but it played over and over.

I stayed with friends for most of the summer holidays and only went home every few days. I no longer cooked with Granny or helped my father in the vegetable garden. Sunny afternoons were spent at The Sun. When someone new was introduced to our group, Simon, a friend of Paul's who was always the life and soul of the party, would lead a spirited game of spitfire in The Sun's car park if it was warm enough.

About six of us would stand, drinks in hand, and represent the engines of a spitfire plane and the guns. Simon would stand at the front as the pilot and at the top of his voice call out, 'Start the engines.' We would all make noises as if the engines were indeed being fired up. We followed Simon's instructions as he led us up into the air. We leaned left and right in response to his commands and fired the guns with a loud 'Rut-a-tut-tut.' After a couple of minutes, Simon would shout, 'Fire, fire!' to alert us to a fire in one of the engines—always the engine that our new friend had been asked to play—and we would throw our drinks over the engine to extinguish the fire. It was light-hearted fun and was always met with good humour.

I went home for the ball and the fete in August—I would not have missed them. Shortly after my seventeenth birthday at the end of the summer holidays, I returned to Alton College. Against my mother's wishes, I had abandoned any plans of completing my A levels and, therefore, of securing a place at university. I had left the convent and enrolled in a secretarial course. I didn't want to be a secretary, but I didn't know what else to do, and I thought typing would be a useful skill. I was keen to pass my driving-licence test as soon as I could, so I drove to college every morning with my mother, who then continued on to work.

Blackadder III, set in the Regency era when Jane had been in Chawton, was screening on television and was very popular. Everyone at college loved it. I was excited and impressed when my father told me about the dedication

of *Emma* to the Prince Regent. I was also a little confused—why had Jane
dedicated one of her precious works to such a foppish idiot as played by
Hugh Laurie in *Blackadder*? But Jane had not liked the Prince at all and wrote
candidly to Martha Lloyd on 16 February 1813 in support of the Prince's
estranged wife, Caroline of Brunswick-Wolfenbüttel:

> I suppose all the World is sitting in Judgement upon the Princess
> of Wales's Letter. Poor woman, I shall support her as long as I can,
> because she *is* a Woman, & because I hate her Husband—but I
> can hardly forgive her for calling herself "attached & affectionate"
> to a Man whom she must detest—& the intimacy said to subsist
> between her & Lady Oxford is bad—I do not know what to do
> about it;—but if I must give up the Princess, I am resolved at least
> always to think that she would have been respectable, if the Prince
> had behaved only tolerably by her at first—.

But the Prince Regent was a fan of Jane's, and a couple of years later, she
was invited to view the library at Carlton House, his London residence. It was
early October 1815, as *Emma* was being prepared for publication, and Jane
travelled to London to stay with her brother Henry in Hans Place. Henry fell
ill, and Dr Baillie, who just happened to be the Prince Regent's physician, was
called in. Dr Baillie mentioned to Jane that the Prince was a great admirer of
her works and that he had a set of them in each of his lodgings and read them
often. Dr Baillie had therefore thought it right to inform His Royal Highness
that Miss Austen was staying in London, and the Prince had instructed Reverend Clarke, the librarian of Carlton House, to show her the library.

The invitation was accepted, and Jane visited Carlton House on 13 November 1815. I was in awe—to think of Jane going to the Prince's mansion.
While she was there, Reverend Clarke said he had been asked to convey that if

Miss Austen had any other novel forthcoming, she was at liberty to dedicate it to the Prince. What a tricky position Jane must have been in. Two days later, Jane wrote to Reverend Clarke to ask to what extent she was obliged to comply:

> SIR,—I must take the liberty of asking you a question. Among the many flattering attentions which I received from you at Carlton House on Monday last was the information of my being at liberty to dedicate any future work to His Royal Highness the Prince Regent, without the necessity of any solicitation on my part. Such, at least, I believed to be your words; but as I am very anxious to be quite certain of what was intended, I entreat you to have the goodness to inform me how such a permission is to be understood, and whether it is incumbent on me to show my sense of the honour by inscribing the work now in the press to His Royal Highness; I should be equally concerned to appear either presumptuous or ungrateful. (Nov 15th 1815)

Reverend Clarke responded the very next day:

> DEAR MADAM,—It is certainly not *incumbent* on you to dedicate your work now in the press to His Royal Highness; but if you wish to do the Regent that honour either now or at any future period I am happy to send you that permission, which need not require any more trouble or solicitation on your part.

Jane eventually decided she would dedicate *Emma* to the Prince Regent and added a 'perfectly proper' dedication. Her exaggerated deference would have no doubt pleased the Prince but also revealed her true feelings to those who knew her.

TO

HIS ROYAL HIGHNESS

THE PRINCE REGENT,

THIS WORK IS,

BY HIS ROYAL HIGHNESS'S PERMISSION,

MOST RESPECTFULLY

DEDICATED,

BY HIS ROYAL HIGHNESS'S

DUTIFUL

AND OBEDIENT

HUMBLE SERVANT

THE AUTHOR.

In later correspondence, Reverend Clarke went on to suggest the subject matter of Jane's next novel. In March 1816, he wrote: 'Perhaps when you again appear in print you may chuse to dedicate your Volumes to Prince Leopold: any Historical Romance illustrative of the History of the august house of Cobourg, would just now be very interesting.' Jane replied firmly and ended her letter:

You are very, very kind in your hints as to the sort of composition
which might recommend me at present, & I am fully sensible
that an historical romance, founded on the House of Saxe Cobourg might be much more to the purpose of Profit or Popularity, than such pictures of domestic Life in Country Villages as
I deal in—but I could no more write a Romance than an Epic
Poem.—I could not sit seriously down to write a serious Romance under any other motive than to save my Life, & if it were
indispensable for me to keep it up & never relax into laughing at
myself or other people, I am sure I should be hung before I had
finished the first Chapter.—No—I must keep to my own style &
go on in my own Way; And though I may never succeed again in
that, I am convinced that I should totally fail in any other.—

I loved it! Jane had been so brave and articulated her rebuke so wonder-
fully. I, too, wanted to 'keep to my own style & go on in my own way'. I just
didn't know yet what way that was. I knew I didn't want to work in a shop
or in a factory or at a job that would be the same every day. I wished I had a
passion—Jane had written since she was a young girl.

If we had to leave Chawton, I wanted to travel and see the world. Edward
Austen Knight had travelled around Europe, my father had travelled to
Australia, and my mother and brother had travelled to England. Perhaps
I would travel the world one day. As Jane had written in *Northanger Abbey*,
'If adventures will not befall a young lady in her own village, she must seek
them abroad.'

I had no idea what I wanted to do, but I was determined to do something
I enjoyed and at which I could excel. After all, it was possible I would not be
as fortunate as the Bennet sisters had been. I might not find a rich man, fall
in love and marry—I needed a backup plan.

CHAPTER SEVEN

'It is as if I had lost a part of myself.'
Letter to Fanny Knight on 20 July 1817 from Cassandra Austen

ON TWO OR THREE OCCASIONS in my teens, I had noticed Bapops absent from his library chair for a couple of days. 'Bapops is unwell,' my father would say and reassure me that he would get better. The details were not shared, and I did not ask. Bapops stayed in his bed for a few days, with regular visits from his doctor. Granny would tell me to make myself scarce, and I would leave my grandparents' quarters in good time so as not to be in the way. Within a week or two, Bapops would take up his daily routines once more, and the incident would not be mentioned again.

A month or so into my secretarial course, my father suggested I visit Bapops who was ill and confined to his bedroom. It was such an unusual request that I didn't need to ask why—there was only one possible reason. As I wondered what I should say to Bapops, I felt a knot of apprehension tighten in my stomach. I asked my father when I should go, how long I should talk to Bapops and how this visit was to be arranged. We agreed that I would see Bapops when I got home from college the following afternoon, and my father would let Granny know of my plans.

It was early October and autumn was setting in. The morning passed at college without incident—I pushed Bapops to the back of my mind. I arrived home with a false air of normality and tried to convince myself this was like any other day. I dropped my bags in my room and went to see Granny, who was sitting in her chair in the library. The chair beside her was empty. Her smile was as warm as ever, and she betrayed nothing of her inner thoughts or of the inevitable change she was about to endure. 'Bapops is expecting you,' she said. I smiled, walked out of the library, turned immediately left and walked up the main staircase.

The sloping stairs creaked with my every step, and I held the inner rail firmly as I purposefully walked towards the first floor of my grandparents' quarters. I stepped off the staircase onto the first-floor landing and, with a lump in my throat, stood for a moment outside Bapops's bedroom on the left. Opposite his bedroom door, behind a curtain, were the stained-glass windows and a screen obscuring the southern end of Suicide Alley. Bapops had lived in the house the longest, so I assumed he knew where everything in Suicide Alley had come from—who had owned the old shoes and when the furniture had been broken.

I had been in his bedroom only briefly before, when I dropped off linen to help Granny. I wasn't sure who changed his bed linen—he would not have done it himself, that was for certain. Granny did have a woman who came in a couple of hours a week to help, so perhaps she did it. I was suddenly struck by the peculiarity of his choice of bedroom. My grandparents' quarters had five bedrooms: Granny's large bedroom above the library at the back of the house; Uncle Robert's bedroom, also known as the Oak Room, at the front of the house; and two large bedrooms above the Great Hall that shared magnificent views down the front drive. These were the childhood bedrooms of my father and Aunt Ann, and they had not been used for decades, other than for the occasional guests. Yet Bapops preferred to sleep in this small dark oak-panelled room overlooking the lawns to the south-west.

The room was so small that I imagined it had been intended as a dressing room, but an inventory of the 'Goods & Chattells of Sr. Richard Knight' in the back of Montagu's book lists a 'little Chamb. at ye staire head'—I had been mistaken. There was room for only a single bed, bedside table, small desk, chair and small wardrobe. The south-west face of the house was covered in ivy that turned a vibrant red in the autumn. The ivy was regularly cut back from the windows so as not to obscure the light or the views, but not from Bapops's bedroom window, where it was left overgrown. I couldn't see out of the window, and the daylight struggled to get in to brighten the dark room.

I wondered why Bapops slept in a cupboard, which is exactly how it felt in comparison with the other bedrooms in the house. Surely, as squire, he would have had first choice of room. How long had he slept in this room? Even if he had not wanted to move Granny or Robert from their bedrooms, two other grand rooms lay empty just across the hall. I stood outside the room and pondered his choice for the first time. Bapops had slept in this room for at least the whole of my life, and I had never considered it, never wondered why a man of such privilege and position would shut himself away and spend his days in either a poky dark bedroom or the corner armchair of the library. I had never seen him walk about the house, and he never came to our quarters. Chawton House had so much life: the resident family and tenants, visiting family and guests, the tea room, community events, parties and celebrations. But other than quiet attendance at private family lunches and traditions, Bapops didn't join in.

I breathed slowly in and out to calm my nerves, lightly knocked on the dark oak door and pushed it open. Bapops lay in his bed, supported by pillows, with his cotton pyjamas buttoned up to the neck. I remember it as if it were yesterday. 'Hello, how are you?' I asked.

'Hello,' he responded but ignored my enquiry about his well-being. Why did I ask how he was? What a silly question to ask someone who is very sick.

No one had specifically said Bapops was dying, but it didn't need to be said. Why else would he want to see me? It then occurred to me that I couldn't be sure he wanted to see me. Perhaps this visit had been Granny's or my father's idea. I ignored the thought and chose to believe that Bapops had instigated it.

As my eyes adjusted to the poor light, I could see his frailness under the blankets. I sat on a wooden chair that had been placed next to the bed, and we exchanged awkward superficial words about the weather while I struggled to think of something more interesting to say. I didn't know what he knew about me, and I didn't know anything personal about him. We had lived in the same house for seventeen years, but I didn't know his likes or dislikes. We didn't share any interests, and other than immediate family, we didn't know the same people.

I looked around the room and noticed on his desk an ornate leather-covered box with a brass lock. It was beautiful, and I stood up to admire it. 'Can I look inside?' I asked. I carefully undid the brass latch at the front, and the lid hinged backwards to reveal compartments for writing paper. Next to the box lay what appeared in the dim light to be a large matching leather book. I picked it up and discovered it wasn't a book. It was a hard leather document folder with fabric lining which had been used as a writing blotter—it was covered in small ink stains. I admired the writing set; its brown leather was highly embossed with an ornate gold pattern, a little faded with signs of use.

Bapops said he liked it too, but he didn't tell me where it had come from. Had it been a gift to him from someone special, his mother perhaps, or had it been in the family for generations? It had been manufactured by Dreyfous of London, Paris and New York, according to the gold writing embossed on the rear of the box. I later discovered that it was likely to have been made towards the end of the nineteenth century, around the time Montagu became squire, so perhaps it had been his. What letters had been written while leaning on the folder? Is this where Bapops had signed the many documents authorising the sale of the estate's assets over the years?

I placed the document folder back on the desk and continued to make polite but somewhat awkward conversation about my college courses. Bapops's contribution was limited to acknowledging my words. He seemed calm, with no signs of distress either physically or mentally. He appeared comfortable with my presence and content with my chatter but offered no opinion or words of guidance. He tired after a few minutes. Neither of us made mention of his health or said our goodbyes in any way, and we didn't acknowledge the reason for my visit. 'Well, I need to go and help Granny', I said, and he nodded, happy to let me go. 'Take care, and see you soon,' I said cheerfully and left the room. I walked downstairs to let Granny know I was finished. She didn't ask how it had gone or what we had talked about.

I attended college as normal for the next few days and occasionally thought about the interaction with Bapops—I hoped our conversation had not disappointed him. I felt numb and didn't know what to think. On the Tuesday of the following week, I was in a shorthand lesson at college. The morning had passed without incident, and I had entered the class in good spirits. As the teacher, a kind woman, turned from the whiteboard, she noticed the tears streaming down my face. Without warning, I was overwhelmed with emotion and sobbed, unable to stop. She took me into a nearby empty room and asked what had happened. 'My grandfather is dying,' I said.

'I'm sorry to hear that—you are obviously very close,' she said. I didn't know how to begin to explain. No, we were not close; we had never really spoken, but I didn't want to admit that. I barely knew him, but I loved and respected him as the head of our family. His death would spell change for Granny and Robert, for my family, for Penny and her family and for Richard, who was to inherit a house in need of significant repair and investment that was full of tenants and his resident half-siblings. This inevitable change was more than I could imagine or come to terms with and brought a fear I had learnt to ignore.

'I just wish it was over,' I said. I was surprised at my words, but the wait had become unbearable. The teacher could see I was horrified by the words I had uttered, and she told me it was to be expected and that I should not feel bad. I didn't know what to expect; no one I was related to or was close to had ever died. I had never even been to a funeral.

Three days later, on Friday, 8 October 1987, my mother told me when I awoke that Bapops had passed away that morning. 'Oh, right,' I said. It had been expected, so I wasn't surprised—I didn't know what I felt. My mother and I spoke for a few minutes; she asked whether I was OK, and I asked when the extended family would arrive. Bapops was still in his bed, she said. The doctor had confirmed his death, and the undertakers would be coming in the afternoon. I decided to be elsewhere when they arrived.

I washed, dressed and walked through to the library to see Granny, who was sitting in her chair. Robert and my aunts were keeping her company, and I leant down and gave her a hug. She smiled, but her eyes were red from recent tears. I had never seen such emotion from Granny, and I struggled not to cry. The conversation was kept superficial—who was coming for lunch and what was needed from the shops.

Everyone was calm in the days after Bapops's death. There were no hysterics and no outward signs of grief, and if any disagreements over arrangements did occur, they were discussed in private, out of my earshot. Over the next few days, a slow but steady stream of close family and friends came to see Granny and give their condolences. Meals were cooked, shopping was done, and the mantel clock ticked as always, but the atmosphere in the house subtly changed. Chawton belonged to Richard now, and it was unavoidable: our time at the manor was coming to an end. What would happen to Granny? Where would we go? My parents planned to buy a house in Alton. I simply couldn't imagine living as a family of four in an ordinary house, without our extended family, the portraits of our ancestors and the freedom to roam the estate.

My parents answered my questions as best they could. Yes, we would eventually have to leave, but Richard had not given a firm indication of when that would be. It wasn't likely to be soon, however, as there was a lot to be sorted before he would know. The house was in such poor repair, and although Richard was a successful farmer, he did not have the millions needed for renovations. With so many affairs to be sorted and the financial challenges of the estate to be faced, it would be some months before any of us would have answers—perhaps longer. But whatever happened to Chawton House, my parents reassured me we would settle well in a new home. I listened but was not wholly reassured. I didn't want to live anywhere else. I so desperately wanted to stay.

The funeral was arranged for Thursday, 15 October, to be held in the church, followed by a burial in the Knight family corner of the graveyard, opposite Montagu's grave. A couple of days before the funeral, I missed a deadline for an assignment at college and asked to see the teacher (a different teacher from the previous week's outburst) after class to apologise and agree to a new deadline. Before I could speak, she said, 'It's all right, Caroline, I know what's happened.' I was very grateful I didn't have to explain.

The funeral was planned for eleven o'clock. I had breakfast, washed, and dressed in a dark dress and coat for the day. I had seen funerals on television, so I had some idea of what to expect. I wasn't looking forward to Bapops being lowered into the ground—I imagined this to be the most difficult part. At a quarter to eleven, my parents, Paul and I walked together through the Great Hall, out of the main entrance and down the front drive. There were already many people in the church; the pews were almost full. We walked calmly down the centre aisle of the church to take our place in one of the Knight family pews at the front. We sat on the left-hand side.

The coffin was already in place, resting on wooden stands in the middle of the nave in front of the pews. I thought about Bapops lying in the coffin, there, right in front of us. Paul briefly held my hand and smiled, as best he could, to comfort me. Bapops had never held my hand. I couldn't recall him ever touching me.

The church continued to fill, and as I looked about, I saw many familiar faces from the village and many I did not know. After a short time, Granny entered and walked up the central aisle to take her position in the front pew on the right. She didn't talk to anyone or make eye contact with the congregation. I saw her attempt to take her seat at the front as quickly as she could manage—her arthritis slowed her down. She sat and leant forward, her head in her hands.

It was as if I were in a film. Time seemed to move quickly and slowly simultaneously. I can't remember any details of the service. I was in a daze. Hundreds of people were packed into the church to pay their respects to Edward Knight, the fifteenth squire of Chawton House. The pews were full, and many had to stand. All I could think about was Bapops lying in the coffin, there, right in front of me. I would never know him now. The service passed without incident, and the family maintained their dignity throughout. After the final prayers, the coffin was carried out of the church. Granny led the procession, followed by her children and grandchildren and other family members before the rest of the congregation poured out of the church.

As we left the church and turned towards the Knight section of the graveyard, I struggled to keep my composure. I stopped my mother and quietly told her that I couldn't do it—I couldn't watch as Bapops was lowered into the ground. Aunt Ann's husband offered to escort me back to the house, which I gratefully accepted. I broke down in tears as soon as we left the churchyard.

As we walked slowly to the house, I gradually regained my composure. We waited in the Great Hall for the rest of the family to return. My parents were quick to find me when they arrived and hugged me in quiet comfort—no words were necessary—before we joined the family around Edward Austen Knight's grand dining table once more for lunch. It was such an extraordinary occasion and yet so completely ordinary. I had conflicted emotions and many questions, but this was not the time to express them. I couldn't mourn Bapops as a person because I hadn't known him. Yet I was devastated he had gone and fearful of the future. Who would we be if we were no longer the Knights of Chawton? That was now the rightful privilege of Richard and his children.

When I went to bed that night, I felt drained. It had been a difficult day, and I was relieved the funeral was over. I usually enjoyed the hustle and bustle of visitors and events, but not this time. We were all exhausted and needed time to recover.

At five the following morning, I was woken by voices in our kitchen. I poked my head out of my bedroom door to see what was happening. There had been a storm overnight, a windstorm, the strength of which had not been seen in the south of England for centuries. The council had already been on the telephone—every tree surgeon in the county was needed to clear trees from the roads. My father made a cup of coffee for Paul, who looked bleary-eyed. I pulled on jeans and a jumper and, after Paul had set off, joined my father on a walk around the grounds. Everywhere we looked, in whichever direction we turned, was mass destruction. The forces of nature had left their mark. Ancient oaks had been torn up by the roots. Most of the trees in the South Lime Avenue that Montagu had planted on the parklands a hundred years earlier had been ripped out of the ground. The air was still—the calm after the storm.

It was difficult to take in the level of destruction. After the events of the previous day, the effects of the storm seemed to heighten the magnitude and apocalyptic nature of Bapops's death and this moment in Knight family history. In playful reference to our motto, *Suivant Saint Pierre* (Follow St Peter), the family joked that Bapops must have created havoc when he got to the gates of heaven.

The estate was eerily quiet, except for the distant sounds of chainsaws. Cars had been crushed and houses damaged, but fortunately no lives were lost in Chawton or the neighbouring villages. Other areas were not so lucky. In just three hours, eighteen lives had been lost in England and four in northern France as strong wind gusts reached 115 miles an hour. The storm brought down fifteen million trees, including historic trees in Kew Gardens and Hyde Park. Six of the seven oak trees after which the town of Sevenoaks is named were blown over. It was the worst storm since 1703—Elizabeth Martin Knight's first year as squire. What a shock it must have been for her to wake to devastation across the estate and what a challenge to clear thousands of fallen trees before the invention of tractors and chainsaws.

Every road in Hampshire was closed. Home Secretary Douglas Hurd called it the 'worst, most widespread night of disaster' since the Blitz. A cross-channel ferry, the MV *Hengist*, was driven ashore near Folkestone, and a number of ships capsized. London was blacked out for six hours, and hundreds of thousands of people were left without power, in many cases for several weeks. Three people were killed when their chimneys toppled. Others died on the roads or when struck by falling trees. A fisherman was killed in Hastings when a beach hut hit him, and two men in Dover died when their ship sank.

Schools and colleges throughout the area were closed, and the following week was half-term, so I didn't return to college for about ten days. The aftermath of the storm lasted for weeks, longer in some regions. Paul worked around the clock for the council, and my parents cleared fallen trees and branches on the estate.

The obituary in the local paper of 'The late Major Edward Knight of Chawton' reported that Bapops 'always held the village cricket club dear to his heart':

Major Knight, who was 77, was a cricket enthusiast from an early age and made history as the only first-year boy at Sherborne School to play for its first eleven. Major Knight, who inherited Chawton House in 1932, played cricket for Alton. His sporting interests also extended to hunting as a member of the Hampshire Hunt and to polo. An A.D.C. in Kenya in 1932–34, he played for the Kenya Polo Club. He had been in the Territorial Army before joining the Queen Victoria Rifles, serving in the Second World War in France before being seconded to the 17th–5th Jat Regiment in India.

The obituary mentioned only his military service and the sporting achievements of his youth, but I suppose there was little to say about his later life.

A few days later, my father said he had something that Granny had asked him to give me. In his hands was the Dreyfous leather writing box and document folder I had admired in Bapops's bedroom. I was astonished and didn't know what to make of the gesture. It was hard to believe that Bapops had remembered our conversation and specifically asked Granny to give it to me, but how else would she have known? What did it mean? Did he regret not knowing me better and want me to know that he cared after all? I was overjoyed to have something so personal of his, but I was also saddened that this was all I would ever have of Bapops now. I knew I had to treasure it, but I didn't want such a personal reminder of the relationship I had missed having with Bapops—or of his death—in my bedroom, so I asked my parents to look after it until I was older.

At the beginning of the following year, my father confirmed that beyond all doubt we would have to leave our ancestral home. Richard would have to find a way to make the estate viable or find a buyer. It was hard to imagine summer without events to organise and Christmas Eve without Snap-Dragon.

I didn't like the thought of Chawton House in the hands of another family or of it being run as a business. It was hard to comprehend that four hundred years of history were coming to an end. I thought about the prospect of saying goodbye, of the day when we would close the door to our north-wing quarters for the last time and drive away. Jane wrote of the very moment in *Sense and Sensibility*:

> Many were the tears shed by them in their last adieus to a place
> so much beloved. "Dear, dear Norland!" said Marianne, as she
> wandered alone before the house, on the last evening of their
> being there; when shall I cease to regret you?—when learn to feel
> a home elsewhere!—Oh! happy house! could you know what I
> suffer in now viewing you from this spot, from whence perhaps
> I may view you no more!

I wasn't sure whether Jane shared the sentiment or whether she was mocking Marianne's oversensitivity, but that didn't matter. I couldn't bear the thought of it and resolved to be away from home when that day came. I didn't want to say goodbye, and I certainly didn't want to watch Granny leave for the last time. According to what my father had told me, Granny had always known this day would come. Richard was, and always had been, the rightful heir to the Chawton estate, but Granny had spent decades as mistress of Chawton House. She had worked tirelessly and had little to show for it, other than her memories. It was sad to think of Granny in a small bungalow or apartment somewhere, which seemed the most likely outcome. It wasn't Richard's fault she had to leave. There was just no way she could stay. The house was in desperate need of investment, and he had inherited a heavy responsibility: to find a way to preserve Chawton estate for future generations if it were at all possible. What a challenge that was going to be.

I resolved not to enquire about the fate of the house any further, as it upset me. I would not dwell on it—there was no point. If it were to be turned
into a business or sold to a private family, I didn't want to be informed of the
details until it was all over, and I certainly didn't want to know on which day
Richard would be parting with the house. I didn't want to experience Anne
Elliot's sorrow:

> and now Anne's heart must be in Kellynch again. A beloved
> home made over to others; all the precious rooms and furni-
> ture, groves, and prospects, beginning to own other eyes and
> other limbs! She could not think of much else on the 29th of
> September; and she had this sympathetic touch in the evening
> from Mary, who, on having occasion to note down the day of
> the month, exclaimed, "Dear me, is not this the day the Crofts
> were to come to Kellynch? I am glad I did not think of it be-
> fore. How low it makes me!"

Anne Elliot, the Dashwood sisters and the Bennet sisters—all had to secure a future because they could not stay in their family home. Jane herself
had experienced the loss of her childhood home in Steventon, although Jane's
real-life approach to securing her future differed greatly from the solution she
gave her characters. Her heroines always found long-term security and happiness with an advantageous marriage based on genuine affection and love.
Jane refused her only offer of marriage and set out to make some money as an
author. The conflict between her stories and her actions was a puzzle. Jane was
a realist and, like the rest of her family, practical in her approach to money.
She wanted her novels to appeal to the reader of her day and to be circulated
by travelling libraries. But did Jane truly believe in happy endings? Perhaps
she was dedicated to her novels above all else and didn't want to compromise

her writing time with the responsibilities of a husband and children. Perhaps she just never found her own Mr Darcy.

There and then, I decided I would be financially independent. I wanted to be in control of my own destiny and not beholden to a wealthy husband. I would earn my own money, pay my own bills and make my own way in the world. I would decide where I lived and when I moved. I had no idea what I wanted to do or what career I would have. I couldn't go to university as I had dropped out of my A levels, but I was confident I would be able to secure some job or other and make something of myself.

I had plenty of female role models to draw upon. Elizabeth Martin Knight had been one of the most significant squires in our history. Granny ran the house and the tea room and was landlady to the tenants. When I was little, my mother had taken an evening course in business administration at Basingstoke College, and she passed the diploma-level course with distinction. She had tired of her job at the hospital and wanted to develop her career. When I left school, she took a leap of faith and resigned from her job at the hospital, unsure of where fate would take her—a good decision in the end. She was much happier working in the office of a local business. Trish also left the hospital and built an extension on the side of their home for a private physiotherapy practice. It was one of the first in the area and became a huge success, so much so that Dennis left his career to help Trish run the business.

And, of course, there was Jane. Against all odds, she went on to write six books which are so extraordinary that she has attracted a continuous following for nearly 200 years, is hailed as one of the best female classical writers of all time and has brought joy to millions. What an inspirational achievement and legacy. To think that a member of my family had created such iconic stories and characters! A poem written to Jane in 1813 by James Edward Austen Leigh (James Austen's son who later went on to publish *A Memoir of Jane Austen* in 1870) summed it up perfectly. He was fifteen and had discovered that his aunt was the anonymous author of *Sense and Sensibility* and *Pride and Prejudice*.

> To Miss J. Austen
>
> No words can express, my dear Aunt, my surprise
>
> Or make you conceive how I opened my eyes,
>
> Like a pig Butcher Pile has just struck with his knife,
>
> When I heard for the first time in my life
>
> That I had the honour to have a relation
>
> Whose works were dispersed through the whole of the nation.
>
> I assure you, however, I'm terribly glad;
>
> Oh dear! just to think (and the thought drives me mad)
>
> That dear Mrs Jennings's good-natured strain
>
> Was really the produce of your witty brain,
>
> That you made the Middletons, Dashwoods, and all,
>
> And that you (not young Ferrars) found out that a ball
>
> May be given in cottages, never so small.
>
> And that though Mr. Collins, so grateful for all,
>
> Will Lady de Bourgh his dear Patroness call,
>
> 'Tis to your ingenuity really he owed
>
> His living, his wife, and his humble abode.
>
> Now if you will take your poor nephew's advice,
>
> Your works to Sir William pray send in a trice,
>
> If he'll undertake to some grandees to show it,
>
> By whose means at last the Prince Regent might know it,
>
> For I'm sure if he did, in reward for your tale,
>
> He'd make you a countess at least, without fail,
>
> And indeed if the Princess should lose her dear life
>
> You might have a good chance of becoming his wife.

I was particularly amused by the suggestion that Jane might seek notice of the Prince Regent, given her opinions of him.

I returned to college after half-term and was at home less and less frequently. I didn't go to see Sir Richard in the church again or look at the pedigree book, the stained-glass windows, the bookplates or any of the portraits. I didn't go to Jane's cottage or sit in her garden.

My mother dropped me at college each day on her way to work and collected me on her way home, unless I got a lift home with a college friend. I spent a couple of hours at home and normally went out after having dinner with my parents. A quiet evening at home would usually initiate a restless night of nightmares in which I was homeless, so I went out as often as I could. As long as I was busy, in the pub or at a party, I could ignore my thoughts, and that was all that mattered.

It was as if I had lost a part of myself.

CHAPTER EIGHT

'And sometimes I have kept my feelings to myself,
because I could find no language to describe them in.'
Sense and Sensibility – Chapter 18

AT THE BEGINNING OF the summer of 1988, I left Alton College. I still
didn't know exactly when we would leave Chawton, but as our inevitable departure drew nearer, I worked harder at my studies and passed the secretarial
course with a distinction. It was four hundred years since John Knight had
put the iron fireback, with the date 1588, in my grandparents' quarters, but
it didn't seem appropriate to mention the anniversary—there wasn't much to
celebrate. My relationship with Phil came to an end, and I spent the first few
weeks of the summer with college friends. I had passed my driving test earlier in the year and sometimes borrowed my parents' only car, a Suzuki jeep.
When the car was unavailable, I stayed overnight at a friend's house.

I wanted—needed—to leave Chawton before moving day, so I bought a
copy of *The Lady* magazine and searched the Situations Vacant for nanny jobs
close by. Within a couple of weeks, I had secured a job as a live-in 'mother's
help' for a family twenty miles away, near Midhurst—I shall call them the
Millers. I liked children, although I was in no hurry to have my own. I had no
intention of making childcare my career, but this live-in position offered safe

ABOVE Paul, me and my mother in the Great Hall, Chawton House, Christmas 1985

ABOVE My mother and me in the Great Hall, Chawton House, Christmas 1986

ABOVE My father and me in the dining room, Chawton House, 1988

LEFT
Me trying on
Granny's diamonds
in the dining room,
Chawton House, 1988

ABOVE My eighteenth birthday dinner in full flow at Edward
Austen Knight's dining table, the Great Hall, Chawton House, 1988

ABOVE Austen Knight dinner service made by Wedgwood in 1813

ABOVE The Great Hall as shown in *Chawton Manor and its Owners: A Family History* by W. Austen Leigh and M.G. Knight, published by Smith, Elder & Co. in 1911

ABOVE Montagu and Florence Knight's twenty-fifth wedding anniversary carving from 1895, above the fireplace in the dining room, Chawton House

LEFT
Heraldry
windows in the
picture gallery,
Chawton House

ABOVE The stables at Chawton House

ABOVE St Nicholas Church, Chawton

ABOVE Jane Austen's House Museum, Chawton

ABOVE Jane Austen's writing desk,
at Jane Austen's House Museum, Chawton

Chawton House Library

Chawton House Library preserves a unique collection of early women's writing (1600–1830). Visitors can enjoy the 'Great House' referred to in Jane's letters, relax in the tranquil gardens and find inspiration in the lives and works of the library's women writers.

Chawton House Library is open to the visiting public from March to October; anyone who wants to read the books can make an appointment at any time. For further information, event programme and admission prices, visit www.chawtonhouselibrary.org.

ABOVE Dining room

ABOVE Front entrance

ABOVE Old kitchen

accommodation, my own bedroom and bathroom, a car and a small wage. I was excited but nervous—this would be my first move away from home. I thought I would perhaps stay for a year and save some money to move to London or to buy my own car; I wasn't sure.

Mrs Miller didn't work, but she was heavily pregnant and needed help with the household chores. I washed and ironed, cooked, kept the kitchen clean and helped care for her two young children. She had high standards, but she was a nice woman, and we got on well enough. Mr Miller was a silver-haired man in his fifties. I saw him briefly most days before he left for work as I swam laps in their pool in the early morning, but we rarely spoke.

I went home most weekends and enjoyed the annual summer events as usual, particularly the Summer Ball. I had made a strapless dark-green taffeta dress with a tight-fitting bodice for the evening, and I asked my mother whether I might borrow some costume jewellery to wear around my neck. My father suggested I might like to try on Granny's tiara before its imminent sale. I didn't know Granny had a tiara, and I was intrigued. My father returned a few minutes later and opened a velvet-covered box to reveal a beautiful necklace, with minute rows of diamonds strung together like lace. He hung it around my neck and closed the clasp. I looked in the mirror in amazement as the necklace twinkled in the light. It was the most luxurious thing I had ever seen. I had seen old photographs of Granny dressed in expensive clothes, but I hadn't realised just how fancy she had been. I wondered whether she ever looked at it now and remembered the glittering parties that she had once attended.

'I thought you said it was a tiara,' I said, confused, as my father took a photograph of me in front of Montagu and Florence's anniversary carving. My father explained that the jewellery was designed to be versatile, and the diamonds could be worn as a necklace or attached to a headband and worn as a tiara.

Granny once had a lovely collection of jewellery, but it had been sold off gradually over the years. The tiara was Granny's last keepsake of the prosperity she had enjoyed as a young woman. It must have been terrible for her to let go of the last vestiges of the life she had once known. She had lost her husband and her home, and now she would have to give up something so personal and precious—to be sold at auction. I couldn't imagine how heartbroken she must have been feeling, but she never let it show.

Alas, I wasn't allowed to wear the necklace for the evening; the diamonds were far too valuable. I took the necklace off, put it back in the velvet box, closed the lid and handed it back to my father. I never saw the diamonds again.

After the weekend of the annual Fete and Horticultural Show at the beginning of August, I returned to Midhurst. Mr Miller was due to catch a train and asked me to drive him to the station. He usually drove, so it was an unusual request. The conversation was a little stilted, but we talked politely for most of the car journey. As we neared the station, he told me I was pretty and that he had watched me in the pool. I didn't know how to respond and wasn't sure I had heard him correctly, so I remained quiet. He went on to say how much 'fun' we could have together while his wife was in hospital giving birth—she was due in a couple of weeks.

When we reached the station, he stopped the car and leant over to kiss me. Time went into slow motion. I firmly pushed him away and told him in the strongest voice I could muster to go and get on the train. I didn't swear or scream and told myself not to panic. I needed to be calm and assertive. He smiled and told me there was nothing to be scared of. I repeated my words, and he released his grip, grabbed his bags and cheerfully said goodbye as if nothing had happened.

I was bewildered and sat in the car for a few minutes with the doors locked. I was supposed to drive straight back to Midhurst, but I couldn't face his wife. How could I tell such a heavily pregnant woman that her husband had tried to make plans with the live-in help? But I couldn't pretend it hadn't happened; I was scared of what he would do when she did go into hospital. I decided to visit my mother at work and tell her what had happened; she would know what to do. My mother drove me straight back to Midhurst and, while I packed, spoke privately to Mrs Miller. Before we left, Mrs Miller said how sorry she was but didn't seem as surprised as I had expected. She may have been in shock and determined to keep calm, just as I was, I supposed. I heaved a sigh of relief as my mother drove us away.

My mother took me straight back to Chawton House and insisted I stay at home for the next few days. I didn't want to, but I agreed. It was a horrible end to my first home away from Chawton, but I was determined not to let it affect me. My eighteenth birthday was only a couple of weeks away, at the end of August, so I focused on the plans for my celebration. I had attended many events and parties in the Great Hall, but none of them had been held especially for me. My life in Chawton was at an end, and this was my one and only chance to host a dinner party for my friends in the grandeur of our home, just as generations of Knights had done before me. I was not going to miss it.

My parents happily agreed to my birthday plans, and my mother designed the menu: smoked mackerel pâté and toast; pheasant casserole, cauliflower cheese and roasted potatoes; pavlova; and cheese, biscuits and coffee to finish. My invitation list included Paul, my cousins Fiona and Robin, Martin and Simon, a few friends from college and the pub, and a couple of Chawton House tenants, most with partners.

Edward Austen Knight's dining table was not quite big enough for my twenty guests. To make one long dining table, we used another table of the same height and width and covered both tables with blankets and large white linen tablecloths. I wasn't allowed to use the Austen Knight china, as the risk of damage was too great, but I wasn't disappointed—at least I would not be worrying about it all evening. The table was laid with cutlery, side plates and wine glasses—the latter holding folded pink napkins. Pink flowers and gold candles in white porcelain holders adorned the centre of the table.

The dress code for the evening was black tie. I didn't have the time or inclination to make myself another new dress, and I didn't want to wear one that I had worn before, so I borrowed an off-the-shoulder blue taffeta gown from a friend. I felt a touch of sadness as I walked into the Great Hall. It was difficult to imagine that this could be our last celebration in our family home, but I quickly pushed such thoughts to the back of my mind.

Everyone dressed accordingly, and I felt very grown-up. Some of the men owned dinner jackets; others had borrowed one from their father or a friend. My father served drinks as the party gathered around the fireside in the Great Hall. We were in good spirits, and the room was filled with voices and laughter. My parents had asked Jake, Amber, Trish and Dennis, who already knew many of my friends, to help deliver silver service at the table. Everyone was delighted to hear that our friends would be 'waiting' on us. What fun!

I sat at the head of the table, beside my new boyfriend, and enjoyed every minute of the evening. The food was delicious, the wine and conversation flowed, my guests all seemed to enjoy themselves, and I had never been happier. For just one night, I pretended I was at Chawton House in its heyday. It was such a treat to be served by our 'wait staff', who went from one guest to the next, serving pheasant casserole and vegetables onto each warmed plate. I thought of the thousands of guests and many dinners and parties that had been hosted over four centuries; it was such a joy and privilege to entertain guests in our own home and on a grand scale. I knew this might be the last Knight family celebration at home in the Great Hall—I didn't know what the future held for Richard.

I was determined that one day I would be able to host dinner parties in my own home, so for my eighteenth birthday present, I had asked for linen and table settings to host a dozen guests. I had asked my parents for a canteen of antique silver cutlery. I had always liked the classical 'bead' design, and so my parents spent months attending antique fairs to find dinner and dessert forks, dessert and serving spoons, and bone-handled knives to match the pieces that were already in the house and to complete a set of twelve. My father restored an oak box and painstakingly renovated the interior with intricate blocks of wood covered in bright-red felt to hold the cutlery in place in neat rows—it took him weeks. The top of the box was complete with an inlaid brass shield engraved with the Greyfriar. The cutlery shone, and I was grateful for the time and effort my parents had invested.

Granny gave me a dinner service that had long been in the house. It was white with a cobalt-blue border, edged with gold leaf. There were serving plates of various sizes for meat and fish, many lidded serving dishes for vegetables, a gravy boat and a condiment dish, but only a couple of dinner plates. Most of the plates had been broken and thrown away years before, but I didn't care. I was thrilled to have it, and I quickly found a set of modern plates with almost the same design. With birthday money from other friends and relatives, I bought enough dinner plates, side plates, dessert bowls and coffee cups and saucers to entertain a dozen. My dinner party set was completed with new white linen tablecloths and napkins with an ivy design to remind me of the ivy that grew on the south-east face of the house and turned a beautiful deep red in the autumn. I had no idea when I would get to use my dinner service, but that didn't matter—I wanted to make sure I was ready.

Within a couple of days, the euphoria of my birthday celebrations had dissipated, and I was forced to face reality. Where were we going to live? My parents had raised enough money to buy a modest home in Alton. Richard had not yet asked us to leave Chawton, but prices were rising so quickly that it was a race to secure a suitable property before they were out of reach. House prices in Britain rose twelve per cent in 1988, and properties sold for more than advertised as buyers outbid each other. Aunt Ann helped Granny and Robert find a house to share, and Penny and Dougie were on the hunt for a home large enough to accommodate their family.

I went on a few house-hunting excursions with my parents to look at show homes on new property developments and a few older houses that were for sale. Older character properties were sought after and expensive, but it was difficult to imagine life in a new house where we would be able to hear each other all the time. It was harder still to imagine a small garden as our only outdoor space. I understood compromises had to be made, but it didn't make it any easier. My parents remained positive about our future and assured me they would find us a home. They found a couple of suitable houses but were outbid; it was an anxious time for all of us.

Fortunately, by the end of the summer, my parents had bought a detached three-bedroom four-year-old house in a quiet close in a housing development in Alton, not far from Chawton. I was as determined as ever to leave home before my parents moved. If I couldn't live at Chawton House, I wanted to be somewhere completely different. My parents planned to move most of their furniture and pictures to the new house, and I didn't want to be surrounded by reminders of our former life.

Before long, I had found another live-in nanny job with a family in Liss, a large village nine miles away. I knew the family, so I wasn't worried despite my previous experience. I had use of a car and went home at weekends to spend time with my friends, at the pub or going to parties. I returned to Liss every week with a boot load of possessions until I had everything I wanted from Chawton with me: my clothes and shoes; my guitar; and my David Bowie, Prince and Blondie tapes. I didn't take my dinner service, silver cutlery or the Dreyfous writing box. I wasn't sure where life would take me and asked my parents to look after them until I was settled.

I decided not to visit Chawton for the few weeks before my family moved—I didn't want to see the house as it was being packed. It never occurred to me that they might need my help. On 30 September 1988, my parents left Chawton. When it was all over, I went to my parents' new house for the weekend. The front door opened straight into the sitting room, behind which lay a dining room, small kitchen, utility room and downstairs toilet. A staircase led up from the sitting room to two double bedrooms, a single bedroom and a compact bathroom. It had been well looked after and, by modern standards, was big enough for our family, but in comparison with Chawton the rooms were tiny. My father, however, had plans; he always did. The dining room would be extended to encompass the kitchen space, and the utility room would be extended behind the garage for a new kitchen. I struggled to sleep in the smallest of the three bedrooms; it was claustrophobic, and I wasn't used to a single bed or to hearing Paul on the other side of the wall.

In my mind, I had succeeded in my goal and completely avoided the trauma of leaving Chawton. I didn't take a final walk around the house or the grounds or say goodbye to Sir Richard, Elizabeth Martin Knight or Jane Austen. Within a couple of weeks, Granny and Robert had moved into a house around the corner from my parents, and Penny and Dougie had a property close by.

I went to see Granny and Robert in their new home. Granny couldn't manage stairs anymore and was restricted to the four rooms on the ground floor: a bedroom, bathroom, sitting room and kitchen. Robert slept in an upstairs bedroom. The garden was small, and Granny hadn't brought any of her chickens—I wonder what happened to them all? She didn't drive any more and relied on Robert to drive her to the shops and to the post office to pick up her pension. Granny never mentioned Chawton House or all she had left behind. Perhaps she saw her departure as the natural order of things— making way for the new squire. She must have known there was no practical way she could remain in the crumbling manor with no income or means to maintain it, but she couldn't hide the sadness behind her smile. Her active life at Chawton was over, and for most of the day, Granny sat in her chair and read or watched television.

A few months later, in the spring of 1989, Paul decided to put his tree surgery business on hold and travel to Australia to see his birthplace and my mother's family. He intended to travel around the country and work to fund his plans. 'I can climb trees down under,' he said excitedly. Although I didn't want him to go and knew I would miss him terribly, I understood his need to get away and wholeheartedly supported his plan.

Cousin Robin and Simon were looking for a new house to rent in South London along with Simon's sister, Stella. I saw my opportunity and asked whether I could join them in sharing the house. We found a large three-storey Victorian terrace to rent in Clapham with five bedrooms and a small garden. My mother lent me enough money for my share of the security deposit and my rent for the first month. Before we moved in, I left the family in Liss and stayed with a friend in London for a couple of weeks to find a job. I went to an employment agency, and within days I was offered a job as an administrator in an office. I was on my way.

This was London in the late 1980s. It was the height of the 'yuppie' era—money and champagne flowed freely. I was eighteen and loved my life in London, but I couldn't settle in a job. I worked as an administrator in an estate agent's office in Twickenham, as a receptionist for a textile wholesaler in Great Portland Street and in telesales at Oxford Circus. I often had a boyfriend, but they didn't last very long either. Six months seemed to be about the longest I could stick at anything. Most weekends I went to Alton. I liked nothing more than the distraction of doing something new and accepted as many invitations as I could. I attended parties all over London and often slept for only a few hours before going to work the next day. In June, I went to Glastonbury Music Festival for a week, the first of many annual visits to the festival. I don't remember much about it.

I was torn. During the week when I was in London I missed home, but when I went to Alton, I wanted to be somewhere else. I dropped in to see Granny every few weeks or so, but I didn't stay for long. We had never really talked about ourselves, and without cricket teas, events to prepare for and endless cakes to bake, I didn't know what to talk about. I didn't want to ask her about her youth, Chawton or the years that had followed, and I didn't want to tell her about the chaos in my own life—but that was selfish. I didn't think that she might have wanted me to stay. I had spent so much time with Granny when we lived in Chawton, and I loved her dearly, but there was a part of her that I didn't know. Was she happy? Did she accept her duty or resent the path her life had taken and the burdens she had carried? Perhaps it was for the best that I didn't know.

On one visit home, I was shocked and saddened when my father told me that Chawton House had been burgled. Brass door handles, light switches, firedogs and other fittings had been removed—I felt sick to my stomach. I hadn't taken anything from Chawton House; nothing was mine to take. The only keepsakes I had were Bapops's Dreyfous box and the dinner service Granny gave me. I was upset to think that other people had stripped Knight family heirlooms from Chawton House.

The following year, I left London and moved to Four Marks, a village just outside Alton on the way to Winchester, with a new boyfriend, Kevin, and some of his friends. I got a job as an assistant in an estate agent's office in Alton. I was nineteen and thought I was ever so mature—a proper 'working girl'. I was financially independent, paid my own rent and bought a cheap car for myself—a Renault 5.

A few weeks after Easter in 1990, I woke up in hospital, with my parents at my bedside. I asked what had happened but instantly forgot what I was told. I knew that I had been asking the same question over and over, but I couldn't seem to hold on to the answer.

On my way home from work, I had crashed my car into the left side of a flatbed truck that blocked the road ahead of me. An iron, on the parcel shelf in the back of my car, had struck the back of my head and split it open. I was covered in small cuts and bruises, and fragments of glass were embedded in my face, shoulders, left knee and ankle. I had stitches in my head, face and left hand, but my physical injuries were largely superficial—no broken bones or internal damage. As I lay in hospital unable to think straight, the doctors reassured me that my confusion would pass. I was in shock and had a mild head injury. I was taken back to my parents' house to convalesce for a couple of weeks, and my memory returned within a few days.

I wanted to see the wreckage of my car. Kevin took me to the yard where it was being stored until the police had finished their investigation, when it could then be destroyed. We pulled up at a farm, beside a big metal enclosure with about forty or so damaged cars lined up in rows. I was on crutches, and it took me a while to get out of Kevin's car as he spoke to the farmer just around the corner. I heard the farmer ask whether I had survived. I was speechless. I hadn't realised how serious the accident had been. I couldn't see my car among the wrecks so thought it must be in another enclosure, but I was wrong. We were led over to a crumpled pile of metal, and I couldn't believe my eyes. Every window had gone, and every panel was twisted beyond recognition. It was hard to tell what make of car it had been. I felt a chill down my spine—it seemed a miracle I had survived.

I obsessively read all the witness statements and reports from the police, ambulance service and fire brigade. There were no street lights and, despite the road being pitch black, the truck had no lights on or reflectors in place. Evidence from the crash scene indicated that I hadn't seen the truck at all. My car hit the truck at about fifty miles per hour, bounced off into the line of traffic still flowing in the opposite direction, where it was struck by a car and propelled across the road.

When I was well enough, I left my parents and returned to work. Not long after, the company closed the office where I was working, and my relationship with Kevin ended. I got a new job with another estate agent in the area. I enjoyed the thrill of a sale. The 'win' was an adrenaline rush—it was something I could do, and I loved the moment I telephoned the vendor to share the good news.

After about nine months, I was restless again. It was time for a change, and I decided to go overseas. Within a couple of weeks, I was booked on a flight to Switzerland; I had got a job as an au pair through an agency in London. I was nervous as I boarded the flight but excited at the adventure of it all. But from the moment I arrived, I felt desperately homesick and was home within a month, just in time for the Easter of 1991. I quickly secured a live-in position with a family in Chiswick, in the western suburbs of London. I had a spacious bedroom, one young child to look after and a nice family to work for, and I soon made new friends at the local pub to keep me amused in the evenings.

At the end of August 1991, I celebrated my twenty-first birthday. I wanted to have a party, but I had neither the money nor the luxury of Chawton House to host an event, so I organised a dinner for about twenty guests in the function room of a local pub. I had high hopes for the evening and borrowed a blue floral dress for the occasion. I was excited as guests started to arrive, but the service was slow, the lighting too bright, the food less than delicious and the atmosphere a little strained. I was bitterly disappointed and embarrassed. My guests were not having a wonderful time, and I couldn't wait for the evening to be over. It was the first party I had hosted since leaving Chawton, and it was a disaster.

Three years had passed since I left Chawton. I had worked ever since. I always had somewhere to live and paid my own way. I felt proud of my independence. But deep down, I knew that, other than day-to-day survival, I had achieved very little. I led an unhealthy lifestyle—poor diet, no exercise and too many late nights. I had gained twenty kilograms and didn't look my best. I had few qualifications and was a long way from having a career, independent financial security or a home of my own. Bapops's Dreyfous writing box was still in my parents' dining room, and the presents I had received for my eighteenth birthday were still packed in boxes in their attic.

I moved from one job, home and group of friends to another. I didn't mean to; it just happened—over and over. The only constant in my life was my guitar, which I played every day. I needed to find a job that inspired me to stay beyond the first six months and a place that felt like home. I lacked the qualifications for a proper career. Employers were put off by the number of jobs on my CV, and who could blame them? I knew I would not stay for more than a few months, but I had to convince a new employer, and myself, that I would. I was embarrassed and avoided my parents' attempts to talk about it. There was no explanation I could give for my behaviour—I didn't understand it myself. I was ashamed and didn't want to discuss it. When I went home, I always took a friend with me because I knew my parents would not raise the topic in company. I never stayed long.

I continued with my nanny job as best I could but was on the hunt for something else to do. I had no idea how I could find a sense of home again, but I remained determined. I was going to figure this out myself and did not want a wealthy husband to support me. Some of my friends had rich boyfriends and wanted to get married and have children, but I couldn't risk being beholden to someone else for my home and financial security. I *had* to be independent.

As if by good fortune, I met a businessman who owned a shipping insurance firm in the City of London, close to Simon and Robin's offices. It was a firm of average adjusters, who assessed the validity and value of insurance claims for cruise ships and cargo liners. He offered me a job as a junior in the office, with the potential to train as an average adjuster. It was a great opportunity to get into a profession, and I jumped at the chance. I moved into my parents' house for a couple of months and commuted to London with the boss, who lived just outside Alton. We sat in the same seats on the train every day and often stopped for a drink at the pub on the way home with his wife, who picked him up from the station every evening.

In the spring of 1992, I was very excited to become an aunt. Paul and his girlfriend, Sue, had a beautiful baby daughter they named Melissa. Millie, as she was known, was my parents' first grandchild, and we were all smitten. Around the same time, on a visit to The Sun, I met Sarah, a local girl about five years older than me who had her own small business. She was full of life and liked to party, and we struck up a friendship. She rented the annex of a large house in Chawton village, next to the village hall, a couple of hundred yards from the pub, The Greyfriar, and offered me her spare bedroom to rent. I could almost see Jane's cottage from the annex.

I wasn't sure whether it was a good idea or not, but perhaps Chawton was exactly where I needed to be. The village had given Jane the security and stability she needed to achieve her ambition; Montagu had written in his book that it was 'probable that the first six years of her residence at Chawton were as happy as any part of her life'. I accepted Sarah's invitation—what did I have to lose? Sarah and I went to the pub most evenings after work and often had friends round.

Sometimes I would spend the afternoon with Simon and his insurance-broker friends, tour the pubs of Leadenhall Market behind Lloyds of London, head off to a restaurant or late bar, and not make it back to Chawton at all. I was rarely on my own and had little time to think, but that suited me just fine; I didn't like being alone with my thoughts and jumped at every opportunity to have fun. I enjoyed nights out all over London, weekends at festivals and parties, and in May 1992, I didn't hesitate to accept an invitation from a shipping insurance colleague to attend the Monaco Grand Prix.

I carried on commuting from Chawton village to London. At the other end of the village, I could see scaffolding on the front of Chawton House, all the way to the roof. It was impossible to ignore. My father said that Richard was to retain the freehold, but a long lease had been granted to a country club and golf course—the most viable option. I didn't want to talk about Chawton House so didn't ask for any details.

I realised I hadn't seen Bapops's grave before we left Chawton House, and so I walked up to the church one Sunday to visit the graveyard. Sarah and I had been to the pub at lunchtime, and some friends had come back to our house for the afternoon. I didn't tell anyone where I was going and slipped out. I walked to the other end of the village and along the front drive of the house to the church on the right-hand side. The latch seemed to 'clank' louder than ever before as I opened the door and walked into the familiar church. I was relieved to see that nothing had changed. The font where I had been christened and the pews where I had left the doll during the nativity were still in place, and Sir Richard still lay in the chancel.

I walked into the graveyard and towards the Knight family graves, but I couldn't bring myself to go over to them. I could see blue plastic sheeting covering the roof of the house. I realised I could no longer go through the secret gate from the back of the churchyard to the south-west lawns; I had been 'degraded to the condition of visitors', like Mrs Dashwood and her daughters, and for the first time in my life I needed permission to enter. I was winded by the knot of pain in my stomach and overwhelmed with emotion. I missed my extended family, the library, our ancestors and the safe cocoon that Chawton House had provided. I missed being part of the centuries of tradition, the annual events and Christmas Eve celebrations in the Great Hall. I missed the Summer Ball and cooking with Granny.

I walked home with a heavy heart. But I couldn't go back in time, so I joined the party, poured myself a drink and pushed it to the back of my mind.

I stayed in Chawton for another few months but spent more and more time in London. I didn't want to live in Chawton any more. The renovations at Chawton House had ground to a halt. My father said the company behind the golf course was in financial difficulties and did not have enough money to finish. The house was left with its roof off, covered in plastic.

Once again, the future was uncertain—for Chawton House and for me.

CHAPTER NINE

'Give a girl an education, and introduce her properly into the world, and ten to one but she has the means of settling well, without farther expense to anybody.'

Mansfield Park – Chapter 1

I ENJOYED THE ATMOSPHERE of the city and decided to move back to London—it would be easier to go out after work if I was living close by. My new boyfriend had a flat in Wimbledon Village, so I moved in with him for about a year. Simon rented a spare room for a few months, and we often talked late into the night. I returned to Alton every other weekend or so to see my friends and family and to play with my niece.

A few months later, in July 1993, my father called to tell me that Granny had died early that morning, peacefully in her bed. She was seventy-eight. I didn't like to think of Granny dying alone, but at least she was at home and had not spent years in a hospice or care facility. I wished I had stayed longer when I visited her.

The family reunited at Chawton Church for the funeral. It was the first time we had all been together in Chawton since we had left Chawton House and our family had crumbled five years previously. Penny had died a couple of years after we left Chawton following a long battle with cancer, and

Dougie had died unexpectedly of a heart attack only eighteen months later. Aunt Ann and her husband had divorced, and Uncle Richard and his wife had separated. I felt numb, disconnected from my emotions, and I have no memory of the service at all. I didn't watch Granny's coffin being lowered into the ground, and I left Chawton village as soon as it was polite to do so. I didn't see Sir Richard in the church or stop at Jane's house in the village.

At the end of the summer, I became an aunt again. Robin was a large baby who was always happy and sociable. I liked going to Paul and Sue's house to play with my niece and nephew—I could relax, have fun and forget about everything else. Since Granny's death, my sleep had been disturbed by nightmares in which I wandered the streets homeless. My relationship with my boyfriend soured, and I moved into a share flat in Islington with some Portuguese people I had met some months before at the Trocadero in Piccadilly Circus.

I was uninspired by shipping and the fine print of insurance policies and damage reports. I didn't want to be an average adjuster, but how could I leave after being so proud of getting a 'proper job' with career prospects? I would need to find a compelling alternative. I met Simon in Leadenhall Market for lunch one day and mentioned that the father of the family I had worked for every Saturday when I was at Alton College was a Lloyds of London underwriter. Simon, an insurance broker, knew of him and that afternoon took me into Lloyds. He had the required pass to get through security. I waited in line with the brokers to see the underwriter. He didn't recognise me at first—it had been six years—but it didn't take much explanation for him to remember. He asked what I was doing for work, and I told him about the adjusting firm. He asked what type of degree I had. 'I don't have a degree,' I responded. 'I didn't go to university.'

'Well, I can't offer you a job then,' he said, unable to hide his disappointment. We had shared some good conversations when I worked for his family, and he had once commented on how intelligent I was. I realised he was cross because he thought I had not fulfilled my potential. I also realised how limited my prospects were due to my lack of higher education—even someone who knew and liked me had closed the door.

There was a university almost on my doorstep, and I often saw students of all ages as they walked to the tube station or between campus buildings. I lacked the required A-level qualifications to gain entry to university, the discipline to succeed academically or the financial means, but I was curious nonetheless. One night at the local pub, I talked to some students and was enlightened. At twenty-three, I was considered a 'mature student' exempt from the A-level entry criteria, as long as I had relevant work experience and interviewed well. My tuition fees would be fully paid by the government, and I could apply for a grant to cover my living expenses and top up my spending money with a student loan.

It was the perfect plan. University was a credible reason to leave my job. The thought of not having to work full time for a full three years appealed to me, and even as a full-time student I would have only a few hours of lectures a week to attend. I could live just as well on the grant money if I got a part-time nanny job. It would be a big adventure. Three years was a long time, and in my heart I knew I would not finish or gain a degree, but it solved my immediate dilemma, and I could cross that other bridge later.

I looked at a number of universities in London. I had no idea what I wanted to study, so I sat down with some prospectuses to see what my options were. The first brochure opened at a marketing degree. The course would teach me to understand what people wanted and to present products and services to them in a way that would appeal and ultimately lead to a purchase. Peppered with words like 'advertising' and 'PR', marketing sounded exciting. 'I could do that,' I thought, and the decision was made. I was accepted into three universities. I chose the University of North London, also known as

UNL, because it had the highest proportion of mature-age students and over half were from ethnic minorities. I hadn't had much exposure to different cultures and wanted to broaden my world view.

It was the beginning of the summer, and my course didn't start for a couple of months. I left my city job and became a part-time nanny for a wonderful young family in Highbury, a short walk from UNL. The mother was an author and editor who worked part time from home. The father was a political editor for *The Sunday Times* newspaper, and they had two young boys of whom I was very fond. By the end of the summer, they had asked me to continue working part time while I was at university in return for the use of a studio flat on the top floor of their house and a small wage. It was perfect. A job and a family I loved, a roof over my head, enough money to cover my expenses and the anticipation of a new adventure at university.

At the end of September 1994, I attended the first lecture of the Marketing and Human Resource Management joint degree programme. In the first term, I studied four modules, including International Marketing. I bought all the required textbooks and attended every lecture and study session. Ninety people were enrolled in the course, and there was a great diversity of students, many of whom seemed much cleverer than me.

For my first assignment, I was required to write a report on the issues to be considered when launching a product in a new country. I spent a day in the library reading numerous articles to supplement the information in the textbooks. I wrote the best report I could about the cultural, practical and regulatory issues that would need the most attention. A week later, I stood on the side of Holloway Road holding my marked report, which I had just collected from the faculty office. I gingerly opened the envelope, hopeful of at least a 'C' grade for my first attempt but prepared to accept the inevitable 'D' and 'could try harder' comment, or even worse. At the top of the page were the words: 'A – great report, showing real insight into the issues, well done.' I read the comment multiple times to make sure I wasn't mistaken, but it was true—I had received an 'A' for my first assignment. I whooped with joy and smiled for so long my cheeks hurt. I was elated and could hardly contain myself. For the first time, I believed I could actually get a degree; it wasn't just a silly idea.

Despite my mother's best efforts to persuade me, I had never before realised how important education was. Now it was important for me, as it had been important for Jane. Jane Austen's success was dependent upon her education. In his book, Montagu had written enthusiastically:

> the usual English course of education for the two sexes was
> inverted in this family—the boys were brought up at home and
> not sent to school, while the girls got a good deal of teaching
> elsewhere. While Jane was still a young girl she had passed a year
> at Oxford under masters, she had gone through a course of sim-
> ilar studies at Southampton (where she had a fever of which she
> nearly died), and had afterwards gone with her sister to a school
> at Reading. If the subjects of her books are strictly confined
> to one sort of society, it was self-control rather than ignorance
> which dictated the limitation.

Montagu was mistaken with some of the details. Jane didn't study under masters at Oxford—she attended a school run by Mrs Crawley, the widow of the principal of Brasenose College, Oxford, but it was true that Jane was better educated than most women of her time.

In Jane's time, nearly sixty per cent of women in England were illiterate, and she was lucky to be born into a family that highly valued learning, even for girls. Her father encouraged her to read books from his library, to expand her mind and to have views and opinions, albeit within the boundaries of social norms and acceptability. I imagined her as she pored over the books, soaking up knowledge and perhaps critiquing the writing style, structure and flow of each book as her literacy skills developed. It was hard to imagine how different our family would have been if Jane had not been educated. She would not have written her books and become a world-famous author, her cottage would not be a museum, there would be far less interest in the Austen and Knight families, and Chawton village would not attract tens of thousands of visitors each year. Perhaps Granny's tea room would have attracted only a handful of patrons, if any. How would I have earned my pocket money?

None of my Chawton family had gone to university, so I hadn't known what to expect. But if Jane could study at Oxford, which sounded very impressive, and could write such masterpieces, then there was no reason I could not get a degree. I resolved not only to complete the course but also to achieve a high-grade degree with honours.

Before each lecture, I read the suggested chapters in the coursebook, and I listened intently in class. Halfway through the semester, we organised ourselves into groups for a marketing project. I teamed up with Gina, a beautiful and intelligent ex-model in her late twenties, and Rosie, a bright and sporty Canadian in her early twenties, both of whom I worked with from time to time over the next three years. For our first group assignment, we researched the fashion industry's preference for tall, skinny models and the effects of this on young girls, their body image and self-esteem. I was nervous as we stood on the stage to present our findings to the ninety-strong group, but as soon as I started talking about the frustration of buying clothes in larger sizes, I completely forgot myself as I went into a 'zone' and passionately articulated my points. I involuntarily stomped my foot when I said, 'I am not prepared to be overlooked just because I am overweight.' I surprised myself—I didn't know I felt so strongly about the dire selection of clothes from which I had to choose in the shops. I loved presenting.

That first year at university was blissful. I lost weight, excelled academically and developed a real love for learning and exploration. I was finally working towards a career. I enjoyed my nanny job immensely. I had enough money to go out with other students and have fun, as well as to pay for my textbooks and a computer to type up my course work. Paul's daughter, Millie, occasionally came to stay with me for the weekend. On her first visit, I got a fright when I woke up at five in the morning and she was gone from her bed. I ran through the house in a panic and found her downstairs in the family's play room, grooming the rocking horse. In my second term, I met Andrew, a law student from another London university. He was from a good family, and he was intelligent, handsome and fun, with a bright future. Andy was more steady and traditional than most of my previous boyfriends, and at last, I felt stability in my life. We became inseparable. Andy loved his navy and cream Citroen 2CV, and I bought a red and white one for myself.

For the last assignment of the academic year, I worked with Gina and Rosie to develop a marketing plan for a luxury golf course in northern France and was astounded to be given a mark of eighty per cent—an A+. It was the perfect way to end the first year of my university education. I was in no doubt I would complete the course, and I was thrilled—I had finally found something that inspired me. For the first time in my adult life, I felt proud of what I was doing and was excited about the possibilities.

Andy's mother was Slovenian, and his family had a second home in Kranjska Gora, a town on the Sava Dolinka in the Upper Carniola region of north-western Slovenia, close to the Austrian and Italian borders. In the summer holidays, we drove our cars in convoy to the 2CV world rally which, coincidentally, was being held in Slovenia that year, and we visited Kranjska Gora—a beautiful town surrounded by snow-topped mountains. It was the happiest I had been for years, and I didn't want the summer to end. But I was also excited to return to university. I continued to work for and live with the Highbury family. Andy began the final stages of his legal training at a law firm in the west end of London and lived in his parents' London apartment, a stone's throw from the world-famous Madame Tussauds wax museum and Regent's Park.

On 24 September 1995, at the start of my second year, BBC Television began screening an adaptation of *Pride and Prejudice*, with Colin Firth as Mr Darcy and Jennifer Ehle as Elizabeth Bennet. All of a sudden, the words 'Mr Darcy' were on everyone's lips, and I was constantly reminded of Chawton—I had thought London was far enough away to forget about it. Friends, who had no idea of my connections, encouraged me to watch the series. I resisted at first but eventually borrowed a videotape recording, and one Sunday afternoon sat down to watch it, alone.

I paused for a minute before pressing 'play', wondering whether it was a good idea. I didn't have good memories of reading *Pride and Prejudice* as a teenager. I decided to pretend in my mind that it was a new story I had never before heard and written by a great writer I didn't know. From the moment it started, I was spellbound. The story, the dialogue, the characters, the setting and the production were perfect, and I loved it. It was witty and joyful, despite the challenges faced by the characters, and it was far from the novel I remembered. Alison Steadman's portrayal of Mrs Bennet made me laugh out loud, and Lady Catherine de Bourgh was exactly as I had imagined her. However, Colin Firth was not at all what I had expected for Mr Darcy. I quickly realised this was because his portrayal painted a more compelling character than I had been able to imagine. By the end of the first episode, I had completely forgotten what my Mr Darcy looked like.

At the same time, though, I was reminded of estate life and of living in a large house with acres of parklands and avenues of trees. It reminded me of the grand fireplaces, portraits and traditions of the landed gentry. It reminded me of country walks and summer balls, and it reminded me of Chawton. This was Jane's work, and I was overwhelmed with pride and appreciation of her talent. But it was also a reminder of what I missed so dearly, and my heart ached as much as it always had. I still couldn't think about Chawton without getting a knot in my stomach.

I watched all six episodes that Sunday, with the last episode finishing close to midnight. I had to be up early the following morning, so I went straight to bed but lay awake for hours and thought about the entail that saw Mr Collins inherit Longbourn. The legal challenge to Edward Austen Knight's succession was evidence that conditions of inheritance existed, but what were they? Elizabeth Martin Knight proved a woman could inherit the house in the eighteenth century, but Bapops had inherited it instead of Aunt Betty, and Fanny Knight had been overlooked. My father said Richard was heir to Chawton because he was the firstborn son, but Montagu was the fifth surviving son. It didn't make sense.

I gained more weight in my second year at UNL and was diagnosed with polycystic ovarian syndrome. As my professional and academic confidence grew, my self-esteem declined. I was embarrassed by the poor physical shape I was in, yet seemed paralysed to do anything about it. I loved learning and the university atmosphere, and I wished I could study at UNL forever. I enquired at the faculty about continuing my studies but lacked the money to do a master's degree—there were no grants to cover the cost, and I didn't want to get into debt.

Andy and I married halfway through my final year, in the middle of January 1997, in Chawton Church. I wanted to be married in the church I had spent so many hours visiting as a child, among my ancestors. I ignored Chawton House at the top of the drive. Richard had joined forces with American executive and philanthropist Sandy Lerner, co-founder of a successful multinational technology company, Cisco Systems. Sandy had a passion for early women's writing and owned a world-class collection of books written by women between 1600 and 1830 that she had put together over many years. My father said that a trust had been established, funded by Sandy's charitable foundation, and the house had been leased to the trust for 125 years. Richard was on the board of trustees, so he would be involved long term. The house was being fully restored and would eventually be open to the public as Chawton House Library, a UK-registered charity. It would house Sandy's collection, which she donated to the charity, as well as the Knight family collection of books. I didn't know when or how they had met, or the details of the restoration—I didn't want to know. It was certain that Chawton House would never be our family home again—not in my lifetime, anyway.

The following week, Andy and I had our wedding blessed in the church in Kranjska Gora to share the happy occasion with his Slovenian relatives and friends. My mother had made me a luxurious midnight-blue velvet cape to keep me warm, as the village was deep in snow and the air was crisp. In keeping with local traditions, before the church service, Andy and I were taken in a horse-drawn open-top carriage through the village and halfway up a mountain for a shot of schnapps to warm us up before we made our way back to the church. People waved and cheered as we passed and wished us well for our future together. Andy was fluent in Slovene and translated for me.

I finished my degree in June 1997, two months before my twenty-seventh birthday. I was one of the top three performers and achieved first-class honours in Marketing and upper second-class honours in Human Resource Management. I possessed a new-found professional confidence and could now work in a team, research, write reports, create marketing plans, pitch my ideas and present to groups of up to a hundred people. I now understood the terminology in job advertisements for marketing positions, and I was excited to have a goal and the qualifications I needed to pursue it. Most of all, I had learnt that I could stick at something for three years and finish with honours. I had learnt to believe in myself.

Andy and I wanted to travel before we started our careers, and we began planning a round-the-world trip. Andy qualified as a solicitor at the end of the summer. We left Heathrow Airport late September 1997, headed for Singapore. We spent three months in South East Asia travelling by land across Malaysia, Thailand, Cambodia and Vietnam. We lived on a shoestring, staying in cheap accommodation and loving every minute of it. The architecture, people, history, culture and countryside were so different from anything I had ever known. I wanted to experience and learn as much as I could, and we made the most of every day. We trekked through the mountains of northern Thailand, wandered the markets in Bangkok and spent a day at the prisoner of war camp museum in Kanchanaburi beside the bridge over the River Kwai—made famous by Hollywood. We visited spice plantations deep in the forest and the extensive network of underground hideouts in the Mekong Delta that were used by the Viet Cong in the Vietnam War. We travelled by bus to the ancient Angkor Wat in Cambodia and snorkelled with stingrays, turtles and tropical fish off the islands of Malaysia.

From Asia, we flew to South Australia to see my mother's family, and we stayed with her youngest sister, Annette, and her family for a few weeks. We planned to stay in Australia for six months. We bought an old camper van and drove across to Melbourne, then up the east coast to Sydney and Brisbane before taking the long drive to the Northern Territory and down the red centre back to Adelaide. I wanted to extend our stay in Australia and work for a year, but Andy was keen to continue our journey as planned. We had agreed before we left that we would not change our travel plans unless both of us wanted to, so I accepted his decision without question. My grandfather Alf decided he wanted to join us in New Zealand for the next leg of our trip. The three of us drove around the South and North islands and marvelled at Milford Sound, the hot mud pools, the glaciers and the marine wildlife. It was a treat to spend six weeks with Alf—I had only ever seen him during his visits to Chawton.

Alf returned to Australia, and Andy and I continued our journey through Fiji and on to Rarotonga in the Cook Islands. We stayed at the private beach chalet of the governor of the island for a few glorious weeks due to a chance meeting at the airport. His gardener taught Andy how to open fresh coconuts straight from the tree, and we bought fresh fish and produce from the local markets. We walked miles on pristine white sands and swam in the warm tropical lagoon at the foot of the chalet. We rented scooters and took day trips on the twenty-mile road, circumnavigating the island.

Our final destination was America—a week in Hawaii and a couple of months in the south-western states. We drove south from Los Angeles to the old cowboy town of Tombstone in Arizona, north to the spectacular Grand Canyon and the bright lights of Las Vegas, and over the Hoover Dam to San Francisco before heading back to Los Angeles to catch our flight home. I had a heavy heart as we boarded the plane for our last flight. It was the end of 1998, and I hadn't worked full time for over four years. I loved every minute of my studies and travels and hoped I would find a marketing career equally as rewarding.

Andy was soon employed as a solicitor for a firm in Guildford, and I landed a job as an account executive with a field marketing agency. We rented a flat nearby and started our life together. I worked on the agency's Vodafone account and was soon promoted to account manager. I loved my job and worked hard to do well. I had a husband, a career and high hopes for the future. But after just a few months, my relationship with Andy was in tatters—we had such different expectations of married life, and we didn't know how to make it work. The following year we separated. I was shattered—I had thought that this time would be different.

I bought a small flat in Bordon, a village not far from Paul and Sue's house, and lived on my own for about a year, but I was rarely home. I was promoted to business analyst for the Britvic Soft Drinks account. I could feel my motivation slipping, and after a year and a half at the agency, I was looking for something new. A chef friend had started a luxury catering company for lavish parties thrown by his contacts in the music industry, and he needed help to organise an event.

I continued my day job at the agency but threw all my spare time and energy into the preparations to cater for a three-day-long 'eclipse party' for Roger Taylor, the drummer from British rock band Queen. Most of England would see a partial eclipse of the sun on 11 August 1999. Roger had invited a hundred or so of his friends to his country estate in Falmouth in Cornwall, on the south-eastern tip of England, to see a once-in-a-lifetime total eclipse. We joined about twenty music and support crew on-site for a week, which included a couple of days to set up and clear down when the party was over. Most of Roger's guests camped in luxury tents and marquees in the grounds, where they were treated to a few days of live music and jam sessions with Roger, Brian May and other musicians in a large marquee on the lawn.

The catering demands slowed by midnight, so we joined the party and watched the live music. On the night of the eclipse, I sat on the floor of the marquee with about thirty people and listened to the jam session on stage. I recognised Pink Floyd's David Gilmore, but I didn't know who the other musicians were and didn't ask; I felt I should have known and didn't want to embarrass myself or appear rude. Roger took to the stage to introduce a very special drummer—his eight-year-old son, Rufus Tiger Taylor. Rufus bounded onto the stage and smiled as he took his seat behind the drums and confident-ly played the iconic drumbeat of 'We Will Rock You'. He was soon joined on stage by Brian May on lead guitar, and the audience, thrilled to witness such a proud moment in the young boy's life, clapped in time with the drumbeat. The marquee erupted into cheers and roars of delight at the end. Rufus gave a confident bow and left the stage. It was the highlight of an exciting week which ended all too soon; I was back at work the following Monday.

A few months later, I celebrated New Year's Eve 1999 quietly with friends and wondered what the new millennium would bring. I was nearly thirty, and I had thought that by now I would be settled in a career and a happy relationship. Instead, I had a failed marriage, which I deeply regretted, and had lost interest in the career I had studied for before it had even got going. When was I going to find a job that could hold my interest? I was intelligent, adventurous and determined to have fun, and I just couldn't find anything exciting enough for me—at least that is what I told myself. I didn't realise I was my own worst enemy and stood in the way of my dreams. I couldn't admit that the problem was me.

By the end of 2000, I had left my marketing career, sold my flat and moved to a seaside town on the south coast of England to manage a bar for a friend. I enjoyed hospitality. The town attracted holidaymakers throughout the summer, and we worked flat out for three months to take enough money to pay business expenses as well as the wages for skeleton staff over the quiet winter months.

I loved the hustle and bustle of the summer but struggled with the long winter. On wet and windy days, I would often stand behind the bar all day to serve only three customers. I saw an advertisement in the local shop window for a singer and musicians to form a band, and I jumped at the chance. I had played my guitar and sung on my own for years, but never with other people. We wrote and performed our own songs, influenced by breakbeat and trip hop. I was the lead singer and wrote lyrics and melodies—I loved every minute of it. I set up a home studio in the spare room of the flat I was renting, and within a few months, we recorded our first and only album. We played a few live gigs at the pub to a packed house. I loved being on stage, in 'the zone', singing my heart out—I felt free.

One afternoon, I answered the phone in the bar. There had been a car accident in Slovenia, and Andy had been killed. He had gone to Slovenia to complete his national service, which was required to retain his nationality. On a weekend off from his army duties, he had accidently driven his car off the road and was killed instantly. We hadn't spoken for months. My legs gave way beneath me. Andy was the only person I had found stability with, and despite our separation, I cherished the four years we had shared together—it was the happiest I had been since leaving Chawton. He had supported me and encouraged me to study hard for my degree, and I owed it to him to do the best I could. I could do so much more with my education.

At the end of 2002, I moved back to Alton. Uncle Robert had moved into Granny's old bedroom on the ground floor, which left the two upstairs rooms of the chalet bungalow empty. I decorated both rooms and moved in for a few months. I used one as a bedroom and the other as a sitting room. I fell back on my nanny experience to get a part-time job locally while I made a plan. I decided to return to marketing, the field I had so enjoyed at university and for which I was best qualified. I approached some agencies, and the following year, REL Field Marketing, an agency in Bracknell, offered me a role as an account manager to grow their business with Sainsbury's Supermarkets. I couldn't muck it up this time. I was thirty-two, and I owed it to myself, my family and Andy to make something of my life.

Later that year, the renovations to Chawton House were completed. Richard's eldest son, Adam, was an architect and his daughter, Cassie, was a landscaper, and both had worked extensively on the restoration project, my father said—I hadn't seen my cousins for years. The house was opened to the public as Chawton House Library, The Centre for the Study of Early Women's Writing, 1600–1830. Academics and researchers from all over the world were expected to visit to study the books, some of which were not available anywhere else. I was pleased to know that the house was saved for future generations—it was the best possible outcome in the circumstances. But I stayed away. I didn't take a tour. I didn't read any media articles about the opening or ask how it had gone. I didn't want to know any more about it. I was grateful my parents had decided not to christen me Jane Austen Knight after all—my connections would have been much harder to conceal.

But, unfortunately, I couldn't escape them. I had moved out of Robert's house into a rented property in the grounds of a larger country house, closer to work. One Sunday morning my landlady, a well-to-do retired woman, rushed excitedly to me with a Sunday broadsheet newspaper in her hand. 'Is this your family? You said you were from Chawton,' she said and proceeded to read an article aloud to me; it was about the restoration and opening of Chawton House Library.

The article said that the previous family—my family—had lived in squalor and had allowed the manor to crumble. I was horrified. Some parts of the house that we hadn't used were full of dust, but our living quarters had been well kept, clean and tidy. It was deeply upsetting, but I kept my feelings to myself and smiled as I answered her questions. She was clearly impressed by my family heritage and, from that day on, encouraged me to meet her son, as we were a perfect match. I humoured her but was a little insulted that it was only the knowledge of my family connections that had made her enthusiastic towards me. I never did meet her son, despite her best efforts.

CHAPTER TEN

'What have wealth or grandeur to do with happiness?'
Sense and Sensibility – Chapter 17

ALMOST TEN YEARS LATER, I looked in the mirror and hoped the fifth gala outfit I had tried on wasn't too tight. I had gained fifty-five kilograms since leaving Chawton, and I was the heaviest I had ever been. I was forty-two and had been obese for over a decade. I had a poor diet and didn't exercise. Although I was a very busy person and usually on my feet, my knees ached all day, and I was concerned I would develop diabetes or heart disease. I smoked and had dull hair and blemish-prone skin, exacerbated by polycystic ovarian syndrome. I had wanted to lose weight for a long time but hadn't even got through the first day of a diet. In the moment, after a stressful day at work, the comfort I felt when I ate outweighed any good intentions I had to prevent future illness or disability. This is not a unique story, of course.

It was September 2012, and I had been selected as a finalist for the Telstra Business Women's Awards in Australia. The awards gala lunch was to be held at the glittering Crown Entertainment Complex on the Yarra River in the centre of Melbourne. I had relocated to Australia for work in 2008 and was living on the outskirts of the city. I had been nominated for the award by a business associate, and I had already completed an extensive questionnaire about my background, career and work achievements—I didn't mention Jane Austen or Chawton. My boss and other colleagues had provided references, and I was one of eighteen finalists selected from 4,500 nominations. I was interviewed by a panel of judges, and I reflected on the years since I had joined REL Field Marketing in the United Kingdom. I had become the CEO of Australia's largest food-sampling and product-demonstration agency, responsible for over 1,500 staff, and a board director of two not-for-profit organisations.

How had I become so fabulously successful at my job, yet so horribly unhappy with myself? Back in England in 2003, I had accepted the job at REL Field Marketing and worked with over forty suppliers of household brands. I grew the Sainsbury's Supermarkets account tenfold in eighteen months and won a gold award at the Field Marketing Awards in the United Kingdom, and I was soon promoted to sales director. I spent my annual bonus on the down payment for a three-bedroom farm cottage in a beautiful village on the Hampshire–Berkshire border, about forty minutes from Alton. At last, I had my own house in a village and with a garden that backed on to open fields. I threw myself into decorating, and my father remodelled the kitchen to incorporate a stainless-steel cooking range. I made friends at the local pub and was happy enough. The house was nice, and the villagers were friendly, but it didn't feel like home, and I didn't expect to be there for more than a couple of years.

The year after I moved in, Richard had organised a family reunion at Chawton House. My aunts, uncles and cousins had all been invited for a picnic on the lawn. I had said I would go, but I was not looking forward to it. I didn't want everyone to see me so overweight and unhealthy, and I didn't know whether I would have the courage to visit Chawton House—I felt anxious just thinking about it. I didn't want anyone to see me upset. The morning of the reunion, I woke with an intense headache. I had suffered migraines before, and I knew the only option was to lie down in a dark, quiet room and wait for it to pass, so I rang my parents and made my excuses.

At the end of summer 2006, I decided to buy a horse and keep it with a neighbour who had a three-acre property with paddocks and stables, one of which was empty. I had liked riding as a child and wanted something to keep me busy, other than work. I searched a two-hundred-mile radius and bought Phoenix, a twelve-year-old grey, that I had ridden a couple of times. He seemed safe but with a fun spirit. Although I had never been a talented rider like Paul, I enjoyed it a lot and looked forward to riding across the rolling fields that surrounded the village. Millie, my niece, was fifteen and a gifted horsewoman. She helped me settle Phoenix into his new yard after the transporters had delivered him. After a long and tiring day, we walked up to the local pub for dinner before falling into our beds.

We woke early the next morning, eager to see Phoenix after his first night. He seemed to have adjusted well to his new surroundings. I led him into the riding school and mounted for a gentle walk. After only half a length, he started to buck violently. I tried to hang on, but as we neared the railing, he twisted to the right. I flew off to the left and landed on the thick wooden railings surrounding the school.

I limped into work a few days later. I had not broken any bones but had badly injured my right shoulder. I was bruised black and blue from the middle of my back to almost my knees. I didn't know what to do with Phoenix while I recovered. If no one rode him for weeks, he would likely be even more of a challenge for me to ride. Roger, a data analyst who also worked at REL, overheard me sharing my dilemma with a colleague and offered to ride Phoenix at weekends. Both of us had worked at the company for a couple of years, but we didn't know each other well. In his youth, Roger had worked with horses in New Zealand and at Rosehill Gardens Racecourse in Sydney. Roger was of average height and build and didn't look like a jockey. 'That was the problem,' he explained, 'I was a small kid but shot up at sixteen and got too big.'

For the next few months, Roger came to the village to ride, and we became friends. Then, out of the blue, Phoenix bucked the full length of the riding enclosure, and Roger damaged his hand when he was thrown into the fence. I knew I would never ride Phoenix again. At the beginning of December, I advertised him for sale. He was potentially dangerous, and I couldn't take the risk that someone else would be hurt, so I told prospective new owners exactly what had happened and sold him to a very experienced horsewoman for a fraction of what I had paid.

Roger and I spent time together over the Christmas holidays. He had an accent that was difficult to place. He was New Zealand born, spent his junior school years in America, returned to New Zealand for his senior years, went to Australia in his late teens and moved to England in his mid twenties. His mother lived in a retirement village in Queensland in Northern Australia. His father was a runner and had represented England at the Helsinki Olympics in 1952 in the 880-yard foot race, but he had passed away a decade earlier. Roger was five years older than me and great fun, and he stayed true to his values. He was intelligent and had a strong sense of who he was, which I admired. It became obvious we were destined to be more than friends, and when we returned to work in January, he resigned from the company.

I needed to do things differently if I wanted this relationship to work. Roger knew me as a driven career woman, and I wanted him to know that my capable exterior hid the truth—my personal relationships didn't last long. I also wanted Roger to see where I had come from, so my father took us to a public open day at Chawton House. The lawns were freshly mown, and neat edges bordered the new gravel on the driveway. The Victorian extension— and with it, my bedroom—had been demolished, some of the stonework above the main entrance had been replaced, and the ivy had been removed from the south-west face. But the Knight coat of arms remained untouched above the front door, and I was reminded of the eternal connection I will always have with Chawton, no matter what the house is used for.

As I walked into the Great Hall, I was struck with how similar it looked. The walls above the panelling were freshly painted, but otherwise, the same antlers were on the walls, and the smoke-stained stone mantel was still above the fire. I walked through the large oak door at the far end into what had been my family's living quarters. Montagu and Florence's wedding anniversary carving still stood proud above the fireplace in our sitting room, but the room had been furnished as it would have been in Jane's time—as a dining room with Edward Austen Knight's grand dining table in the centre.

'But it looks just the same,' I said to my father quizzically. I had heard about an extensive restoration, and I was puzzled. My father smiled and led me through to the original house kitchen where we had kept the freezers. I couldn't believe my eyes. The eighteenth-century kitchen bench that the cooks had used to prepare meals in Jane's time was no longer covered in mountains of dusty boxes, and the old cooking range had been restored and polished. The flaky walls had been plastered and painted. The whole room was bright and had been dressed with old cooking pots and utensils. It looked spectacular, and as we walked from room to room, I could see just how much restoration had been necessary. I hadn't realised the need when I lived there.

I had so many emotions. I felt numb, as if in a sort of dream world. I was pleased to see the house in such good condition, but it felt difficult to be a guest. The open day was hosted by the team who worked at the house, not by a Knight. My father pointed out historical features of the house to Roger as we walked back to the Great Hall. I was only half listening; I didn't find any comfort or joy in reminiscing, and I didn't want to stay any longer than necessary.

A woman overheard my father talk about the old fire buckets that hung high along the entrance hall wall, and she asked whether he had been a

Barnardo's child. Barnardo's was a charity that had evacuated children from London to the safety of the countryside during the Second World War to avoid air raids from enemy fighters. Chawton House had taken in Barnardo's children when my father had been an infant. 'No, I grew up here. I'm Jeremy Knight,' my father explained, and the woman curtsied, bowed her head low and said how honoured she was to meet him. I had seen all sorts of reactions from Jane Austen fans over the years, and so I wasn't surprised, but I could see the shock on Roger's face. He hadn't expected it at all. We left shortly afterwards and laughed all the way back to Alton.

In 2007, REL Field Marketing was sold to the Photon Group, a large Australian group of advertising, public relations and field marketing agencies. I immediately saw a chance to expand my business experience in a new market and to return to my mother's childhood home. I was ready for a new professional challenge, and I had wanted to stay in Australia when I travelled with Andy ten years earlier. Roger was also keen to be closer to his mother in her twilight years. In March 2008, we went to Australia for a holiday to visit both our families and to decide whether we wanted to emigrate. I visited a couple of Photon's field marketing agencies in Melbourne and spent a day at each business, hosted by the CEOs. There were variations in the business models, driven by geographical, cultural and infrastructural differences, but the fundamentals were the same. I was confident I would adapt to the market quickly enough. I was excited at the opportunity to leave England behind and start a new life in Australia, far away from all reminders of Chawton.

A few months later, Roger and I married in a Berkshire register office in front of our family and friends, followed by a party at home for more than sixty guests. As well as a wedding celebration, it was a farewell, as Photon had offered me a job in Melbourne. The flights were booked, and eight weeks later we packed up our belongings and moved.

At the beginning of 2009, after a six-month tour of Australia in a camper van, I started work at DemoPlus, a family business that Photon had bought a couple of years earlier. The business was very successful and had over a seventy per cent share of its primary market. The founder and CEO wanted to retire and needed to appoint and induct her successor. She had remembered me from my holiday visit earlier in the year.

At the end of 2009, the founder retired, and I became the new CEO. I felt validated, as if I were finally living up to my family name and could now hold my head up among my ancestors. I was 'head of the firm', just like Elizabeth Martin Knight, and I wanted to make my family proud. I gave it my all and worked tirelessly to ensure a smooth transition and to implement the change I thought was necessary to grow the company and build on the founder's impressive record. Profits shot up, and in my first full financial year as CEO, DemoPlus delivered the biggest growth of any of Photon's fifty-plus agencies. I received a handwritten note of congratulations from the head of Photon and was overjoyed. I was thrilled that the head of the entire group had taken the time to recognise my achievements, and I whooped with delight. But the thrill was short-lived. Within a couple of days, I was worried about how I would maintain the company's performance—and my success. I was still putting on weight.

My professional network grew, and I was invited to join the board of Life Education Victoria, a charity that empowered children and young people to make safer and healthier choices through education. I had made some very poor health choices over the years, and it seemed like the right thing to do, but I was nervous—it was my first charity board position, and I didn't know what to expect. I enjoyed the commercial business sector, and I had heard the not-for-profit sector was full of people who couldn't make it in corporate business. But that couldn't have been more wrong. The chair of the board, Paul Wheelton, was successful in business and, having built his fortune, spent his time on philanthropic endeavours. Paul used his self-made wealth to support charities and causes he felt would improve the community and particularly the lives of children in Australia and the Indonesian island of Bali. Every board member was a professional, highly skilled in their area of expertise, who wanted to give children the best possible chance of success in life. I was inspired.

At the beginning of 2011, Photon appointed a new head for the field marketing division, to whom I reported. Within the year, he had formed an investment team with the agency CEOs and bought the division, with the major financial backing of a Malaysian private equity firm. In October 2011, the Blueprint Group was launched, comprising five agencies in Australia and a couple in the United Kingdom, including REL Field Marketing.

I was excited to be part of it and had to pinch myself; it was hard to believe I could hold my own in such senior levels of business. But the more senior I became, the less I was involved with the grass roots of the business: the people we employed, the individual clients we served and the solutions we delivered. My focus was now cost control, business restructures and financial commitments. The job was stressful and had grown into something I didn't enjoy nearly as much as I had when I was working my way up the corporate ladder. I started to vomit before work every morning. But I wasn't going to leave and risk the future I had worked so hard to secure. Instead, I decided to broaden my horizons elsewhere, and at the beginning of 2012, I accepted an invitation to join the board of the Australian Institute of Management, Australia's largest membership organisation for managers and leaders, and a training partner to over half the companies on the ASX200—the Australian Stock Exchange.

Roger and I had lived in a rented house since we arrived in Melbourne. We had planned to invest in our own property within the first couple of years, but I hadn't found anything I liked enough to view, despite hours of searching online. Then one day I saw a large character house in a pretty village northeast of Melbourne. It had spacious rooms, high ceilings, an open fireplace and a mature rambling garden complete with lawns, fruit trees, a vegetable patch, rose bushes and a chicken coop. I was curious and arranged a viewing. It needed considerable work and probably wasn't the best investment, but I didn't care—it felt like home, and by the end of the day we had made an offer. We moved into our new home just before Easter 2012.

It was a few weeks later that I was nominated for the Telstra Business Women's Awards. I was honoured to be considered. I hoped that Bapops would have been proud of me, and I wondered what Jane would have thought. What might she have achieved if she had had the same opportunities? In Jane's time, women were not encouraged to participate in commercial pursuits, and there I was, taking part in a high-profile national awards scheme that celebrated and publicised the success of women in business. The novels published in Jane's lifetime didn't even identify her as the author—they were written by 'A Lady'. By the end of Jane's life, many in the local community were said to have known she was the mystery authoress, and she probably enjoyed a little praise and recognition from her neighbours. But Jane was able to celebrate her success with only those closest to her; there were no awards, no speeches to write—no public recognition.

Like Jane, I worked in the minority—only fifteen per cent of board positions in Australia in 2012 were held by women. I was keenly aware of the sexism often inherent in the culture and structure of corporate businesses. But while fifteen per cent is a small proportion of the total, many women had come before me, and although it could be challenging, it was a well-trodden path. There had been other women writers who Jane could look to for lessons and inspiration, and Jane had had the support of her family. But she had not had access to the wide range of resources that I had been able to draw on. I had been university educated and supported by mentors, a professional coach, management and leadership publications, courses and online resources. I had listened to Stephen Covey's *The 7 Habits of Highly Effective People* and networked with many women and men who had overcome extraordinary setbacks to succeed.

Jane must have been aware that she was a success. Her novels, especially *Pride and Prejudice*, were well reviewed. She was sought out by the best London publisher, John Murray, and not many writers would have been asked to dedicate a novel to the Prince Regent, nor invited to view his library. It is a pity that Jane didn't know just how popular her novels would become.

I had become more professionally successful than I had thought possible, particularly given the late start to my career, and I had relished each new challenge and responsibility. Roger and I were happily married, and we had our own home. I should have been basking in my achievements, but deep down I felt lost and disconnected.

I defined myself by my job, and my self-esteem depended on my success as an executive. The more I achieved, the more anxious I became that it would all come crashing down—it was a double-edged sword. Who would I be if I were no longer the CEO of DemoPlus? I couldn't bear the thought of losing my identity again. I took the responsibilities of leadership very seriously and believed that when I took a break, even at the weekends, I had failed in my duties. I rarely went on holidays, and for more than a year, I had been physically sick before work every day. I had ballooned to over a hundred and twenty-five kilograms and didn't know what to do.

Roger and some friends joined me at the Telstra Awards gala lunch and clapped proudly as I walked up to the stage to collect my finalist's plaque and have my photograph taken. I had squeezed into a blue tailored dress with matching jacket and was embarrassed by my appearance but nonetheless smiled enthusiastically. It was the best and the worst moment of my life. I was at the top of my career, but a part of me was at rock bottom.

The following week, a trusted friend and colleague came into my office and found me crying uncontrollably. 'You need to see a counsellor,' she said firmly, 'I am not taking no for an answer.' I usually prided myself on making my own decisions, and I had resisted Roger's attempts to help me, but I didn't have any fight left in me and agreed. I needed to pull myself together, or I risked the career for which I had worked so hard. I found a highly recommended counsellor, Marilyn, not too far from home and booked an appointment.

In the first couple of sessions with Marilyn, I told her about the course of my life—growing up in an extended family, my heritage in Chawton, the car accident, years of instability, university, Andy's death, and my career. I remained detached and unemotional throughout, as if I were telling a story about someone else. I told her that I was professionally successful but often felt anxious. Despite my success, I thought I was failing in my responsibilities. I had heard it said that therapy was like 'peeling back an onion' and other such clichés, but I didn't understand what that meant. I didn't think I had any layers that needed peeling back. Fear of failure drove me to succeed, but I was exhausted, and my resilience was low. All I needed was help to worry less, so I could focus more on my work. I was sure it would not take too long to resolve.

As I told my story, Marilyn listened and spoke only occasionally to pose a question or make an observation. I thought I could easily explain my thoughts and actions, but it wasn't long before I realised I had never talked honestly to myself before, let alone anyone else. I began to see patterns in my behaviour and thought processes that were not at all logical. I wanted to make my ancestors proud, but they were all dead, and I would never hear the acceptance I craved. I was lonely, but I didn't let anyone in. I wanted to be fit and healthy, but I had sabotaged every effort I had ever made to improve my diet or exercise. I wanted to be happy, but I told myself repeatedly that I wasn't good enough. I was depressed and felt powerless. Even in the quietest moments, my mind raced—it never stopped. I focused on poor decisions I had made in the past and feared what the future might bring—I was particularly afraid of being homeless. I rarely stopped to 'smell the roses' and to appreciate what I had achieved.

After a couple of months of weekly sessions with Marilyn, I recognised that I worried about the past and the future so much that I ignored the present. I had a husband and a home I adored, loving parents, a great job and an impressive résumé. I had risen to the top of my career in nine years and been happily married for four. It seemed so obvious, and yet I had never thought about myself in that way before. I learnt to trust that I could and would survive, whatever life threw at me, and to accept failure as a necessary part of exploration and growth. I focused on my talents and achievements, cleared my mind of pointless worry and enjoyed every day. For the first time since I was a young girl at Chawton, I felt calm. I had lived with a knot of anxiety for so long that I had forgotten how it felt to truly relax. A weight had been lifted, and I felt free.

Roger and I settled well into our new home. We cleared the overgrown garden, replaced the bathrooms and redecorated throughout. The main bedroom was huge with a high cathedral ceiling, and I slept soundly—I have not dreamt of walking the streets without a home to go to since. It was a great home for entertaining, and I asked my parents to pack my Dreyfous writing box, canteen of cutlery, dinner service and linen and ship them to me. My father asked whether I also wanted Granny's kitchen scales. 'Yes,' I said, without any hesitation, hardly able to contain my excitement. When making cakes with Granny in the kitchen at Chawton, I had weighed ingredients on those cast-iron scales on more occasions than I could remember. I was excited when they arrived, and I displayed them on a dresser in the dining room.

In November of 2012, Millie, who was twenty, came to Australia for a year with her boyfriend and stayed with Roger and me for the first couple of months. Just after New Year, my mother joined us from England for a few weeks. 'We want to lend you these to add to your collection,' my mother said as she handed me a tatty brown cardboard box. I opened the top and peeled back layers of bubble wrap to reveal two plates from the Austen Knight china that Jane had described: 'the pattern is a small Lozenge in purple, between Lines of narrow Gold;—& it is to have the Crest.' I hadn't thought about the china in years and was overwhelmed by my parents' trust in me.

For the first time since I had started working at DemoPlus, I took three weeks off. I forgot about work; I relaxed and enjoyed every day with my family. I went to the shops with my mother and cooked from scratch with the freshest of ingredients. Millie liked to keep fit and exercised regularly. I was inspired and started swimming again. I had always been comfortable in water, and swimming was one of the few exercises I could do without hurting my knees. I discovered a new Olympic-size pool only five minutes from home, and I began to swim regularly. The combined effect of a break from work, the company of my mother and niece, the warm summer sunshine, a healthy diet and regular exercise was dramatic. I jumped out of bed at the crack of dawn every day to open the chicken coop so that our chickens could roam about the garden for the day. I started to look to the future and feel excited about the possibilities.

After my mother returned home to England, my father called to say that he had met a woman from the Jane Austen Society of Australia at Jane Austen's House Museum, where he had volunteered as a guide since his retirement a few years earlier. The bicentennial of the publication of *Pride and Prejudice* was approaching, and my father suggested I attend the celebrations in Australia to mark the occasion.

Other than the BBC Television production in 1995, which I hadn't watched since my university days, I had avoided Jane Austen for years. I hadn't watched any other films or documentaries about Jane, or read any articles about her. I didn't like to be reminded of my former life. None of my work colleagues, fellow board members or friends in Australia knew anything about my upbringing or family heritage. I wasn't on social media and used the Internet for business purposes only. I was filled with horror at the thought of going to a Jane Austen event. I didn't want to talk about who I used to be. I caught myself thinking the words, 'who I used to be', and I felt sick in the stomach. In an attempt to protect myself from the sense of loss, I had become estranged from my heritage and Jane, but it hadn't worked—it was as painful as the day I had left. I knew what I had to do.

I found the contact details for the president of the Melbourne society and spoke to a very pleasant woman, Mercia, who said she hadn't been to Chawton recently, but she would be thrilled if I could attend the *Pride and Prejudice* anniversary celebrations in March. She then went on to explain that there were three Jane Austen societies in Australia and that my father had probably spoken to the president of the society based in Sydney, but not to worry as she was also due to attend the March event.

I was happy to dress for the occasion. I had lost fifteen kilograms and had a wide choice of clothes in my wardrobe that fit. I had been swimming two-hundred laps a week in the pool and walking the dogs twice a day with Roger. I hadn't smoked for months, my skin was smooth, and my knees didn't hurt any more.

It had been a long time since I had talked about Chawton or Jane Austen, and I was very nervous as Roger and I drove across Melbourne with the Austen Knight dinner plates. When we arrived, I was surprised to discover that one of the speakers was Sandy Lerner, whom I had never met. Sandy financed the restoration of Chawton House, and I hoped she hadn't planned to talk about Chawton; I couldn't bear it. I was relieved to learn that Sandy had written a sequel to *Pride and Prejudice* called *Second Impressions*. Sandy had painstakingly analysed Jane's writing. She spoke about sentence structure, rhythm and individual word choices, and discussed what these said about

Jane's characters. I was fascinated and gained a new perspective on Jane's genius—I hadn't given it much thought. Sandy explained that after she had deconstructed Jane's writing, she used the same techniques to write her novel, which had just been published. I sat quietly at the back and didn't tell anyone of my connections.

The other speaker discussed the popularity of Jane's most famous novel and the explosion of Jane Austen fandom over the twenty years since Colin Firth had played Mr Darcy. Jane's novels had been translated into more than thirty-five languages, and Jane Austen societies all over the world were meeting regularly to discuss and celebrate all aspects of Jane's life and works. The Jane Austen Society of North America had grown to over seventy branches. Thousands of online sites and social media profiles were dedicated to Jane, and there were many games and apps from which to choose. Jane's work had inspired seventy movies and major television productions, and more than ten thousand fan-fiction works. A plethora of Jane Austen merchandise was available, and over one hundred thousand Janeites made the pilgrimage to Jane's homes each year. 'Austenmania' had swept the world—a term I had never heard before.

I was shocked. I had no idea Great Aunt Jane had become such a global star, and while I didn't doubt the speaker, it was hard to comprehend. Jane had always been famous and appreciated by academics and book lovers, but this was a new type of 'fandom' that reached the four corners of the world and attracted people from all walks of life.

Mercia thanked the speakers and thanked me for my attendance. I had intended to stay anonymous, and as she announced my identity to the audience, I recoiled, unsure of how people would react to the granddaughter of Edward Knight III, the fifteenth squire of Chawton, who allowed the house to fall into such disrepair. But, for the second time that day, I was surprised as people approached me with enthusiasm to ask what it was like to grow up in Chawton—Jane's literary home. They listened intently as I talked about Snap-Dragon in the Great Hall.

'You're like a missing link,' said a middle-aged woman. She had been to Chawton the previous year and had wondered what it must have been like as a family home. 'You're an Austen and a Knight and grew up at Chawton House—how fascinating!'

Mercia asked if I would be willing to speak at Janefest, the largest annual event of the Jane Austen Society of Melbourne, held in November. I hesitated for a moment but accepted—I was a practised public speaker, and the society members were keen to hear more.

I felt excited and fearful in equal measure. Later that day I opened my laptop and typed 'Jane Austen' into Google. The more I clicked, the more flabbergasted I became. There were thousands of sites, discussion groups and interest groups documenting, analysing and celebrating Jane: her novels, her characters, her life, her family, her legacy and every place she had ever been. There was more merchandise than I could fathom: mouse pads, clocks, aprons, air fresheners and handbags—even a Jane Austen action figure! I found details of hundreds of Jane Austen events, festivals and exhibitions around the world. I felt so proud—Jane had always been a role model to me, and now she had inspired millions of others. Jane was a star.

CHAPTER ELEVEN

'Till this moment, I never knew myself.'

Pride and Prejudice – Chapter 36

IT WAS ASTOUNDING TO discover online seemingly never-ending research, assumptions, commentary and opinions about the history of Chawton House and the Austen and Knight families. Students, academics and authors had combed the records and registers filed at the Hampshire Record Office and other source materials and written all manner of material about my ancestors and Chawton estate. It was uncomfortable looking at our history laid out for all to see and pass judgement—we had been such a private family. I leapt to Edward's defence as I came across an article titled 'Edward Austen Knight: A Tightwad or a Man with Heavy Responsibilities?' which speculated about why it took until 1809 for Edward to provide accommodation for his mother and sisters, four years after their father had died. I couldn't help but be dismayed to see Montagu's bookplate for sale online.

At my next session with Marilyn, I told her about my intention to speak at Janefest. 'What are you going to say?' she asked. I hesitated for a moment; I hadn't thought about the details of my speech. We talked through a couple of options—perhaps I could talk about cooking with Granny or about the

Jane Austen AGM we used to host on the lawns at Chawton House, but every topic brought me to tears. I couldn't even think about our lives in Chawton without becoming emotional, let alone deliver a public speech on the topic.

I was on the verge of cancelling my speaking engagement when, on 24 July 2013, the Governor of the Bank of England announced Jane Austen as the face of the next ten-pound note, most likely from 2017—the bicentennial of her death. I couldn't quite believe it and checked a number of news sources, including the BBC: 'Jane Austen certainly merits a place in the select group of historical figures to appear on our banknotes. Her novels have an enduring and universal appeal and she is recognised as one of the greatest writers in English literature,' the Governor said. I was speechless. Jane—our Jane—had become so revered that she was going to feature on British currency. I couldn't think of a higher honour than this and was ecstatic. Jane was finally receiving the 'award' she deserved.

All of a sudden, there were references to Jane Austen everywhere I went. Talks on Jane's life and work were advertised in Melbourne, and Austen-related questions were asked on television quiz shows. The Jane Austen Tea Room had opened only twenty minutes from my house in Melbourne, and the movie *Austenland* was due for release. I had thought Australia would be far enough away for me not to be reminded of Chawton, but Jane's popularity had spread to the other side of the world, and it was impossible for me to avoid.

The more I thought about Jane and my connection with her, the more I became aware of the philanthropic opportunities I could pursue, and an idea began to form in my mind. One hundred million children across the world do not receive an education and face an uncertain future. How different our lives and the literary world would have been if Jane Austen had not been able to read and write or to fulfil her dream to be an author. If so many people around the world loved Great Aunt Jane, there had to be a way to harness that collective passion to help improve literacy rates in the world's poorest communities. It was difficult to imagine just how challenging everyday life must be for the 775 million adults around the world who are unable to read or write. Applying for a job or housing, completing a form, reading dosage instructions on medicine, using the Internet, voting at elections or writing a shopping list—all would be a challenge. It was impossible to comprehend the talent that would never be discovered and the skills that would be wasted.

I had to prepare my speech for Janefest. I wanted to give the audience an idea of what it was like to live at Chawton House, and I planned to share photographs of my family. I needed time to talk to my parents, research and read, and that would be impossible with a busy CEO role. I knew it was time to take a break from my career. I was terrified of giving up the security and status of the position I had worked so hard to achieve, but I simply had to do it. I resigned from the Blueprint Group and started my own consultancy business, The Greyfriar Group, where I could work part time and invest time in my new project in honour of Jane and my heritage.

It took some time, but I eventually became accustomed to the articles online about my family, and I started to piece together the stories I had heard as a girl into an accurate timeline, although so much of the information online was either inaccurate or conflicted. I spent hours on the phone to my parents as they patiently answered my never-ending questions and encouraged me. *Country Life*, the magazine I had flicked through many times in the library at Chawton, ran a feature on Jane Austen and Chawton House, which was published on my birthday at the end of August. It seemed an extraordinary coincidence.

I started to read Jane's novels again, in the order of their publication, and I watched movies and television productions of each. I was able to look at Jane's work through different eyes, and it was magnificent. It was a challenge to capture the brilliance of her words on screen, but I enjoyed most of the filmed adaptations. I wasn't too concerned about the minor alterations to the stories and Jane's dialogue. I enjoyed the films that best captured the essence and experience of the characters she had so skilfully created. I loved Emma Thompson's *Sense and Sensibility* and the 2003 BBC Television adaptation of *Persuasion* as well as the 1995 *Pride and Prejudice*, which I watched again.

I downloaded a couple of films about Jane herself. *Miss Austen Regrets* portrays Jane in Chawton. In one scene, Jane and Edward discuss the legal challenges to Edward's ownership of the Chawton estate. Jane is dismayed that the security of their home is not settled. I had become used to Jane as public property, but I felt a little nauseated watching an actor play Edward Austen Knight, *my* fourth great-grandfather. It was hard to watch the drama-tisation of my family's challenges. In another scene, Jane watches her brothers play cricket on the family's pitch in the middle of Chawton. It was a delight to watch, and I was reminded of the many joyful afternoons I had spent as a child, sitting on the edge of the same pitch while my father, uncle and brother played. The Austens are joined by Henry's wife, Eliza, who laughs without restraint as they play.

By this time, I knew a lot about Jane Austen's family. Jane was very fond of Eliza de Feuillide—her cousin and sister-in-law—and dedicated an early novella, *Love and Freindship* [sic], to her. Eliza had fled to England during the French Revolution in 1790, leaving her first husband, Jean-Francois Capote Feuillide, in France. She feared London had become unsafe and fled to the Austen's in Steventon in 1792 in the bloodiest months of the gruesome period. The September Massacres of that year saw the Tuileries Palace stormed and fourteen thousand people slaughtered. Priests, political prisoners, women and children were among the victims. France abolished its monarchy and formally established a republic. The details were well reported in the English press, and Eliza was terrified for her husband. Her worst fears were realised when, in 1794, Jean-Francois was arrested for conspiracy against the republic and guillotined. To think people believed Jane led a dull and sheltered life!

Jane's life wasn't dull at all. She lived in a time of wars and cultural and political change. She travelled extensively in the south of England and was a frequent visitor to friends and relatives in the country and London. Jane was educated, well read, intelligent and witty. William Austen Leigh in *Jane Austen: Her Life and Letters, A Family Record*, published in 1913, wrote about Jane's good humour. Jane and her niece Anna 'could joke so heartily over their needlework and talk such nonsense together that Cassandra would beg them to stop out of mercy to her, and not keep her in such fits of laughing.' Jane's nieces and nephews remember her fondly as a 'favourite aunt'—Jane was generous with her time and her talents, mentoring her nieces Fanny and Anna, both of whom were budding authors. But Jane never played with the serious responsibilities of life. In Montagu's book, a niece of Jane is quoted as saying, 'When she was grave, she was *very* grave.'

I had always known Jane was a remarkable woman. She had stuck to her guns to achieve her dream and, against all odds, had become a successful author. But, as an adult myself, the more I thought about Jane, the more impressed I became by her self-belief, resilience and approach to her 'business'. 'There is a stubbornness about me that never can bear to be frightened at the will of others. My courage always rises at every attempt to intimidate me,' Jane wrote as dialogue for Elizabeth Bennet, but the words seemed to reflect Jane's own determination and perseverance. Her strong rebuke to the Prince Regent's librarian, Reverend Clarke, at his suggestion for the topic of her next novel was proof of her resolve: 'No—I must keep to my own style & go on in my own Way; And though I may never succeed again in that, I am convinced that I should totally fail in any other.'

While Jane no doubt wrote for her own satisfaction and in her own style, she wanted her books to be commercially viable, to appeal to the audience of the day and to make some money. Jane weaved her contemporary commentary on the culture of the day into a romantic story to increase the chances of her books being circulated by travelling libraries that catered to the genteel women of the growing literate middle class.

Jane wrote with wit and masterfully painted the essence of her flawed characters, often in just a few carefully chosen words of dialogue. Montagu wrote:

> There were depths in the quiet, self-contained nature of the author which were not easily fathomed; and the idea that she was in any way deficient in emotional consciousness (though they would not have used that phrase) would have been scouted by all her family as preposterous.... hers was an emotional nature, capable of deep feeling.

Jane contained her writing to characters, situations and surroundings that her audience would be familiar with but provided only the scantest of details, allowing her readers to paint their own mental images. Jane reveals only that 'Mr. Darcy soon drew the attention of the room by his fine, tall person, handsome features, noble mien'. The readers project their own secret fantasies to imagine Mr Darcy's face, hair, eyes and clothes. Jane doesn't ask us to picture her idea of a perfect man but to imagine our own. Perhaps this is one of the reasons many consider Mr Darcy one of the best romantic heroes of all time.

From an early age, Jane wanted to be a published author. I had read about the power of envisioning goals or 'beginning with the end in mind', as Stephen Covey called it. Jane had done just that and had kept going, even in the face of challenges and disappointments. It is believed that in 1795 she wrote *Elinor and Marianne*, an epistolary novel in the form of letters from one character to another, the first incarnation of *Sense and Sensibility*. Like so many 'facts' about Jane, this is an assumption based on the available evidence and is subject to conjecture. She began writing her second novel in 1796 and a year later had a finished work she titled 'First Impressions'. Her first attempts to publish this work failed. Her father's approach on her behalf to publisher Thomas Cadell with 'First Impressions' was ignored. In hindsight, that may have been a blessing, as the maturity and skill she brought to the revisions of her earlier manuscripts led to the *Pride and Prejudice* that has been cherished by readers and academics for two centuries, but Jane would not have known that at the time.

In 1803, George Austen sold the copyright of *Susan*, Jane's first complete narrative work for £10 to Benjamin Crosby, who promised to publish the novel, but failed to keep his word. Six years later in desperation, Jane wrote to Mr Crosby under the pseudonym Mrs Ashley Dennis—M.A.D. for short. She implored him to publish the novel, or she would have no alternative but to seek publication elsewhere. After only two days, she received a quick response informing her there was no obligation on Mr Crosby's part to publish the book, and action would be taken to stop sales if publication were attempted elsewhere. I could only imagine how frustrated Jane must have been.

Jane could have decided not to subject herself to such disappointment and to give up, but she didn't. Despite her limited funds, Jane paid for *Sense and Sensibility*—the first of her works to be finished in Chawton and prepared for print—to be published on commission, which guaranteed that her book would be printed and available for sale. Jane would share in the profits from any sales of the book but also carry the financial risk if it didn't sell. Jane backed herself and made a profit of £140 (the equivalent of about £5,000 today)—no doubt a welcome boost to the Austen ladies' modest income.

For Jane's second published novel, *Pride and Prejudice*, she again revised an earlier story she had drafted. But this was the last revision of her early works; she never finished 'The Watsons', a story about a clergyman and his daughters. Her father had died in Bath while she was writing it, and as far as we know, she never looked at the incomplete manuscript again. *Mansfield*

Park, *Emma*, *Persuasion*, and the incomplete novel known as 'Sanditon' were all new stories conceived in Chawton.

Jane was resilient. She looked after her body, mind, heart and soul, and was 'sharpening the saw' long before Stephen Covey coined the phrase. Frequent walks kept Jane physically fit, and hours of daily practice at her piano cleared her mind of the issues of the day, allowing her to write creatively and productively. 'Composition seems to me Impossible, with a head full of Joints of Mutton & doses of Rhubarb,' Jane wrote to Cassandra just after she had completed the manuscript of *Persuasion*.

Jane was clearly the talent and the driving force, but it was a family affair. Paper and writing materials were expensive, and without the generosity and support of her father and brothers, Jane would not have been able to afford to pen her novels, and Mr Darcy would never have been shared with the world. Clearly, the household at Chawton Cottage was organised to allow Jane to write for hours each day. Her sister, Cassandra, and friend Martha Lloyd undoubtedly took on more than their fair share of chores. Jane read her stories to her family and sent draft manuscripts to her closest friends and family for comment—much like a modern-day focus group. Her father and her sister, Cassandra, gave her editorial advice and support, while her brother Henry, a banker, acted as her agent. I had been so determined to succeed on my own without any help from anyone and had kept friends and family at arm's length for years. I had thought it a position of strength, but I had isolated myself. 'Other than for Roger, I am lonely,' I told Marilyn at my next session.

After a wet Melbourne winter, September 2013 was the warmest on record—our garden was in early bloom and attracting birds and other wildlife. I had lost another twenty-five kilograms over the winter, and after fifteen years of being restricted to plus-size outlets, I was enjoying shopping for clothes in regular shops. I felt fit and strong and was no longer ashamed of my physical appearance.

Rather than stubbornly doing it all myself, I decided this time I would share my plans with family and friends and ask for help. A few years earlier, a colleague had introduced me to Amanda, who also worked in marketing. We were the same age, both married without children, and we shared a passion for music. I still played my guitar almost every day, and Amanda was the lead singer with a local covers band. I enjoyed her company very much. Amanda was my closest friend in Australia, but I had never shared my heritage or my private thoughts with her. We arranged to meet for a coffee. I was nervous, and to help me get through the conversation, I had prepared a PowerPoint presentation to share my connection to Jane Austen, our family home of Chawton and my plans to start a charity to improve literacy rates around the world. I clicked on the first slide and began to tell Amanda my story as she stirred her coffee. 'What!' Amanda exclaimed and dropped her spoon on the table.

'I am Jane Austen's fifth great-niece, and I grew up in Chawton, where Jane lived and wrote her books,' I repeated.

'I love Jane Austen. Why didn't you tell me?' she asked, clearly excited but a little bewildered that I had kept it secret. I explained as best I could and continued my presentation. As I talked about the idea of a charity to raise money for literacy in Jane's honour, our excitement grew. We considered the size and scale of Jane's audience, the purpose of the charity and the way in which it might operate.

'Do you want to help me?' I asked, but before I could finish Amanda had said 'yes' without hesitation or qualification.

We sat and talked for hours about what we would need to do: register as a not for profit, define the purpose and objectives of the organisation, appoint a board of directors, develop a set-up plan, connect with literacy organisations, establish infrastructure. The list went on and on. I would have to face my fears and immerse myself in the Austen community. I knew it would be difficult at times and no doubt emotional, but it was the only way.

We made some decisions at that first coffee meeting. First, the operating costs of the organisation would need to be kept to a minimum. Perhaps the day would come when the charity was big enough to require paid staff to manage it, but that was a long way off. We would build the organisation with volunteers, including voluntary board members. I had successfully run a company, held charity board positions and developed a strong professional network, but I had no experience of the inner workings of a charity or a literacy organisation. I had much to learn and do and a limited amount of time each week to do it. Second, like Jane, we would take our time, and do it to the best of our abilities.

I knew it would be hard work, would take years and would divert me from my career. I would make mistakes, and no doubt be criticised, but there was no going back. I had a chance to improve literacy rates and couldn't walk away from it, despite the risks. I was excited to be able to honour Great Aunt Jane's success and legacy. Jane Austen had brought pleasure to millions, and perhaps together we could raise millions to teach people to read. But there was a lot to consider, and so I pondered the idea for a couple of months to be sure.

In 2013, my parents were due to join Roger and me in Melbourne for Christmas, but they decided to arrive early, at the end of November, to attend Janefest. The day arrived. I had prepared my speech and a presentation of family photographs of Chawton House and estate, my family and ancestors, and private and public events held at Chawton. I spoke candidly about the joys and privilege of growing up immersed in four hundred years of my family heritage and of the circumstances under which our family home—Chawton House—had come to an end.

From the moment I started speaking, the audience listened to every word—I could have heard a pin drop. I choked with emotion when I said how much I missed Chawton, but it was a relief to share these pent-up feelings publicly. For the first time, I talked honestly about how I felt and a weight lifted from my shoulders. I regained my composure and ended the speech with my intention to establish a literacy charity in honour of Jane Austen. The enthusiastic reaction I received to my story and vision of a charity gave me all the encouragement I needed to turn my vision into reality.

I had given the first-ever public talk about our family and our private lives at Chawton House, and I was keen to know what my parents thought. They were both very positive. Later that evening while I cleared the kitchen after dinner, my father approached me in private. 'I want to talk about something you said in your speech today,' he said and proceeded to tell me how he had felt when we had left Chawton.

I was surprised. In many ways, my father had been relieved—the responsibility of maintaining the house on a shoestring budget for his elderly parents had been immense. He had worked in the garden, mowed lawns, patched the leaky roof, made repairs on all areas of the house, prepared for events and helped Granny. His sleep had often been disturbed by the same nightmare: the house was flooding from the top floor down, and he had to wade through the water to pull out a plug and drain the house. While he had enjoyed many aspects of living at Chawton, he had been happier in the years since. It was a revelation. I had assumed my entire family felt the same as I did. It was a huge comfort to know that my father had not been crushed by it.

I talked endlessly to my parents about Chawton and our family history after that. We reminisced about Granny's tea room, the vegetable garden, the Fete and Horticultural Show, the Summer Ball, and family celebrations held in the Great Hall. My father even lit a Snap-Dragon on Christmas Eve. The familiar smell transported me back to the most joyful night of the year at Chawton House and happy memories of my ancestors and extended family.

My parents went home in the new year, and I set up a board for the charity. It would be a steep learning curve, and I reached out to professional friends and colleagues with the experience to help, including Mercia, an experienced lawyer, and the president of the Jane Austen Society of Melbourne. In February 2014, we gathered around my dining room table and voted unanimously to register the Jane Austen Literacy Foundation as a not-for-profit organisation.

Mercia completed the paperwork and filed the registration, and we held our first board meeting in April 2014. Preliminary research had revealed the huge number of experienced and reputable charities that deliver literacy programmes to impoverished communities around the world, and all needed reading and writing materials to support their teaching programmes. We unanimously agreed that one of the goals of the Jane Austen Literacy Foundation (or JALF as we called it for short) would be to raise funds to buy books and literacy kits in support of these existing efforts. This would be an effective use of our resources and an efficient way to help improve literacy rates.

There was a lot to do, but we were not discouraged. Amanda and I spoke almost daily. We had to create everything from scratch, and with our other work commitments, progress was steady but slow. But it would not matter how long it took us to build the foundation and engage the global Austen community; Jane's fandom continued to grow day by day and didn't give any indication of being a passing fad.

I contacted some local literacy charities and was very impressed with the Australian Literacy and Numeracy Foundation, who, among other things, develop, implement and sustain innovative literacy programmes for Indigenous Australians. I met with the CEO of UNICEF Australia, Norman Gillespie, who was very encouraging. I joined the modern world of social media and opened my first Facebook account. I couldn't believe what I found—hundreds of profiles and pages dedicated to Jane Austen and her books, characters, adaptations and fan clubs, mostly run by fans as a hobby and out of love for Jane and her stories. One of my favourites was 'Elizabeth Darcy', a beautifully written and illustrated story of Elizabeth Bennet and Mr Darcy after *Pride and*

Prejudice. I followed a few pages and joined some groups, and I was fascinated by the depth and breadth of conversation about Jane and her novels, and by the modern-day fandom.

News of the foundation spread. I was invited to attend the World Literacy Summit at the University of Oxford in April 2014 to officially announce my intention to build a charitable foundation to provide literacy support and resources for communities in crisis. It would be an extraordinary opportunity to speak about the foundation at a global event and one I could not miss, even at short notice. It was also time for me to visit Chawton to see the house through fresh eyes, with my new perspective. I hadn't returned to England since I had left for Australia six years earlier and may have delayed it for another few years had it not been for the summit.

Roger stayed at home to look after our animals while I was away. I booked the cheapest flight I could find—it had been a year since I gave up my corporate salary, and our lifestyle had changed dramatically, but Roger never complained. 'My wife left me for Jane Austen,' he would joke, but he knew how important it was for me, and he appreciated the opportunity it afforded to raise money for literacy. He supported and accommodated significant changes in our lifestyle and stood by me every step of the way.

I arrived in England for a whirlwind week. On the first afternoon, Paul and I went to Chawton and walked through the village to the church to visit Granny and Bapops in the churchyard. As we neared the church, I stopped in my tracks. There, on the left side of the driveway, opposite the entrance to the church, stood the newly restored gamekeeper's hut relocated from the woods, and for a brief moment I was terrified—I had spent a childhood avoiding the hut and the witch who my cousins said lived in it.

It was the first time I had seen the gravestone Granny and Bapops shared. The serenity of the estate and the sounds of the birds, different from those I had become accustomed to in Melbourne, brought back childhood memories of playing in the churchyard and riding my aunt's horses in the four-acre paddock in front of the church. Paul and I walked back to The Greyfriar—the pub in the middle of the village—and talked for hours. We reminisced about the fun we had in the stables, cellars and attic rooms, but beneath the laughter was an unspoken sadness we both understood and shared.

The next day, I returned to Chawton with Martin, who had had his eighteenth birthday party in the Great Hall thirty years earlier. We had remained friends, and he had offered to support me with the foundation while I was in England. I had arranged for us to meet with a director at Chawton House. As we walked up the driveway, I could feel my heart pounding. We were met at the front door and led straight up the main staircase to the Cross Room at the very top of the house, above Granny's bedroom, to talk. I enjoyed the conversation, but we were sitting in Cousin Robin's bedroom. My mind was racing, and I was shaking from head to toe—I don't know whether it showed. After we had discussed the foundation and the house for an hour or so, Keith asked would I like to look around. Like Anne Elliot, on her visit to the Crofts in Kellynch Hall, I declined the offer and left the house. Jane wrote of Anne:

> However sorry and ashamed for the necessity of the removal, she could not but in conscience feel that they were gone who deserved not to stay, and that Kellynch Hall had passed into better hands than its owners. These convictions must unquestionably have their own pain, and severe was its kind.

As we passed the library at the bottom of the stairs, I pictured Granny and Bapops sitting side by side in their armchairs. I didn't want to open the door and look inside.

Once outside, Martin and I walked to the top of the neatly manicured lawns. The Bottles on the library terrace had been shaped into cylinders, and the large copper beech tree had gone. The brick and flint work of the library terrace and upper-terrace walk had been restored, and the gravel paths were revealed once more. The rose garden was fully stocked and the hedges clipped. We listened to the birds and walked in silence for quite some time until we reached the walled garden.

We pushed open the ornate iron gates and stepped inside. Vegetable plots had been replaced by large beds of flowers neatly edged with low-box hedges. Many of the fruit trees were still in place, although I couldn't tell whether they were the same trees or had been replanted. The greenhouses had been removed from the north-eastern wall, but otherwise, it looked very familiar. I could vividly remember walking from the house to the walled garden in the summer to help my father plant potatoes or pick runner beans and running away from my father's geese, all the while trying not to be spiked by rose bushes.

Chawton House was the most difficult place for me to be, but I knew I had to let go of the sorrow. I was about to throw myself into the world of Jane Austen, and I needed to feel comfortable when talking about Chawton. I had seen enough that day, but I vowed to return on my next visit to England and spend as much time at the house as I could.

On Wednesday, 16 April, in the Holywell Music Room within the grounds of Wadham College, a constituent college of the University of Oxford, I shared some memories and photographs of growing up in Chawton with Great Aunt Jane and announced my intention to establish the Jane Austen Literacy Foundation in her honour. My family were in the audience, and Amanda watched from Melbourne via video link. The event was a great success and attracted print, television and radio media. I was delighted with the enthusiasm and messages of support I received.

A few days later, I received a call from the organisers of the summit. Simon Langton, director of the BBC Television 1995 production of *Pride and Prejudice*, had made contact and asked them to pass on a message and his contact details. Simon had read about the foundation in *The Telegraph* and wanted to offer his help and support. I had to pinch myself to check that it wasn't a dream. Simon had directed the most popular Austen production of all time, and he wanted to help me raise money for literacy. I was thrilled.

CHAPTER TWELVE

'For a few moments her imagination
and her heart were bewitched.'

Persuasion – Chapter 17

ON MY RETURN TO MELBOURNE, I was excited to tell Amanda about my trip, but Amanda had news of her own. She had been diagnosed with breast cancer and needed surgery and, most likely, a full course of chemo-therapy and radiotherapy. I didn't know what to say. I was devastated and couldn't begin to imagine how Amanda and her husband were feeling; she faced months of gruelling cancer treatment and, perhaps, her own mortality. As a friend, I didn't want to let her down, and I wanted to support her in the best way possible. Amanda was determined to remain positive and to take each day one step at a time. I resolved to do the same and kept my worries to myself. I assumed she would want to take leave from the foundation, but she wanted to carry on working as best she could.

The following month, I met the president of the National Trust of Victoria Foundation at a charity event. She was excited to tell me that a giant statue of Colin Firth wearing a white shirt and striding out of the lake at Pemberley was on its way to Australia from Lyme Park in England. Lyme Park had been used for the exterior shots of Pemberley in the BBC 1995 series adaptation of *Pride and Prejudice*. The statue was to be installed in the lake of a National Trust property in Melbourne, Rippon Lea Estate. Rippon Lea was also hosting an exhibition of wedding gowns with costumes used in Austen movies. I couldn't believe it—Mr Darcy was coming to Melbourne!

A few months later, I returned to England to meet Simon Langton and to attend my father's seventieth birthday party, which was to be held at Chawton House on the day before the end of my week-long stay. I had previously gone out of my way to avoid family gatherings at Chawton, but this time I was determined to be there. I was also determined to overcome the uncomfortable feelings I had had at Chawton earlier in the year, and so I arranged to visit the house a number of times during my stay.

Early in the week, my father and I met Simon Langton at the front door. I immediately felt at ease with Simon—an intelligent, kind man and a gentleman. My father and I talked about our heritage, Jane Austen and our lives at Chawton as we gave Simon a guided tour of the house. We laughed at the memories of Granny waving her stick at picnickers on the lawn and refusing to allow tea room customers to choose their cake. We also marvelled at how busy her life had been—looking after Bapops, the tenants, the tea room, the cricket teas, family lunches and all the events. I asked my father why Bapops had slept in such a small room, but he didn't know.

We looked at the coats of arms in the stained-glass windows and told the story of Suicide Alley. Most of the family portraits had been moved to the picture gallery, as it is properly known, and I was overjoyed to see the familiar face of Elizabeth Martin Knight sitting in her luxurious blue gown. Sir Richard's portrait still took pride of place on the first half landing of the main staircase overlooking the inner hall. Simon was enthralled and curious to hear the details from a family perspective. It still felt strange to be a visitor at Chawton, but it was much easier with my father, as he was so at ease walking around. Old memories came flooding back, and as we neared the Reading

Room, as it is now called, I could see clearly in my mind old Mr Humphries filling the wood cupboard under the main staircase and, behind the door, my grandparents in the library, sitting in their well-worn favourite armchairs. The memories were vivid. As I remembered playing sardines during the holidays and Snap-Dragon on Christmas Eve, I could hear my cousins' laughter.

I still felt conflicted. It was great to see the house in such wonderful condition, but the extended family and heritage I had grown up with was now fading into history. I didn't recognise the new portraits that hung above the panelling in the Great Hall.

Early in the afternoon, my father went home, and Simon and I decided to have a late lunch at The Greyfriar. Simon was particularly curious about my relationship with Bapops and of the sense of responsibility—and perhaps of a need to 'keep up appearances'—that drove my grandparents to continue to host community events despite being in financial crisis. He was also interested in how Jane's fame had brought a continuous flow of tourists to our home and family. 'It's a fascinating story,' he said and suggested I write a book.

Many writers and historians had documented the history of Chawton House and the Austen and Knight families, but there was nothing written about the last years of Chawton as a family home. Montagu had written the last book over one hundred years ago. I had flicked through my parents' copy the night before and had enjoyed every minute. I loved seeing the photographs of the Great Hall, the original plans of the house and the vivid prints of the family portraits. It was such a joy to read. I only wished he had written more about his own life at Chawton. I would love to know whether Montagu knew the estate was heading for trouble or whether it took Lionel and Bapops by surprise.

We talked late into the afternoon about the making of *Pride and Prejudice* (1995). Simon's twelve-year-old stepdaughter thought previous adaptations were 'so artificial'—all the interior scenes were filmed in a studio and recorded on tape instead of film. *Pride and Prejudice* (1995) was filmed entirely on location, and Simon considered this one of the major contributing factors to its success.

Simon winced as he remembered filming Colin Firth powerfully swimming breaststroke underwater for the famous lake scene. This scene was shot at Ealing Film Studios in a tank, which was usually covered by four heavy slabs. Simon instructed that all four slabs be removed, but only three were taken off the top of the tank—he didn't know why, but he was told there was no need to remove the fourth slab. Simon was concerned about safety, but Colin agreed to push on. As Colin dived into the tank, he swam farther than he expected and hit the bridge of his nose on the metal support bar of the offending slab. 'I died for a few milliseconds,' Simon told me 'while the worst scenarios flashed through my head: shut down the filming while the insurers sort it out, recast Mr Darcy and reshoot nearly half the footage or wait until he is fully recovered, with a reconstructed nose!' Luckily, the collision was not nearly as bad as Simon had feared. The swelling on Colin's nose did not stop filming, although Simon avoided profile shots for some time after!

I couldn't help but ask about the most famous clip of all, the most iconic Austen scene ever created—Colin Firth as Mr Darcy in the wet shirt. I was surprised to hear that the scene wasn't in the script and hadn't been planned at all. Mr Darcy had arrived on horseback and decided to take a swim in one of his lakes, but after his swim, his horse was nowhere to be seen. Towards the end of filming, Simon realised this was a continuity problem and imagined young daughters complaining that Mr Darcy had simply abandoned his horse. Colin Firth gamely had a bucket of water thrown over him to create a last-minute continuity scene—Mr Darcy walking away from the lake carrying his outer clothing, while a convenient estate worker leads his horse.

Simon spoke of Jane Austen with fondness and great respect and was humble about the success of his production and its influence on the modern-day fandom of Jane Austen. The number of visitors to Chawton doubled to fifty-four thousand the year after its release, and almost twenty years later it was still the most loved Austen adaptation of all time. Simon was enthusiastic about my vision for the Jane Austen Literacy Foundation, and when I asked him to be the foundation's first ambassador, he didn't hesitate to accept. I planned to eventually launch an online journal for the foundation called 'Pride & Possibilities', and Simon agreed to write about 'shooting Jane', as he called it, for the first issue.

The next morning I met with the librarian of Chawton House to visit the Knight family library and view the books I had grown up with. Our books, now owned by Uncle Richard, were kept in storage in the basement. My first bedroom in the converted boiler room was gone; it was part of the removed Victorian extension. The other basement rooms had been converted into book stores, not open to the public, with rows of shelves and controlled temperature and humidity. The Knight family library was in the middle room, which had once been our bathroom.

Despite the change of location and order, the books were very familiar, particularly the largest sets with long rows of matching spines decorated in gold leaf. I was delighted to see Edward's, Montagu's and Thomas's bookplates and flicked through Montagu's photograph albums, intrigued by every detail of the black-and-white pictures. I was very surprised to see some of our childhood books: *Winnie the Pooh*, a children's book of science experiments to try at home, and a guide for art and craft projects. I was thrilled that we were part of this historical collection.

The next room, where we had huddled around the open fire and played giant dominos when the power was off, now housed a variety of books from the main collection at Chawton House Library. I opened the cover to the pages of the original manuscript of Sir Charles Grandison, written in Jane's hand, an adaptation of one of her favourite books by Samuel Richardson into a play. Just as I had been as a child, I felt overwhelmed with pride to call Jane *my* aunt.

Over the next few days, I returned daily to walk around the grounds, see Sir Richard, read the family plaques in the church and visit the Austen and Knight gravestones that Fiona and I had cleaned when we were children. Although I now lived on the other side of the world, I would always be connected with Chawton and consider it my home. The house had seen numerous changes over its four-century history, from one squire to the next and from one branch of the family to another. From the mid eighteenth to the mid nineteenth century, Chawton had been the squires' second home. At times in its history, the house had been rented or leased for short periods. During the war, it had welcomed children evacuated from London, and it had housed paying tenants in its wings.

I was relieved and grateful that Richard had not sold our house outright. The house was on a long lease with ninety-nine years remaining, but the freehold of Chawton Great House, which hadn't been sold since the house was built in 1585, was still owned by my family. I realised this was simply a new chapter in its long and varied history—a history I will always be a part of. Perhaps Richard's descendants will one day use the house as a home again, and the time when the house was leased to a charity will be a distant memory.

For my father's birthday party, my mother planned a delicious buffet: coronation chicken, baked ham, new potatoes and fresh salads to be followed by a metre-long pavlova, coffee cupcakes and fruit fools—gooseberry and rhubarb—in decorative jam jars. I jumped at the chance to help with the catering. My father made a wooden stand for the pavlova, complete with a lip to keep it in place. My mother baked the meringue base in sections and stripped the cooked chickens while I chopped and sliced the salad ingredients, iced the coffee cakes and mixed the dressing for the coronation chicken.

On the morning of the party, we loaded the food and drinks into my parents' cars, drove the few miles from Alton to Chawton and parked at the rear of the house. The servants' hall had been divided and converted into toilets, a storage room and a modern catering kitchen leading into the back of the original house kitchen. Meat, coleslaw, tomato, and green salads were transferred from plastic tubs to the serving plates and laid out on the kitchen bench. The desserts created an impressive display on the dresser at the end of the room.

As the guests arrived, I was delighted to see so many familiar faces. It was wonderful to host a party at Chawton and be with aunts, uncles, cousins and friends I had known as a child, even if it was just for a few hours. The sun was shining, and a harpist played in the courtyard. That night after the party, I sat at Trish and Dennis's kitchen table with Jake, Amber and my parents and talked into the night, as I had done many times in my youth. For the first time in twenty-five years, I felt happy and relaxed in Hampshire, almost at home. It was the perfect end to my stay.

It had been an emotional and exhausting week, and I was pleased to return to Melbourne, Roger and our dogs. My father rang a few days later. A second-hand book dealer, whom my father had never seen before, had approached him in Chawton to ask whether my father was interested in buying an old book. It was an original copy of Montagu's book, published in 1911, in near-perfect condition, complete with Montagu's square bookplate embossed in gold on the front cover. My father had bought it for me. It seemed such an extraordinary coincidence. I could hardly believe it. I was so excited to have my very own original copy of Montagu's book that I whooped for joy.

I updated my profile on LinkedIn, an online business network, to include my role as founder and chair of the Jane Austen Literacy Foundation, and soon after, I was contacted by a colleague I had worked with at Demo-Plus, who had not known of my connections. He offered to introduce me to his uncle, John Wiltshire, a Jane Austen scholar and author who had taught about Jane Austen at a Melbourne university for many years. Coincidentally, John lived less than five kilometres from Roger and me.

It was as if fate had intended it. John had spent weeks in Chawton and decades reading, studying and teaching about Jane Austen, as well as writing and editing books for Cambridge University Press. John encouraged me to record my memories and offered to mentor me as I wrote. I had many attempts at the first few chapters, and we met for coffee often to discuss each draft at length. I began to research and fill in the details of the stories I had heard as a child. I enjoyed sharing new titbits of information with John and pondering what Jane may have thought. One day, the cafe owner asked me what John and I talked about; the staff were bemused by the roars of laughter, occasional tears and conversation that flowed seamlessly from one century to another.

I had a lot of work to do to, but I was determined. It felt right, more so than anything I had ever done. I worked three to four days a week as a consultant and divided the rest of my time between writing, setting up the foundation and other board responsibilities. On 30 October 2014, the anniversary of the date Jane first became a published author, the website of the Jane Austen Literacy Foundation was launched. Within a few short weeks, we had received our first donations and funded our first literacy materials—a literacy kit to teach forty children for a temporary school, run by UNICEF in Syria. We still had much to learn, but we were on our way. Amanda finished her chemotherapy treatment towards the end of the year. We had often talked non-stop on the days when I had kept her company in the chemo room at the hospital. But sometimes we had just sat in silence together. Chemotherapy was followed by daily radiotherapy, which finished on Christmas Eve. We celebrated the end of Amanda's treatment with a lunch overlooking the water; she was on the road to recovery.

The foundation's priority for 2015 was driving awareness and getting to know the Jane Austen community. I used Skype to talk with hundreds of Austen enthusiasts, or Janeites, from all over the world. I was keen to understand what drove their passion and interest. I became fascinated with the modern-day Austen fandom and the desire of her followers to immerse themselves in every aspect of Jane's life, works and times, as well as the modern adaptations. It seemed Jane Austen had reached all four corners of the earth, and she was enjoyed in many different ways. It is a unique fan culture, unlike any other.

I began to piece together what had happened to the 6,800 acres in Hampshire, distributed through thirty-four parishes, which Thomas Knight had left to his son, Thomas Knight II, in 1781, as well as Godmersham Park in Kent. I had always believed that Lionel and Bapops were responsible for the demise of the family fortune, but I wanted to know the truth.

When Thomas Knight II died in 1794, he left his estates to his wife, Catherine, for her life and confirmed Edward Austen to be the eleventh squire of Chawton. But four years later, Catherine passed over the estates to Edward to run, rather than have Edward wait until her death for his inheritance:

> Catherine Knight out of her love and affection for Edward Austen and in order to advance him to their present possession of the estates which were settled on him and his issue in remainder under the will agreed to convey all the estates unto and to the use of Edward Austen during the joint lives of him and her Catherine Knight subject to a rent charge or clear annual sum of £2,000 clear of all deductions and taxes to be reserved and made passable.

It was supposedly a generous act, but the burden and responsibility of managing the estates had also passed to Edward as well as the risk of the income falling short.

Jane did not hide her views on Catherine's actions. On 8 January 1799, she wrote to Cassandra:

Mrs. Knight giving up the Godmersham Estate to Edward was no such prodigious act of Generosity after all it seems, for she has reserved herself an income out of it still;—this ought to be known, that her conduct may not be over-rated.—I rather think Edward shews the most Magnanimity of the two, in accepting her Resignation with such Incumbrances.

Edward made Godmersham his primary residence and took an active role in the community, including taking up the office of High Sheriff of Kent in 1801. He served for several decades as a magistrate, and his name often appeared in newspapers as among the organisers or supporters of charitable and civic endeavours. Edward made annual visits to Chawton for up to five months at a time. Jane wrote to her brother Frank in July 1813: 'We go on in the most comfortable way, very frequently dining together, & always meeting in some part of every day.—Edward is very well & enjoys himself as thoroughly any Hampshire born Austen can desire. Chawton is not thrown away on him.'

I asked my parents endless questions during our weekly phone calls. They answered as best they could, but they didn't know all the details of Edward's finances or exactly when each property and landholding was sold. Early in May 2015, my father called to say he had put a book in the post for me that I simply had to read. Linda Slothouber had stayed in Chawton for a few weeks the previous year and had researched the family archives to understand Edward Austen Knight's management of the Chawton estate. I was excited and impatient for my copy to arrive.

I was not disappointed. Linda's book *Jane Austen, Edward Knight & Chawton: Commerce & Community* was a revelation. I was fascinated to read how Jane and Cassandra had helped Edward perform the duties of the landowner. There were details about Edward's financial affairs when Jane lived in Chawton and about estate management that I had never considered. I hadn't realised to what extent running an estate was like running a business. I contacted Linda to thank her, and we talked at length about Edward and Chawton in Jane's time.

Linda estimated Edward's annual income at around £8,000. This may sound like a lot (not far short of Mr Darcy's £10,000), but there were many financial demands to be met. Between a quarter and a half of Edward's gross earnings were spent annually on expenses, including labour, repairs, professional fees, tithes, transport, taxes and rates. Catherine Knight received £2,000 a year for thirteen years until her death in 1812, which was equivalent to nearly sixty per cent of the net profits of his Hampshire estates. Perhaps Jane had been right; the early passing of the estates to Edward by Catherine was not such an act of kindness.

Edward also provided financial assistance to his mother and his sisters, Jane and Cassandra, after his father died and took over the financial support of his disabled brother, George. He lent Chawton Great House to his naval brothers and extended his hospitality at Godmersham to his siblings and their guests. He provided significant financial support for Henry's career as a banker and as an army agent. He created annuities for his siblings to help them manage their savings, and he paid his lawyers to handle the legal business of the family. He provided for six sons variously with military commissions and university club memberships, as well as European tours and allowances for five daughters—four of whom married, so there were settlements to pay.

With privilege came responsibility, and estate owners extended support to the community, particularly to the poor of the parish, and Edward made many provisions for the welfare of Chawton residents. Edward gave an Alton apothecary and surgeon £10 a year to attend to the health needs of the poor, and he added two tenements, or houses, to the six he had already made available in the parish. Cassandra and Jane took up the duty of home visits when the Knights were away. Edward made small customary donations to the most needy, and he gave Jane and Cassandra £10 each year to provide small comforts for the poor in the village.

Edward paid for schoolmistresses for Chawton and Steventon to provide basic education for the poor. In September 1813, the same month that Jane and Edward had visited Wedgwood in London to commission the Austen Knight dinner service, Jane made a charitable donation to The Society for Promoting Christian Knowledge, an organisation that established Sunday schools throughout the country, which for many was the only opportunity to learn to read and write. I was thrilled to know I was continuing a family tradition by contributing to literacy and the education of those who would otherwise miss out.

Most of Edward's income from his Hampshire estates came from land rental and payments related to use of the land. He let houses, farms, mills and labourers' cottages. Rent provided a steady income, which Edward supplemented by working in the woodlands. Wood was routinely cut from the 900 acres at Chawton, and Edward sold the same range of wood that Elizabeth Martin Knight had sold a century earlier: firewood, hop poles—cut from slender branches to support growing hops—and fencing rods harvested through coppicing—that is, cutting wood from a tree without killing it. Trees were cut down or topped and the timber sold, and bark was sold to one of the several tanneries in Alton. Edward relied most heavily on the coppices that supplied underwood, the most renewable resources after 1812 when Catherine died. Income from timber had been up to ten times higher in her lifetime, perhaps to pay her annual stipend.

Edward was fastidious. He kept bank clerks on their toes, correcting mistakes in their ledgers, and he took swift and firm action to collect money where he was owed. He met with his steward annually and inspected the accounts in detail. 'He must have been more his own "man of business" than is usual with people of large property, for I think it always was his greatest interest to attend to his estates,' Caroline Austen recalled. However, despite careful management of his financial affairs, Edward decided to sell the Abbots Barton estate in 1811 after thirteen years of stewardship. Through the sale, Edward was able to cut running costs by selling land that was expensive and difficult to maintain and to release capital to finance expenses, such as improvements to Godmersham.

Edward's finances were put under further pressure by Henry Austen's business affairs. In November 1815, Henry's Alton Bank collapsed, due partly to a countrywide agricultural depression and partly to the actions of Henry's banking partner, Edward Gray, who siphoned the bank's liquid assets to his family and friends, leaving a balance in the bank of only sixteen shillings. Edward Gray was declared bankrupt at the end of December, and Henry borrowed £10,000 from Edward on a promissory note. But in March 1816, Henry's London bank also failed, and he too was declared bankrupt. He wasn't blamed personally, but he was embarrassed, as several of his nearest relatives had acted as his guarantors. Edward suffered heavy losses of more than £20,000.

From the time of his inheritance, Edward's ownership of Chawton and other Hampshire property was disputed, and a number of court challenges were filed by those who believed they had a greater claim on the estates. The affair dragged on for several years, and it was not settled until the year after Jane died. In April 1818, Edward was forced to acknowledge the claims of Hinton and Baverstock for the manors of Chawton, Alton Eastbrooke, Steventon and Shalden, and he settled for £15,000. In order to pay this large sum so soon after the collapse of Henry's bank, a substantial area of timber was felled that, according to a niece writing a half century later, 'occasioned the great gap in Chawton Wood Park, visible for 30 years afterwards, and probably not filled up again even now.' Jane died before the matter was settled and, therefore, she would not have known that her mother and sisters would have a secure home for the rest of their lives.

The Knight estates were reduced again in 1824 when Edward sold a large farm at Colemore in Hampshire. The Manor of Shalden and some farmland at Wivelrod, also in Hampshire, were sold in 1840; it is not clear why.

Edward Knight II inherited upon his father's death in 1852, by which time he had lived at Chawton for twenty-six years. He had taken up residence at Chawton House in 1826, perhaps preferring to be master of his surroundings than living in the shadow of his father in Godmersham, or perhaps he moved away in disgrace after eloping with Mary Knatchbull to Gretna Green in Scotland.

Only three years later, in 1855, Edward II sold the 1,700-acre Steventon property to the Duke of Wellington. Despite the sale, Edward II was listed as one of Hampshire's top landowners in *The Domesday Book of 1873*, owning 5,044 acres. The following year, Edward II sold Godmersham Park to an industrial businessman from Manchester, and Chawton was once again the only country manor of the Knight family.

Land values had plummeted from 1870 as foreign imports undercut home-produced goods. Death duties were introduced in 1894, and changes to estate economy in England were already well advanced by 1900. Estate duties and taxes were crippling for the landowners of England. For many, labour forces had been depleted during the First World War, and after the war, many former estate workers sought alternative employment opportunities. The traditional structure of landed estates all over the country was beginning to fail, and Chawton held out longer than did many others.

I calculated that Bapops was only twenty-two when he inherited Chawton in 1932. Lionel had died suddenly after less than twenty years as squire, so none of Bapops's children had known their grandfather. I asked my father whether the estate was already bankrupt when Bapops became squire. Lionel hadn't finished paying off Montagu's death duties before he died, and Bapops had inherited an estate with significant financial burdens, but my father didn't know the details. The majority of the Chawton properties that were sold by Lionel—and by Bapops in his early years as squire—were sold to pay death and estate duties, to finance the costs of running the remaining estate and to cover living expenses. Inflation had remained largely stable throughout Montagu's ownership, and despite an inflation jump during the First World War, my father thought that Bapops was given advice, which he believed, to the effect that the interest from the money raised would look after the estate into the future. But inflation continued to rise, and by the early 1950s, the estate was practically broke.

It was clear: the demise of the family fortune inherited by Edward Austen began long before Bapops and was, in large part, an inevitable consequence of political, social and economic change throughout the nineteenth and twentieth centuries. The extensive financial pressures borne by Edward Austen Knight had led to more than a century of land, property and asset sales. I needed to discover more about the legal challenge that had cost Edward so dearly, but it would have to wait—I had other work to do.

In March 2015, I was invited to be on the panel of the Australian Institute of Management's International Women's Day debate event, and for the first time, I spoke about Jane, her remarkable achievements and the success of her brand to an audience of women executives. People approached me afterwards, and it was remarkable to see their enthusiasm.

Amanda continued to work on projects for the foundation throughout 2015. Her treatment was complete, but as the months passed, she seemed to be getting weaker, not stronger. The toxic side effects of the chemotherapy had left their mark, and it became obvious that her recovery was going to take far longer than we had anticipated. Amanda had changed physically, mentally and emotionally, and she fought hard to remain positive and as active as she could manage.

In July, we staged our first Jane Austen Literacy Foundation 'High Tea for Literacy' fundraising event, held at the Jane Austen Tea Room in

Melbourne. I shared tales of growing up in Chawton against a backdrop of old family photographs, followed by tea, cakes and scones. It was a great success, and the money raised was used to buy books for a library in an Indigenous community in a remote part of Australia. I was a confident business speaker, but I was only now gaining confidence talking publicly about Jane and Chawton.

I read Montagu's book again and discovered further extraordinary revelations about my family—at least they were extraordinary to me—and both Roger and Amanda indulged me in my conversation. I came across an article online by Christine Grover, an author and lecturer at the University of Winchester, titled 'Edward Knight's Inheritance: The Chawton, Godmersham, and Winchester Estates', which showed Elizabeth Martin Knight's family trees. As I read the article, I came to the shocking realisation that Elizabeth Martin Knight had inherited Chawton from her father's side of the family—Michael Martin was the son of Dorothy from the original Knight family. But Thomas, Elizabeth's chosen heir, was descended from her mother's family (Thomas's and Elizabeth's mothers were first cousins). From what I could see, Thomas had no blood relationship to the original Knights. None of us did. I wasn't related to Sir Richard Knight after all!

I had always thought that despite the twists and turns of the inheritance of the house, we were of the same family. I felt numb. I told myself that it didn't matter or make any difference because we still shared Chawton. But it did matter. Elizabeth Martin Knight may have been a great squire, but this decision had broken the bloodline. Could it be true that the figure I had considered the greatest of all my great-grandfathers wasn't my relative at all?

I looked again at the pedigrees, or family trees, in Montagu's book. I had never noticed, but it was there plain to see. Elizabeth had indeed passed the house from her father's to her mother's family. I had previously misunderstood Montagu's meaning when he had written that Elizabeth 'was the

last descendant of the original family of Knight who reigned at Chawton'
and that 'in making the disposition which she felt obliged to make of her
estate she must have deeply regretted having to nominate persons who did
not belong to the old family of Knight'. I had wrongly assumed we were still
blood-related to the Knights—somehow. But that wasn't the last shocking
discovery I made. Elizabeth Martin Knight was responsible for much more
than breaking the bloodline.

Another article by Christine Grover revealed that instead of leaving Chawton to Thomas 'fee simple', with no limitations on the subsequent inheritance
of the land, Elizabeth had left it by 'fee tail', whereby the estate was entailed
with conditions, which meant the property could only be passed linearly to
each heir. Thomas could not sell or break up the property or leave it to whom-
ever he wished. Furthermore, Elizabeth had restricted the succession to 'tail
male', rather than 'tail general', with the obvious intent of ensuring that she
would be the only female squire of Chawton. I wanted to see for myself
and obtained a copy of Elizabeth's will from the Public Records Office of
The National Archives in London. The hand-written document was a little
difficult to read, but eventually—on the fourth page—I found the words:

> To the use and behoofe of the first Son and all and every other
> the Son and Sons of the Body of the said Thomas May lawfully
> begotten or to be begotten and of the heirs male of his and their
> Body and Bodies lawfully issuing severally and successively one
> after another as they and every of them shall be in priority of
> Birth and Seniority of age the Elder of such Sons and the Heirs
> Male of his body always to take and be preferred before the
> younger of such Sons

It was difficult to comprehend: the entail that set the tradition of eldest male ownership was implemented by Elizabeth Martin Knight herself. I was speechless.

As far back as 1741, only four years after Elizabeth had died, Edward Hinton claimed that Chawton should be his, as he was more closely related to Elizabeth. Thomas Knight filed and won legal proceedings to prove he was the rightful owner under the terms of Elizabeth's will. The terms Elizabeth included in her will also led to the legal battles Edward faced from the time that Catherine Knight died and he became the eleventh squire. Hinton and Baverstock challenged Edward's ownership, as it clearly did not comply with Elizabeth's conditions. I had immediately assumed that this was because Edward was adopted and not a 'Son of the Body'. However, although this also invalidated the entail, the case cited as the basis for the claim that the order of legal procedures in the transfer of the property from Thomas Knight I to Thomas Knight II was in conflict with Elizabeth's will.

Elizabeth may have stipulated such conditions in an attempt to ensure that the Knight lands would not be sold or broken up. Thomas and his successors were life tenants, entitled to use of the land and any rental or investment income, but they were not free to sell Chawton. Elizabeth may have intended to secure the Knight family fortune, but the terms of her will ultimately cost Edward Austen a huge sum, and the resulting financial pressures, perhaps, triggered the start of the sales.

I immediately thought of the scene I had watched in *Miss Austen Regrets* and the conversation between Jane and Edward. Jane was well informed about Edward's legal affairs. 'It is a nasty day for everybody. Edward's spirits will be wanting Sunshine, & here is nothing but Thickness & Sleet,' Jane wrote to Cassandra from Henrietta Street in a letter dated 5–8 March 1814. 'Perhaps you have not heard that Edward has a good chance of escaping his Lawsuit. His opponent "knocks under." The terms of Agreement are not quite settled.'

If Jane knew the details of the case, she must have also known that Elizabeth Martin's actions prevented another woman from being squire. I asked my father, and he was certain Jane would have known about Elizabeth—as well as the legal challenges stemming from her will. Jane likely had access to the family records. Elizabeth Martin was famed for insisting the church bells were rung to mark her arrival at and departure from Chawton. Fanny Knight wrote to her old governess in 1807: 'It is very curious to trace the genealogy of the Knights & all the old families that have possessed the estate, from the pictures of which there are quantities, & some descriptions of them have been routed out, so that we are not at a loss for amusement.'

Did Jane understand Elizabeth's decision to secure the future of Chawton through the traditional male lineage (it was the norm of the day), or was she as flabbergasted as I was? It was hard to comprehend. The woman in the luxurious blue taffeta gown I had admired daily in our hallway, the only celebrated female of the family other than Jane, had broken the bloodline and left an entail that dictated male-only ownership and was the source of Edward's legal battles. I could only guess, as I could find no definitive explanation.

I contacted Linda Slothouber again to ask whether she had learnt anything from the archives and family records. We spoke at length about what the Austen ladies might have thought of the 'grande dame', and Linda wrote an article, published online in 2015, about Elizabeth. In her article, Linda starts with the extraordinary similarity between Elizabeth's visage in a 1730 portrait and that of Queen Anne, who reigned from 1702 to 1714. It may have been due to a conventional pose for portraiture at the time, but they were so similar that it was difficult to believe there was not some deliberate attempt to give Elizabeth a more regal persona.

Linda goes on to provide tantalising clues as to Elizabeth's reputation. On 26 February 1838, Cassandra Austen wrote a letter to her niece describing the funeral of Mary Dorothea, the wife of Edward Knight II, who was interred in the Knight family vault under the church: 'The old vault was opened and is now under repair—It contains at present four Coffins, I suppose those of <u>Lady</u> Knight, alias Betty Martin, her two Husbands and one Brother.' Betty is short for Elizabeth, so I assumed this was merely a play on her name, but there was more to it than that. Elizabeth Martin was not eligible to use the title 'Lady', and it seems to have been underlined in mockery. In her article, Linda said:

> One way to mock the grandeur of the great lady was to inflate her title from 'Mrs.' to 'Lady'; another way was to downgrade her to common 'Betty Martin.' Betty Martin was not just a diminutive form of Elizabeth Knight's birth name, however: It was also part of an idiomatic expression that took different forms over the years. A few examples: That's my eye, Betty Martin (Classical Dictionary of the Vulgar Tongue, 1788); My eye and Betty Martin (from a song of the same name in Ashburner's New Vocal Repository, 1807); It's all my eye and Betty Martin (Hampshire Chronicle, 1810), Oh! My eye, Betty Martin! (Oxford University and City Herald and many other newspapers, 1814), All Betty Martin (A Disagreeable Surprise [play], 1828).

> Whatever its form, the expression was well-known, and its meaning was, essentially, 'That's bunk—I'm not buying your story.' (Who Betty Martin was and how the expression originated are unknown.) Cassandra Austen's words '<u>Lady</u> Knight, alias Betty Martin,' suggest that Elizabeth Knight was a bit of a fraud, and beneath the satin gown and queenly stare was only plain old Betty Martin.

It appears that Cassandra was sharing an old family joke with her niece, as she gives no other explanation for her remarks, indicating that there was little reason to think Jane would not have known the joke too.

I had most of the answers I was looking for. I understood the entail, the decline of the family fortune and the enormous challenge Bapops inherited at such a young age. I knew he had sanctioned many property and asset sales, including Edward Austen Knight's portrait in the early 1950s. A cousin told me that Bapops had reportedly been distressed by the sales, had retreated to the library and had never fully recovered. I don't know whether this is true, but it is an explanation for his reclusive lifestyle and why he didn't celebrate his position as squire with a coat of arms or a bookplate.

The biggest mystery remaining was Lionel, Bapops's father, who started the break-up of the Chawton estate with the sale of 220 acres in 1919. I did find some clues about Lionel in a photocopy of his obituary, sent to me by my mother. The obituary printed in the local paper was titled 'Loss to the County—Sudden Passing of Col. Knight, of Chawton—His splendid public work':

> We deeply regret to announce the death, which occurred suddenly from heart failure at Chawton House early on Friday morning, of Lieut.—Col. Lionel Charles Edward Knight, J.P., c.c. He was only 59 years of age, and his sudden passing came as a great shock to the district, the more so as he had not been suffering from any illness, and was in the very best of health on the day before he died. On Tuesday he presided over the Alton Police Court; on Wednesday he attended a meeting of the Hampshire and General Friendly Society at Winchester, and a meeting in connection with the Hampshire Hunt; while on Thursday he was about Chawton village, looking as hale as one could wish.

It was clear that Lionel didn't shut himself away from the local community—unlike Bapops. 'He has served his generation, and served it well. Firstly by administering the estate which fell to his lot, with its many pressing responsibilities and increasing difficulties in these most difficult days, and with tact, humour and kindness,' the Rector of Chawton said in his tribute to Lionel, indicating the estate was already in trouble and that it was common knowledge. At the end of the tribute, the rector said, 'Finally would we ask God's guidance on those to whom this heritage passes, that they may bear its responsibilities and guide its destinies to the well-being of all concerned.'

The weight of the duties that befell the squire was not underestimated, or the consequences for others if the estate did not prosper. It was important for the whole community. I asked my father whether he knew anything about Lionel, but he had never heard anyone talk about him. Bapops and Aunt Betty obviously would have known him—he was their father. I wished I had thought about it when they were alive, although I would not have had the courage to ask when I was young, even if it had occurred to me.

Out of the blue, at the end of 2015, a Janeite sent me an advertisement for a talk that Diana Shervington was giving in Lyme Regis. According to the advertisement, Diana was from Chawton House and related to Jane. I had never heard of her and was instantly intrigued. I turned to Google and discovered that Diana was descended from a granddaughter of Edward Austen Knight and referred to Montagu as 'Uncle Monty'. Diana was about ninety-five and, from the dates, it seemed that she may well have known Lionel when she was a child.

I was very excited and called my parents immediately. My mother made a few phone calls and arranged to visit Diana at her home in Lyme Regis for a cup of tea. I waited with bated breath for my mother to call me after her visit. Although my mother enjoyed her visit, listening to Diana's memories of staying at the dower house and visiting Chawton House as a child (she hadn't lived at Chawton) Diana had not known Lionel and was not able to offer any enlightenment. I couldn't help but be disappointed; Diana was my last hope. There cannot possibly be anyone else alive who would have once known him, and so Lionel remains a mystery to me.

Awareness of the Jane Austen Literacy Foundation continued to grow, and I spoke at some Austen events in Australia. I continued to be surprised at the level of interest, but I was also delighted at the joy that sharing my heritage and memories of growing up with Jane Austen seemed to bring to others.

On 16 December 2015, I received a wonderful surprise. Rita, the woman behind the very popular Facebook page 'All Things Jane Austen', sent me a photograph of Sir Richard reclining in the church with holly in his hand! She had travelled from America to Chawton for Jane's birthday and had re-membered the family tradition I had told her about. I loved it—and vowed to make sure there was holly in Sir Richard's hand every Christmas, just as Granny had all those years ago.

At the beginning of 2016, I visited a grammar school in Melbourne and spoke to a very enthusiastic group of ten- and eleven-year-old girls who were reading Jane's work for the first time. They were spellbound and listened in-tently to every word. Each had prepared a question. Most asked what Jane may have meant in various passages of her novels, or whether she had ever been in love. But one very sweet girl asked, 'If you are the last Austens to be raised in Chawton, if you're the last one, are you lonely?' She then asked why my surname was Knight and not Austen; I explained but thought how much easier it would be for others to understand the family connection if my par-ents had christened me Jane Austen Knight after all.

Afterwards, the head teacher told me how excited the girls had been in anticipation of my visit: 'They've been talking about nothing but Austen all week!' It brought a tear to my eye.

In the middle of 2016, Amanda took a step back from the day-to-day work of the foundation to focus on her recovery. I fully supported her decision.

She needed a fresh start and went to Queensland with her husband. It was a good decision, and I was thrilled to see her looking stronger and healthier on her visits back to Melbourne.

More and more volunteers came forward to help with operations, and on 30 October 2016, the foundation launched an online journal, 'Pride & Possibilities', with unique content and articles from Jane's family, celebrities, Austen experts and foundation ambassadors. The first article was 'Shooting Jane' by Simon Langton, and the response was overwhelmingly positive—our community quickly began to grow.

At the end of the year, a woman who had heard me speak at a women's event in Melbourne earlier in the year contacted me. Tina, as I shall call her, represented a very wealthy family and wanted to talk to me about Chawton. We met for a coffee, and after the initial pleasantries, Tina said it had become common knowledge that Sandy Lerner's involvement with Chawton House Library was coming to an end and that the family Tina represented might be interested in providing some financial support to the charity. I agreed to contact Uncle Richard and make an introduction.

Tina also said the family were interested in a business venture. She painted a visual picture of me, living permanently in Chawton, hosting events year round and welcoming visitors from around the world for their own luxury Jane Austen experience with Jane's fifth great-niece. It was an extraordinary suggestion and impossible, I was sure. Chawton House was a library that promoted early women's writing, and I couldn't imagine the charity agreeing to it being used in this way. 'But don't you want to go back to Chawton?' Tina asked. 'I assumed from listening to your story, this would be your dream.'

That night, I couldn't help thinking about the possibilities, of the joy of hosting at home again—in the Great Hall. I had missed Chawton House for so long that the thought of returning was intoxicating, and for a few moments I was as bewitched as Anne Elliot had been when Lady Russell encouraged her to accept a marriage proposal from her cousin, Mr Elliot, who was set to inherit her family's ancestral home, Kellynch Hall:

> I own that to be able to regard you as the future mistress of Kellynch, the future Lady Elliot, to look forward and see you occupying your dear mother's place, succeeding to all her rights, and all her popularity, as well as to all her virtues, would be the highest possible gratification to me. You are your mother's self in countenance and disposition; and if I might be allowed to fancy you such as she was, in situation, and name, and home, presiding and blessing in the same spot, and only superior to her in being more highly valued! My dearest Anne, it would give me more delight than is often felt at my time of life!

> Anne was obliged to turn away, to rise, to walk to a distant table, and, leaning there in pretended employment, try to subdue her feelings this picture excited. For a few moments her imagination and her heart were bewitched. The idea of becoming what her mother had been; of having the precious name of "Lady Elliot" first revived in herself; of being restored to Kellynch, calling it her home again, her home for ever, was a charm which she could not immediately resist. Lady Russell said not another word, willing to leave the matter to its own operation; and believing that, could Mr. Elliot at that moment with propriety have spoken for himself! – she believed, in short, what Anne did not believe. The same image of Mr. Elliot speaking for himself brought Anne to composure again. The charm of Kellynch and of "Lady Elliot" all faded away. She never could accept him.

I imagined being at home again at Chawton House. I immediately pictured Bapops sitting in the library, and I imagined cooking with Granny in her kitchen. I thought of playing with Fiona in the cellars, helping my father in the vegetable garden and enjoying family lunches in the Great Hall. But none of my family was there, and the house was now a public building, with stakeholders and a board to report to. The charm of Chawton faded away.

Like Fanny Price when she returned to her beloved Portsmouth, I realised I could no longer call Chawton home. 'When she had been coming to Portsmouth,' Jane wrote, 'she had loved to call it her home, had been fond of saying that she was going home; the word had been very dear to her, and so it still was, but it must be applied to Mansfield. *That* was now the home. Portsmouth was Portsmouth; Mansfield was home.' Chawton was Chawton; Melbourne was home. And with this realisation, I left the past behind.

I will always be Caroline Jane Knight from Chawton, a privilege I cherish. I have embraced my heritage wholeheartedly and can now think of Chawton House with joy and great fondness. But I am now looking to the future. I am happy and settled in a home of my own. I have a wonderful husband and my family, and I have Jane—my 'very great' great-aunt—wherever I am.

This year, 2017, marks the bicentennial of Jane Austen's death. The life and works of one of the world's most famous and acclaimed authors are being celebrated all over the world. I have made many friends in the Austen community and love hearing the stories of how Jane inspires and brings pleasure to people today. With Jane's fame and my determination, I will continue to work to grow the Jane Austen Literacy Foundation. I might not be successful, but Jane's words are clear in my mind: 'I must keep to my own style and go on in my own way; and though I may never succeed again in that, I am convinced that I should totally fail in any other.'

AFTERWORD

On 23 February 2017, a couple of months before the bicentennial of Jane's death, I woke to the most exciting news. A set of Jane's novels from 1833, complete with Montagu's bookplate, had been discovered in Texas, and the owner, Sandra Clark, who had been collecting Austen editions for years, had generously sent them back to Chawton House.

I contacted Gillian Dow, the CEO of Chawton House Library, to find out more. It was an important first edition of a set of Austen novels by Bentley, who, for the first time, had published Jane's novels as a 'complete works'. The set was listed in a 1908 library catalogue that Montagu had compiled, which was the first record of these books in the family collection at Chawton House, but there was no way of being sure when the family had bought the set or when it had left our collection. Montagu had put his bookplate in many books that were bought by previous squires of Chawton, so we could not make assumptions. But it didn't matter. At least one of our family's copies of Jane's books, which I had looked for in the library when I was a child, had returned home.

PEDIGREE II.—KNIGHTS

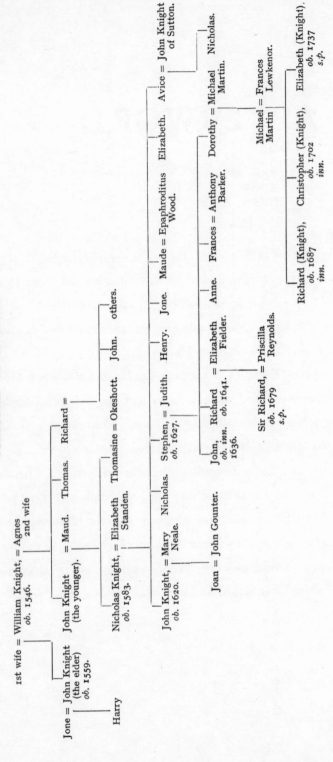

Reproduced from *Chawton Manor and its Owners: A Family History* by W. Austen Leigh and M.G. Knight, published by Smith, Elder & Co. in 1911

PEDIGREE IV.—MAYS

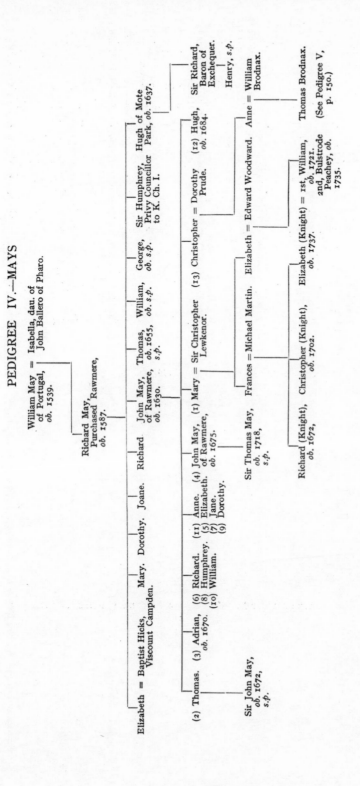

PEDIGREE V.—AUSTENS

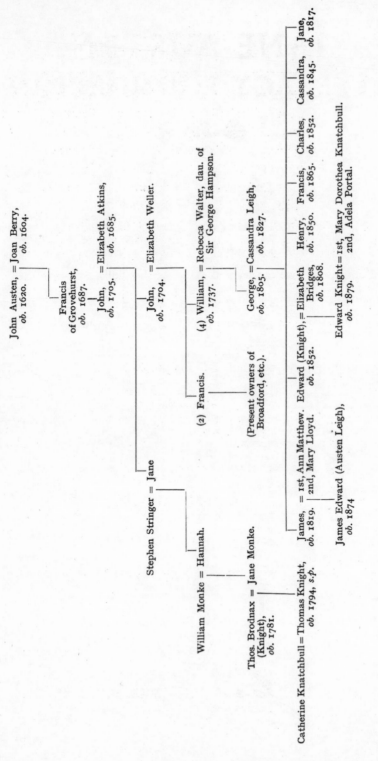

John Austen, = Joan Berry, *ob.* 1620. *ob.* 1604.

Francis of Grovehurst, *ob.* 1687.

John, = Elizabeth Atkins, *ob.* 1705. *ob.* 1685.

John, = Elizabeth Weller. *ob.* 1704.

Stephen Stringer = Jane

(2) Francis.

(Present owners of Broadford, etc.).

(4) William, = Rebecca Walter, dau. of *ob.* 1737. Sir George Hampson.

George, = Cassandra Leigh, *ob.* 1805. *ob.* 1827.

William Monke = Hannah.

Thos. Brodnax = Jane Monke. (Knight), *ob.* 1781.

Catherine Knatchbull = Thomas Knight, *ob.* 1794, *s.p.*

James, = 1st, Ann Matthew. Edward (Knight), = Elizabeth Henry, Francis, Charles, Cassandra, Jane, *ob.* 1819. | 2nd, Mary Lloyd. *ob.* 1852. Bridges, *ob.* 1850. *ob.* 1865. *ob.* 1852. *ob.* 1845. *ob.* 1817. *ob.* 1808.

James Edward (Austen Leigh), *ob.* 1874

Edward Knight = 1st, Mary Dorothea Knatchbull. *ob.* 1879. 2nd, Adela Portal.

Reproduced from *Chawton Manor and its Owners: A Family History* by W. Austen Leigh and M.G. Knight, published by Smith, Elder & Co. in 1911

JANE AUSTEN
LITERACY FOUNDATION

Everyone, no matter their gender or circumstance, has the right to learn basic literacy skills. Many of us are very lucky and have the opportunity to receive an education where we can learn these invaluable skills. However, there are communities around the world where this is not so. Literacy rates in developing, low-income and war-torn countries are staggering and the gap between men and women even more so.

Founded by Caroline Jane Knight, the Jane Austen Literacy Foundation is a registered not-for-profit organisation, created to harness the global passion for Jane Austen to improve literacy rates. The foundation works with the Austen community to support literacy programs and raise funds to provide literacy materials for communities in need across the world—in honour of Jane.

The foundation is run by volunteers. Operating costs are kept at a minimum and are privately funded; one hundred per cent of donations received are used to fund literacy resources. For more information or to make a donation, visit www.janeaustenlf.org.

REFERENCES

Austen Leigh, W. and M.G. Knight, *Chawton Manor and its Owners: A Family History* (London: Smith, Elder & Co., 1911).

Grover, C., 'Edward Knight's Inheritance: The Chawton, Godmersham, and Winchester Estates' [online article], 1997, Jane Austen Society of North America. <http://www.jasna.org/persuasions/on-line/vol34no1/grover.html> accessed March 2017.

Grover, C., 'Pride, Prejudice, and the Threat to Edward Knight's Inheritance', [online article], 1997, Jane Austen Society of North America. <http://www.jasna.org/persuasions/on-line/vol35no1/grover.html> accessed March 2017.

Slothouber, L., 'Another Letter by Cassandra Austen: A Little Nostalgic Humor from Jane Austen's Sister', *Jane Austen, Edward Knight, & Chawton: Commerce & Community* [web blog], 20 July 2015, <http://chawtoncommerceandcommunity.blogspot.com.au/2015/07/another-letter-by-cassandra-austen.html> accessed March 2013.

For the purposes of consistency, the following sources have been used for the exact wording of Jane's work, letters and other family letters:

Brabourne, E. *Letters of Jane Austen* (London: Bentley, 1884). The Republic of Pemberley [website] <http://www.pemberley.com/janeinfo/brablets.html> accessed March 2017.

Le Faye, D., *Jane Austen: A Family Record* (Cambridge: Cambridge University Press, 1989).

Le Faye, D., *Jane Austen's Letters* (Oxford: Oxford University Press, 2011).